FROM SHIP'S COOK
TO BARONET

Sir William Reardon Smith, 1856–1935

FROM SHIP'S COOK TO BARONET

Sir William Reardon Smith's
Life in Shipping, 1856-1935

DAVID JENKINS

UNIVERSITY OF WALES PRESS
CARDIFF
2011
in association with
Amgueddfa Cymru – National Musem Wales

This book is dedicated to the memory of its subject

SIR WILLIAM REARDON SMITH, Bart

and to that of two friends and mentors
ROBIN CRAIG
(1924–2007)
who taught me so much about tramp shipping
and
J. GERAINT JENKINS
(1929–2009)
a roddodd i mi'r cyfle cyntaf

www.uwp.co.uk

British Library CIP *Data*
A catalogue record for this book is available from the British Library

ISBN   978-0-7083-2423-3
e-ISBN   978-0-7083-2424-0

The right of David Jenkins to be identified as author of this work has been asserted by him in accordance with sections 77 and 79 of the Copyright, Designs and Patents Act 1988.

This book has been published in association with Amgueddfa Cymru – National Museum Wales.

Designed by Chris Bell
Printed by the University of Wales Press

Contents

Foreword

E ARLY IN 1921, my great-grandfather Sir William Reardon Smith launched an appeal amongst his fellow shipowners at Cardiff to fund the establishment, initially within Cardiff Technical College, of a department which would provide training for boys between the ages of thirteen and sixteen whose ambitions were set upon a career at sea. By the end of March he had collected the considerable sum of £18,000 and on 3 October that year, the Smith Junior Nautical School accepted its first pupils, or cadets as they were termed. From the outset, a formal class-taught syllabus was combined with practical training, and in 1925 the opportunities available to the cadets were broadened immeasurably when Sir William acquired the racing yacht *Margherita*, which came to serve as both training vessel and family yacht. Every summer, a score of young lads would join her on the Clyde for a voyage that would take them down the Irish Sea and up the Bristol Channel, later rounding Land's End to arrive in the Solent in time for Cowes week – and all under Sir William's critical eye! He was utterly convinced of the value of the experience, and stated:

> Nothing can be a substitute for this. The knowledge of seamanship gained on a sailing vessel cannot be acquired any other way. I want them to experience the delights as well as the duties and hard work of sailing ship training, to train on and become first-class officers.

The Reardon Smith Nautical School (as it was later known) provided a seafaring education for generations of cadets until it closed in 1991, a victim of the sad decline of the British merchant fleet in the latter half of the twentieth century. However, its successor body, the Reardon Smith Nautical Trust, continues to provide encouragement and support for young people who wish to pursue a career in maritime or nautical affairs, ranging from sail training to marine law, and in this way continues to emulate Sir William's original aims of facilitating young people to pursue careers related to the sea.

It is with much pleasure that members of the trust have also provided support for David Jenkins's exhaustively researched study of Sir William. This is the remarkable story of the youngest son of a widowed captain's wife, who went to sea as a teenage cabin boy and cook from his home village of Appledore in north Devon; he ended his days not only as Cardiff's foremost shipowner, but also an esteemed philanthropist whose generosity to many causes in his native Devon and his adopted south Wales – especially the National Museum – assumed a near-legendary status. It is to be hoped that this biography will not only appeal to those interested in maritime history, and the local history of north Devon and south Wales, but that it will also serve as an inspiration to young readers who have a hankering to respond to 'the call of the sea', as the young Reardon Smith did nearly a century and a half ago.

John Reardon-Smith,
Chairman,
Reardon Smith Nautical Trust
2011

Acknowledgements

IR WILLIAM REARDON SMITH was probably the best known of all of Cardiff's great shipowners, and the shipping venture that he founded in 1905, which would eventually become known as the Reardon Smith Line, was likewise synonymous with shipowning at the port until its unfortunate demise in 1985. However, despite that fact that much has been written about the shipping ventures founded at Cardiff by Reardon Smith and his contemporaries, comparatively little is known about the actual shipowners themselves as individual human beings. What were their backgrounds? What had led them to become shipowners? What of their families? What were their religious or political affiliations? What did they think of the issues of the day? These are all themes about which we know surprisingly little, largely because the shipowners themselves – with a few exceptions – never bothered to commit such facts and thoughts to any form of record. What we know about them today comes chiefly from incidental documents which provide occasional tantalising insights behind those moustachioed and bearded faces which stare back impassively at us from a century and more ago. This is why the survival of Sir William's unfinished autobiography is a piece of wonderful good fortune for those who wish to know more about one of the giants of Cardiff's shipowning community and it is a privilege for the present author to bring this rare and fascinating piece of writing to the attention of a wider audience in the following pages.

It would have been impossible to produce this volume without the goodwill of present-day members of the Reardon-Smith family. The present baronet (Sir William's great-grandson) and his wife, Sir Antony and Lady Susan Reardon Smith, have been particularly enthusiastic about the project since its inception, welcoming me to their home to discuss their illustrious ancestor. Sir William's granddaughter, Mrs Mary Davies, similarly welcomed me to her home for a pleasant afternoon of reminiscence. Another great-grandson and a friend of many years' standing – John Reardon-Smith – has also been of considerable assistance, as well as being ever ready with cheerful encouragement over an occasional lunch! And from the distaff side of the family, mere words are almost inadequate to express my thanks to Michael Tamlyn, Sir William's great-nephew, whose grandmother was one of Lady Ellen Smith's sisters. From his present home in Topsham near Exeter, he became to all intents and purposes my research assistant in Devon, ever willing to hunt down snippets of information and interview those who remembered Sir William, on my behalf. To Michael and his wife Mary, a huge and very special thank you!

I asked a number of people, some of them professional seafarers and others experts on the maritime history of north Devon, to read through Sir William's original script and offer comments and suggestions. I wish to thank Andrew Bell, Peter Ferguson, Prof. Alston Kennerley, the late Captain Gwyn Pari-Huws, Owain Roberts and my former colleague Donald Taylor for their valuable observations. Other portions of the text have been read by Dr Roy Fenton and Roger Gagg, whilst the whole work has also been read with consummate thoroughness by Emeritus Prof. Sarah Palmer of the Greenwich Maritime Institute and Captain Roy Jenkins. I am deeply grateful to them all for their encouraging comments and constructive criticisms.

I am also grateful to members of staff of the following organisations who have assisted me in my research: Bideford Community Hospital; Bideford Town Council; Bradford Museums, Galleries and Heritage; Bristol Industrial Museum; British Library (Newspapers), Colindale, London; Cardiff Central Reference Library (Local History section); Cardiff Registry Office; Cardiff University Library; Carlyle Society; Chamber of Shipping, London; Duke of Cornwall's Light Infantry Regimental Museum, Bodmin; Glamorgan Record Office, Cardiff; Guildhall Library, City of London; Jersey Maritime Museum, St Helier; Library and Museum of Freemasonry, London; National Archives, Kew; National Library of Wales, Aberystwyth; National Maritime Museum, Greenwich; North Devon Maritime Museum, Appledore; North Devon Record Office, Barnstaple; Royal Northern & Clyde Yacht Club, Helensburgh; Swansea University Library; University of Exeter; West of England Steamship Owners' Protection and Indemnity Association Ltd, Luxembourg; West Glamorgan Record Office, Swansea; World Ship Society.

Amongst my colleagues within Amgueddfa Cymru – National Museum Wales, I wish to thank Peter Bennett, Dr Richard Bevins, Rebecca Brumbill, Carolyn Charles, Tony Daly, Tim Egan, Mark Etheridge, Oliver Fairclough, Mari Gordon, Lowri Jenkins, John Kenyon, Robert Protheroe Jones, Mark Lewis, Steph Mastoris, Judith Martin, Linda Norton, Mark Richards, Clare Smith, Ian Smith, Phil Smith, Kevin Thomas, Jim Wild, Dr Eurwyn Wiliam and John Williams-Davies.

I also wish to thank the late Bob D'Arcy Andrew, Francis Angwin, Harold Appleyard, Ronald Austin, Mary Bird, Peter Bird, David Burrell, Prof. Ian Buxton, David and Jenny Carter, Peter Christie, David Clement, the late Robin Craig, Hannah Cunliffe, Dr Helen Doe, Sybil Edwards, Philip Ford, Sidney Ford, Dr Glyn Tegai Hughes, the late Richard Jenkins and his widow Bethan, the late Chris John, Dr J. Graham Jones, Julianna Jones, Captain Oliver Lindsay, Elgan Lloyd, Louis Loughran, Lord Morgan of Aberdyfi, Captain Ray Newbury, Kevin O'Donoghue, the late John O'Donovan, Alec Osborne, Tony Pawlyn, Gwyn Petty, Dr Siân Phillips, Mr and Mrs P. J. Powell, Larry Robbins, Theo Rye, Prof. Lars Scholl, Dr Huw Walters, Tom and Elizabeth Waters, and the late Desmond I. Williams.

The publication of this book has been supported by the Reardon-Smith Nautical Trust; I am deeply grateful again to John Reardon-Smith and to his fellow trustees for their altruistic gesture. I also acknowledge a huge debt of gratitude to Sarah Lewis and her colleagues at the University of Wales Press for their efficient and enthusiastic co-operation in the production of this book.

All photographs and illustrations, other than those from the collections of Amgueddfa Cymru – National Museum Wales, are individually acknowledged. All financial sums are given in the pre-decimal sterling currency of pounds, shillings and pence (£-s-d), where twelve pennies equalled one shilling, twenty shillings equalled one pound and twenty-one shillings equalled one guinea. The spelling of overseas place names in the manner current during Sir William's lifetime has been retained.

Any mistakes that may remain are my own; I am indebted to everyone who has been of assistance – *diolch yn fawr iawn i bawb*.

David Jenkins
Senior Curator,
National Waterfront Museum
Amgueddfa Cymru – National Museum Wales
2011

INTRODUCTION

O N THE EVENING OF 23 DECEMBER 1935, the shipowner Sir William Reardon Smith died peacefully at his Cardiff home 'Cornborough', surrounded by his family. He was in his eightieth year and had enjoyed reasonably good health all his life; his final illness had been sudden and brief. News of his death naturally figured prominently in the newspapers of south Wales and his native north Devon, and in shipping journals, but his demise was also widely reported in the national and provincial press, ranging from *The Times* and the *Daily Telegraph* to the *Belfast News-letter*, the *East Anglian Daily Times* and the *Edinburgh Evening Dispatch*. All reports drew attention to his remarkable life story, 'a romance from whichever angle it is viewed', as it was described by the *South Wales Echo*. Having gone to sea from his home village of Appledore as a teenage ship's cook, he had died one of the UK's foremost tramp shipowners, a baronet and a revered philanthropist. His particular munificence to the National Museum of Wales, which he had served as both treasurer and president, was much remarked upon, as was his foundation of the Reardon Smith Nautical School in Cardiff.

Perhaps the most perceptive tribute to Sir William appeared in the shipping journal the *Syren & Shipping Illustrated* on New Year's Day, 1936. In this article, deft comparisons were drawn between the careers of Sir William and his slightly older contemporary, the Newcastle shipowner, Walter, first Baron Runciman (1847–1937). Both were natives of seafaring communities (Runciman came from Dunbar on the East Lothian coast), both had gone to sea in their youth, both became master mariners and, eventually, titled shipowners. Unlike Reardon Smith, however, Runciman went into politics, becoming a Liberal MP, and he also published a number of works of autobiography and maritime history, most notably the memoir *Before the mast – and after* (1924) and *Collier Brigs and their Sailors* (1926), a fascinating firsthand account of the east coast coal trade in the days of sail. Although he shared

Runciman's politics, Reardon Smith never showed any inclination to enter Parliament, and whilst he occasionally appeared in print in the south Wales press and shipping journals over the years, there was no evidence to suggest that he had harboured any further literary ambitions.

Only quite recently did it transpire that Reardon Smith had in fact emulated Runciman by embarking upon the writing of his memoirs in the mid-1930s, shortly before his death. At the end of May 1985, nearly fifty years after his death, the shipping company that had been his life's work went into liquidation, succumbing to one of the most profound periods of depression to hit the tramp shipping industry since the bleak days of the early 1930s. The company's last chairman, Mr Robert Chatterton, was most concerned to ensure that the chairman's personal archive relating to the history of the Reardon Smith Line should be secured for posterity, and therefore contacted Dr J. Geraint Jenkins, then curator of the former Welsh Industrial and Maritime Museum, to see if the museum would be interested in acquiring it. Having given an affirmative reply, Dr Jenkins duly dispatched the museum van to the Reardon Smith offices on Greyfriars Road, Cardiff, where the present author was one of the team that secured the archive and brought it back to the museum. The archive consisted chiefly of photographic albums of the many ships that had flown the Reardon Smith houseflag since 1906, together with copies of genealogical records relating to the family. However, also included was a file of forty-four numbered, typed foolscap sheets, from whose contents it became evident that Sir William had indeed made a start upon writing his life story, albeit never completed. Even more interesting was the fact that the archive also comprised copies of letters from Sir William's personal files which provide some indication as to how and why the elderly shipowner had been persuaded to set pen to paper.

From this correspondence, it would appear that a number of anonymous supplicants had already tried, unsuccessfully, to persuade Sir William to write his life story. However, the available evidence, though not conclusive, would appear to suggest that the person who managed to change Sir William's mind was a fellow native of north Devon, Vernon Boyle. Boyle came from an old Bideford seafaring family known to Sir William, and whilst he pursued a career as a teacher at the Perse School in Cambridge, he returned to north Devon whenever he could, eventually retiring to live in Westward Ho! in 1942. Keen yachtsman, talented watercolourist and knowledgeable local historian, in April 1932 Boyle had published an article entitled 'The Bideford Polackers' in the *Mariner's Mirror*, the journal of the Society for Nautical Research. This article dealt with the characteristics of the unique Bideford polacca brigantines, whose peculiar rig had been developed in the late eighteenth and early nineteenth centuries especially to cope with the vagaries of navigating the notorious bar at the mouth of the Taw and Torridge rivers. Boyle appears to have sent Sir William an offprint of his article, and on 24 June, 1932, he received a reply from the Reardon Smith office in Merthyr House in Cardiff's dockland, in which Sir William noted that he, his grandfather and great-uncle had served in various 'polackers'. He went on to point out a number of shortcomings in the article, and included the pithy line, 'It is impossible for a landsman to write about these vessels'. It would also appear that Boyle had suggested that Sir William should write a book about the 'polackers', for the latter concluded his letter with the line, 'A book could be written on these vessels, but I have not the time'.

Boyle did not give up that easily, however, for on 30 June 1932 Sir William was replying to a second letter from him in which Boyle, amongst other things, had obviously suggested that Sir William should write his memoirs. In his reply, Sir William provided Boyle with further details relating to the peculiar rigging of the 'polackers', but also stated, 'I have been offered large sums to write a story of my life and experiences, but much as I should like to do so, I have other things more serious to think about today – keeping our vessels running and people employed'.

It should be borne in mind that this correspondence was taking place against the background of the depths of the depression of the early 1930s, when nearly 2m. gross tons of British shipping (including some Reardon Smith vessels) were laid up on the Fal, in Milford Haven and in many Scottish sea lochs, so Sir William's preoccupation is totally understandable.Nevertheless their correspondence appears to have continued, for a letter to Boyle, dated 22 October 1932, also noted the amount of Sir William's time taken up by his presidency (1929–32) of the National Museum of Wales. At no point in this correspondence did Sir William commit himself to setting down his memoirs, but he did note in his letter of 22 October that his term as president of the museum was to come to an end in three days. Was this a hint that he might have more time in the future to devote to his memoirs?

As stated above, there is no conclusive evidence as to whether or not it was Boyle who successfully persuaded Sir William to set down his memoirs. In addition to the evidence already quoted, however, some clues lie in the 'Introduction' to Reardon Smith's autobiography, which certainly bears no resemblance stylistically to the remainder of the work; the former is effusive and flowing, in direct contrast with Sir William's plain, matter-of-fact prose. This would appear to be Boyle's work, for in 1952 there appeared a volume entitled *Devon Harbours*, written by Vernon Boyle and Donald Payne; the latter wrote on the county's south coast, whilst Boyle contributed the chapters on the north Devon coast between Hartland and Lynmouth. What is significant is that certain passages from the 'Introduction' are repeated almost word for word in Boyle's chapters on Bideford, Appledore and Barnstaple. Add to this Boyle's evident and understandable desire that one of north Devon's most noteworthy seafaring sons should set down his life story for posterity, and on balance it would appear that it is to Vernon Boyle that we should be indebted for encouraging the genesis of this near-unique script.

Much has been written about Cardiff's shipowners, but chiefly from the point of view of the history of their companies and fleets. There has been only one substantial biography that looks at all aspects of a Cardiff ship-owner's life, namely T. C. Wignall's *The Life of Commander Sir Edward Nicholl, RNR, MP*, published in 1921; cringingly obsequious in its tone, it nevertheless casts valuable light upon Nicholl's decision to enter into shipowning in 1903–4. Hardly any of his fellow shipowners bothered at any stage during their careers to set down their memoirs in their own words, but there have been just a few notable exceptions. In the early months of 1921, Charles Evans, the founder of the coal exporters and (later) shipowners Evans & Reid, published some of his wartime recollections in serialised form in the *Western Mail*; these were later consolidated into the prosaicaly titled *Memoirs of Lieutenant-Commander Charles E. Evans* (1946), a compendium of his own previously published recollections and sections written by an anonymous contributor about his naval career and business ventures. More recently, in 1989, the late Desmond Williams, then chairman of Graig Shipping plc, published *Seventy Years in Shipping*, a fascinating and absorbing personal account of the history of the company established by his father in 1919. A combination of biography, autobiography and company history, it provides countless illuminating insights into the varied facets of operating a family-managed tramp shipping firm during the twentieth century. The fact that Sir William's unfinished autobiography is so rare therefore adds considerably to its historical significance, though the story that it tells is in fact quite typical of the experiences of hundreds of young men from the West Country's coastal communities during the latter half of the nineteenth century. The purpose of this introduction, therefore, is not to retell Sir William's story, but to reflect upon the historical significance of certain aspects of his early life as recorded in this fascinating text.

Sir William's native place, the north Devon village of Appledore, can boast an old-established tradition of maritime activity reaching back to medieval times; it was noted as a centre of shipbuilding and maritime trade by John Leland in 1540, and by the early seventeenth century the village's seafarers were crossing the north Atlantic to participate in the Newfoundland cod fishery. In the mid-nineteenth century the port's trade was dominated by the Yeo family, who maintained transatlantic connections through their shipbuilding business on Prince Edward Island. The Cock brothers and John Westacott were the foremost shipbuilders at the port during the latter half of the nineteenth century, by which time a number of local families, through sheer hard work, had scraped together sufficient capital to own and operate modest fleets of coastal sailing vessels. It was on such vessels that Sir William had his first experiences of seafaring in the late 1860s.

During the nineteenth century, therefore, Appledore was a community in which maritime activity was all-embracing, and the inhabitants' outlook set firmly towards the sea, so much so that the village earned itself a not altogether unjustified reputation for hostility to 'landsmen' who dared venture on to its streets. Indeed, a report of the proceedings of the Bideford Magistrates' Court that appeared in the *North Devon Journal* on 11 February 1869 records that the twelve-year-old William was found guilty, with two others, of throwing stones at a certain Philip Gregory, a stranger to the village who was undertaking some repair work on Appledore quay! A five shilling fine was imposed, though the chairman of the bench expressed the opinion that the young miscreants should have been whipped around the village at a cart's tail! Ironically, the young miscreant was destined to join the Cardiff magistrates' bench in 1923! Clearly it was time to find the young lad some gainful employment, but in Appledore, outside seafaring, shipbuilding or fishing, other opportunities were almost nonexistent. Thus, whilst Sir William states in the opening sentence of his autobiography that he had no overwhelming ambition to go to sea, there were in fact no options: 'Strange as it might seem to some, I did not want to go to sea, but there was nothing else to do at Appledore. So I shouldered my burden, conscious of what others had done before me, and started as cook on board the *Unity*.'

No one could be more conscious than the young William of 'what others had done before him', for he came from a long line of seafarers whose roots lay in both County Cork and north Devon. His Irish paternal grandfather, Daniel O'Riordan, had arrived in Appledore in 1796 as a crew member on board the brig-sloop HMS *Weazle*, stationed locally to combat smuggling in the Bristol Channel. William would have been only too aware of the dangers of the sea; his maternal grandfather, Captain Phillip Green, was lost at sea in 1829, whilst he himself – aged just three – had lost both his father and elder brother when the schooner *Hazard* (of which his father was master) was wrecked off Pembrey whilst bound from Llanelli to Appledore with a cargo of anthracite on 31 October 1859, one of over 300 vessels lost around the British Isles at that time in the so-called 'Royal Charter gale'. This tragic event left his disabled mother Elizabeth to earn a living as a dressmaker, employing a number of other women from the village (probably working from their homes) in her business; the future shipowner clearly inherited both a sense of determination and a degree of entrepreneurial skill from this remarkable woman, who died in 1906 having just lived long enough to see her son acquire his first ship. However, having spent a couple of years at sea, chiefly in the coastal trades of the Bristol Channel, and despite the legacy of his family background, the young William clearly overcame his initial reticence about seafaring. By the beginning of the second chapter, he recalls, 'It was my desire, as is undoubtedly in the breast of every boy associated with ships, to go to foreign lands'.

What becomes increasingly clear, therefore, is that even if William was, initially at least, 'pushed' to sea by economic factors, there gradually developed within him an undeniable 'pull' towards seafaring, prompted to a considerable degree by an eager curiosity about the wider world. Here again he was echoing Walter Runciman, who wrote in an early autobiographical work, *Windjammers and Steam Tramps*,

> [the seamen] were usually the sons of poor parents, living for the most part in obscure villages and small towns bordering on the sea, which sea blazed into their minds aspirations to get aboard some of the vessels that passed their homes one way or the other all day long. The notion of becoming anything but sailors never entered their heads.

Both Walter Runciman and William Reardon Smith participated in a gradual change in patterns of seafaring that emerged during the nineteenth century, reflecting the growth of the British merchant fleet at that time. Between 1850 and 1900, Britain's foreign trade doubled in both value and bulk, and the British merchant fleet was the foremost in the world, controlling some 54 per cent of the globe's entire tonnage in 1870. As the century progressed, it came to be manned to an increasing degree by seafarers whose homes were not in the great port cities, but in some of the UK's most remote, non-industrialised coastal communities. Whether in the West Country, north and west Wales, north Yorkshire, East Lothian or the Western Isles, the same pattern could be identified, whereby seamen from those areas (whose local maritime economies were often in decline as the railway advanced its lines) were drawn instead to crew fleets based at the foremost ports of the British Isles, such as London, Bristol, Cardiff, Liverpool, Newcastle and Glasgow. And it was to one such port, Newport in south Wales, that Reardon Smith travelled in 1872 to undertake his first foreign passage, joining the wooden ship *Ocean Pearl* as an ordinary seaman (OS); she was bound for New Orleans with a cargo of railway rails, a major Welsh export at that time. By the end of his first deep-sea voyage, the young William had evidently acquired a taste for foreign lands and could not wait to go back to sea; he also tellingly mentions that life in Appledore in those days was not as pleasant as one might think whilst wandering its picturesque 'drangs' (narrow alleyways) nowadays: 'There were not the comforts that exist today and food was at that time poor. There was nothing else for me to do but go to sea.'

It was another of the ports of industrial south Wales, Swansea, to which Reardon Smith turned to find a berth for his second foreign voyage, joining the Bideford-built barque *Scout* as an OS in August 1872. Owned by Henry Bath of Swansea, the *Scout* was one of the famed 'Swansea copper ore barques', bound for Chile with a cargo of coal and generals. This voyage would have involved rounding Cape Horn deep-laden in both directions – coal out, copper ore home – but the *Scout's* passages through those infamous seas, which often figure so prominently in maritime writing, are barely mentioned by Reardon Smith; he simply mentions 'making a very good passage'. This may be explained by the fact that the more difficult westward passage would have been undertaken when there was a far better chance of reasonably calm weather off the Horn during the southern hemisphere's summer, for he later makes reference in some detail to a storm and the damage experienced during a subsequent voyage on board the *Viscount Canning*. Also notable is the relatively lengthy period that the *Scout* spent tramping along the Chilean and Peruvian coasts with cargoes of coal and copper ore before finally loading copper regulus for home; it was October 1873 before she passed Mumbles Head once more.

After such an extended absence, three months' coasting in the Bristol Channel as an able-bodied seaman (AB) aboard the schooner *Caroline* provided a contrasting interlude for Reardon Smith before he sailed away deep-sea once more. After a transatlantic voyage from Bristol to Doboy on the Georgia coast on the ship *Viscount Canning* to load timber, he joined the barquentine *Jane* as an AB in August 1874; she was loading coal for Cadiz at Cardiff. Seamen from the West Country were prominent amongst the crews of both vessels, providing a further indication of the growing presence of seamen from the area in the British merchant service at that time; the master and a number of the crew of the *Viscount Canning* came from Appledore, whilst Reardon Smith's surviving elder brother, John, was second mate of the *Jane*. Having discharged her coal cargo at Cadiz, the *Jane* then loaded salt for Newfoundland, destined to be used to salt cod caught on the Grand Banks. Cod – beheaded, cleaned, boned, salted and air-dried, and also known as stockfish – had long been an important element in the diet of many African, American and European countries prior to the advent of refrigeration, especially in warmer climates where the Catholic practice of abstaining from meat and eating fish on Fridays was observed; as stated above, Appledore mariners had been involved in the transportation of this commodity since the early seventeenth century. The fact that the fish had to be loaded in countless tiny creeks (known as 'tickles') on Canada's northeastern seaboard, and the time-consuming and labour-intensive stowage and discharge of this cargo meant that this trade had become the preserve of smaller wooden merchant sailing vessels from Scotland, north Wales, the West Country and Newfoundland itself by the late nineteenth century. At a mere 211 nett tons, the *Jane* was typical of the vessels employed in this trade.

Reardon Smith's next deep-sea voyage saw him involved in the latter days of a remarkable transatlantic maritime business that also had strong connections with Appledore. During the second and third quarters of the nineteenth century, the construction of wooden sailing vessels for the British market was an important business along the north-eastern seaboard of the USA and Canada, and one of the foremost shipbuilding centres was Prince Edward Island. It was to this island that James Yeo (1789–1868), a native of Kilkhampton near Bude, had emigrated in 1827, and by a combination of sheer hard work, ruthless determination and not a little subterfuge, he soon established himself as one of the island's foremost businessmen, combining the skills of timber-feller, farmer, fisherman, merchant, shipbuilder and shipowner. Yeo's three sons – William, James junior and John – joined their father to run his business empire, with William later returning to north Devon and settling in Appledore to act as his father's British agent. A man of single-minded application comparable to that of his father, William Yeo transformed, indeed came to dominate, the economic life of Appledore, building the substantial Richmond dry-dock at which roughly finished vessels from the Yeo enterprise on Prince Edward Island were completed before being sold on to British owners.

William Yeo had died in 1872, but the high freight rates prevailing in the early 1870s saw a rush of orders for new tonnage, leading to what would prove to be the last flourish of large-scale wooden shipbuilding on the island. There was no shortage of timber on Prince Edward Island, but the metal fittings and rigging with which wooden vessels were typically being fitted from the mid-nineteenth century onwards had to be imported to the island from the UK. In April 1875, therefore, the eighteen-year-old Reardon Smith joined the Yeo-owned brig *Lucille* as an AB at Bristol. Fully laden with a cargo of anchors, blocks, cables, castings, fixtures and wire rigging, she also carried a larger crew than would normally have been the case, both to provide gangs to rig the vessels to be completed for Yeo interests on the island that summer and to provide the skilled core of the crews that would sail them on their maiden voyages back across the Atlantic. There were seven Yeo-built vessels awaiting completion on Prince Edward Island in the summer of 1875, all at various locations scattered around Cascumpec Bay and Malpeque Bay at the western end of the island. Living in a bunkhouse near the Yeo homestead at Port Hill, Reardon Smith and his fellow riggers travelled to each vessel in turn, carrying all the fittings required in horse-drawn wagons. He eventually returned across the Atlantic in the barque *Milo*, the last of the seven Yeo vessels to leave the island that year before winter truly set in. Although typically terse and matter of fact, Reardon Smith's firsthand description of shipbuilding on nineteenth century Prince Edward Island is nevertheless a truly unique account of the Indian summer of a once-great enterprise.

Reardon Smith returned to sea as an AB in the barque *Souvenir*, but the voyage merits little attention in his autobiography, despite the fact that the vessel had apparently been given up for lost in a storm in the English

Channel. Upon his return to the UK (discharging sugar from the West Indies at Leith), Reardon Smith took the first step in the progression of his sea-faring career when he applied to take his examination as second mate. Compulsory examinations for foreign-going officers in the British merchant fleet had been introduced on 1 January 1851 under the terms of the previous year's Mercantile Marine Act, and sailors applying to be examined also had to submit a certified record of their voyages to that date to prove their sea-going experience. Although it is not made explicit in the autobiography, it seems likely that Reardon Smith probably spent about a fortnight attending a navigational school at Leith, where he consolidated the knowledge gained from both his practical sea-going experience and detailed study of his prized copy of James Inman's *Navigational and Nautical Astronomy for the Use of British Seamen*. His application brought him success, and by October 1876 he was second mate of the large wooden ship *Vermont*, sailing from Appledore to Cardiff in ballast to load coal for Singapore. Unlike his previous voyage in the *Souvenir*, he describes the eventful sixteen-month passage on the *Vermont* in great detail – the rumours about the Greek crew, running aground in the Bangka Straits and the resulting extensive repair work, sails rotting in the humidity of the Siamese monsoon season and the painfully slow passage home, when his ship was once more given up as lost. Little wonder that he left the *Vermont* at the first opportunity and went to Plymouth to study for his first mate's certificate.

The Plymouth School of Navigation had opened in 1863, and was generally known as 'the Merrifield school' after its remarkable first principal, John Merrifield. Most of its students would have been preparing for masters' and mates' certificates and would have spent just a few weeks at the school, 'cramming' for the all-important examinations. Once again Reardon Smith was successful in his examinations, and in April 1878 he was invited to join the wooden barque *Mary Hogarth*, then loading coal at Penarth dock, as chief officer; 'after a short holiday, I was sent for by a friend to join the *Mary Hogarth* of the firm of Hugh Hogarth and Sons'.

He was destined to remain with this company for the next eighteen years, but it is unfortunate that Reardon Smith is rather vague in his explanation of how he came to obtain a post with Hugh Hogarth of Ardrossan on the Clyde, whose company's traditional preference was for Scottish masters and officers. One can but conjecture as to the identity of the 'friend' who had recommended the young Devonian officer to the hard-headed Scots Presbyterian chandler-turned-shipowner, but it was the beginning of a professional relationship that would last into the 1890s. Over the ensuing years, Reardon Smith would be entrusted with the command, and overseeing the construction, of a number of Hogarth vessels, both sail and steam, an experience which would prove to be an invaluable training for him in his future career as a shipowner. He also appears to have introduced his brother John to the company, for he was made chief officer of a Hogarth steamer, the *Baron Clyde*, in 1888. Hogarth encouraged the efficient operation of his ships by offering officers the opportunity to invest in sixty-fourth shares in the vessels on which they sailed; Reardon Smith was swift to take advantage of this offer, which in turn enabled him to lay down the foundations of the capital that he would one day invest in his own first steamer. Hugh Hogarth came to visit the *Mary Hogarth* at Cardiff at the end of Reardon Smith's first voyage as chief officer and, obviously appreciative of the young officer's talents, he 'spoke very encouragingly to me, stating that if I remained, I would never regret it'.

Leaving the vessel to study for his master's certificate, Reardon Smith once more attended the Plymouth School of Navigation, where he was successful in his examinations on 6 June 1879. He was only twenty-two years of age. He then returned to Hogarth's where, as was often the case at that time with a newly qualified master, he was not immediately given a command, going back to sea as chief officer of the Neyland-built Hogarth barque *Cyprus*. Reardon Smith undertook just one voyage to the Far East in the *Cyprus* before leaving the vessel on the River Tyne to return to Appledore for his wedding. The autobiography is unfortunately most unforthcoming on any details of what must have been a very occasional and intermittent courtship with Ellen Hamlyn of 25 Market Street, Appledore, who was a year his junior. As a fellow native of Appledore she was only too familiar with the lot of the seafarer's wife, bringing up a family alone in the absence of her husband; particularly poignant for her must have been the tragic loss of their first son, Thomas Hamlyn Smith, who died on 12 November 1883, aged a mere sixteen months. He had been ill for twelve days with acute hydrocephalus. Reardon Smith makes no mention of this grievous event in the autobiography, but he does tell us that his wife occasionally joined him at sea, and he also praises her thrifty management of their joint finances, particularly the shares that they owned in various ships of which Reardon Smith was master: 'With such a good wife, it did not take me long to pay off these shares, in fact these ships earned their first cost in five years.'

This was a theme to which Reardon Smith would return many times in subsequent years; interviewed for the *Western Mail* when he had collected some £18,000 towards the establishment of what would eventually become the Reardon Smith Nautical School in 1921, he stated,

> When I married I made a good choice. Living in Devonshire and obtaining a command at an early age, we were soon able to save a little. We invested it in the ships and steamers I commanded, so that we might have a comfortable income when I retired . . . it was the early habit of saving which enabled me to acquire the thirty-four steamers I now control.

Returning to sea after his wedding, Reardon Smith joined the Hogarth barque *Drumadoon* as chief officer in July 1880; he was eventually given command of the vessel in October the following year, aged only twenty-five. He remained her master for a year, undertaking tramping voyages to the Far East and south and north America. Then, in October 1882, he was asked to come ashore to superintend the construction of the iron sailing ship *Macrihanish*, to be built for Hogarth's by Robert Duncan of Port Glasgow.

In 1881, the voyage of the triple-expansion-engined steamer *Aberdeen* from London to Melbourne, with just one brief bunkering stop and achieving prodigious economy in fuel consumption, signalled that the days of the deep-sea merchant sailing vessel were numbered. Indeed, Hogarth's had acquired their first three steamships in 1881–3, but despite this Hugh Hogarth was clearly still convinced of the efficacy of large iron and steel sailing vessels in the deep-sea bulk trades, for the *Macrihanish* was to be the first of six such vessels built for the company over the following decade. As Reardon Smith himself notes, the *Macrihanish* was far and away the best known of these Hogarth sailing vessels, having a reputation for making exceptionally fast passages, and he was particularly proud to have been appointed master of such a fine vessel. However, he undertook just one voyage to the Far East as her master before being sent out to Halifax, Nova Scotia, in September 1884, where he was to assume command of a steamer for the first time, albeit under somewhat unusual circumstances. The vessel had been aground in the area and had been repaired, but her crew had refused to man her on her voyage back to the UK, believing her to be unseaworthy. In the meantime, the mortgagees had seized the steamer to protect their investment and approached Hugh Hogarth to organise her return; he delegated the task to the twenty-eight-year-old Reardon Smith. Reardon Smith does not mention the vessel's name, but it has been possible to deduce that she was the iron steamer *Colonsay*, owned by J. Allan & Co. of Glasgow, and barely two years old at that time. It was a considerable challenge, made difficult not least by the members of her former crew warning of dire consequences should the vessel set sail back across the Atlantic with her cargo of timber. Nevertheless, he succeeded in mustering a crew and bringing the vessel back to Avonmouth with comparatively little trouble, doubtless convincing Hogarth that he was 'a safe pair of hands' in the process.

Having brought the *Colonsay* episode to a successful conclusion, Hogarth sent Reardon Smith back to Robert Duncan's Port Glasgow shipyard to oversee the construction of the next two sailing vessels ordered by the company, the barques *Ochtertyre* and *Corryvrechan*. Representing an owner's interests at the shipyard could be a difficult and exacting task, often involving protracted (and doubtless, at times, heated!) discussions to ensure that his requirements were met to the last letter. The reader is told nothing of this, but Reardon Smith must have been a thorough superintendent, for the two vessels were economically successful, both paying for themselves within five years of entering service with Hogarth's. Appointed master of the *Ochtertyre* in September 1885, his years in command of this vessel were largely successful, though Reardon Smith apparently failed to recall one embarrassing incident that took place on New Year's Day, 1888 (reported in *Lloyd's List* on 6 February that year), when the *Ochtertyre* ran aground on the Baragua Flat off the Irrawady delta; she floated off and arrived safely in Rangoon five days later. More pleasant to recall was an exceptionally profitable voyage from Hamburg to Sydney and back to London in 1888–9, when a dividend of 42½ per cent was earned. He remained master of the *Ochtertyre* for almost five years, his longest period in command of one vessel. It is also interesting to note that some of the facts that Reardon Smith included in his text about Hogarth's sailing ships appear to have been taken from the first volume of Basil Lubbock's classic *Last of the Windjammers*, first published in 1927.

By 1890 there were six steamers in the Hogarth fleet, and in June that year Reardon Smith was appointed to command the largest of them, the 2700 gross ton *Baron Douglas*. He speaks frankly about his regrets at leaving sailing vessels, appearing somewhat ill at ease with the fact that he now had to rely upon engineers and firemen to provide the vessel's motive power, whereas the progress of a sailing vessel under his command had depended entirely upon his judgement of the wind, currents and sea conditions prevailing at the time. He would command two further Hogarth steamers before he left the company in 1896. Whilst his recitation of the barest facts relating to voyage after voyage undertaken in the early 1890s makes somewhat repetitive reading, the number of ports that he visited and the variety of cargoes carried during those years is quite remarkable, reflecting the fact that the development of telegraphy to arrange charters world-wide was as important a step forward in the history of tramp shipping as was the widespread adoption of the efficient triple-expansion marine steam engine. Cotton from New Orleans to Le Havre; cereals from the Black Sea to Rotterdam; jute from Calcutta to Dundee; rice from Rangoon to Bremerhaven; salt from Aden to Calcutta; tinplate from Swansea to Batum: these were the classic trades of the tramp steamer. Knowing when and where which cargoes were ready for export, being aware of the various circumstances prevailing at countless ports world-wide and building up a knowledge of steaming times between those ports were all essential skills for the successful shipowner, enabling him to have his ships strategically placed to maximise their trading potential and profitability. These years truly constituted incomparable training for Reardon Smith's future career.

Reardon Smith's autobiography ceases in 1895; it can only be assumed that he was still writing these memoirs at the time of his death in 1935. It is tantalising to think how much more interesting his autobiography would have been had he been able to complete it, for there are many aspects of his subsequent life (especially the total extent of his activities between his retirement from the sea in 1900 and the establishment of the Instow Steamship Co. Ltd in May 1905) of which the present author would dearly love to know more! However, it would certainly appear that his intention was to finish the autobiography and publish it, for in the summer of 2005, his great-grandson John Reardon-Smith came across a handwritten list entitled 'Photographs for Book' – as many as possible have been included amongst this publication's many illustrations. The editing of Sir William's text has been very light, and extensive footnotes have been provided to explain maritime terms and elucidate certain passages in greater detail. The volume concludes with a comprehensive essay tracing Sir William's life from 1895 until his death forty years later, together with numerous appendices, line drawings and maps relevant to his life and career.

Sir William Recollects, 1870-95

Introduction

SONS OF THE SEA[1]

D EVONSHIRE HAS EVERY REASON to be proud of its maritime record and has been aptly described as the 'forcing house of Empire'. Drake, Raleigh, Grenville, Frobisher and Hawkins are amongst the sons of the sea that have contributed to our illustrious history. The sturdy sons of Devon left their rich land to adventure in far off countries and stout hearts manned 'the King's Navee', taking no mean part in the frustration of hostile designs and in laying the foundation of Empire. Peace hath its victories no less renowned than war, and at the head of many shipowning and commercial firms are Devonshire men whose dominating perseverance and financial courage have resulted in the building up of successful enterprises which have given regular and lucrative employment to many thousands of workers and materially helped to advance the general prosperity of the country.

Sir William Reardon Smith, Bart, the head of the largest fleet of modern cargo carriers in Wales and the west of England, is one of Devonshire's successful men, rising from humble and difficult circumstances to pre-eminence in the shipping and commercial world. Born at Appledore in 1856, he was raised in an atmosphere of schooners, ketches and yawls, imbued with the spirit of the sea and the traditions that this sleepy port still honours. Appledore owed its significance in the early days to the Newfoundland fisheries. The 'silver estuary', as Kingsley described it, is replete with romantic history.[2] Its sons were foremost in beating off piratical raids in the early days. It contributed ships towards the defence of the realm; 'Of the five ships which went over the Bar to join Sir Francis Drake at Plymouth at least one went from Appledore' wrote Phillip Wyot, the town clerk of Barnstaple in his diary in 1588.[3] In Elizabethan days, graceful ships set sail to America and Newfoundland for cod and tobacco until piratical raids and the American War brought this trade to an end. Circumstances, however, never destroyed the spirit of the sea, and small boats ventured forth while sturdy sons forged ahead in consonance with the increasing development of maritime trade. Today Appledore is left behind in [the] great march of progress, but its cobbled streets, it old-world air and its honourable traditions remain to delight present day tourists.

Sir William was born of old seafaring stock; both his father and grandfather were sailors. His paternal grandfather was born in County Cork, his name being Daniel O'Riordan who came of old Irish stock. The O'Riordans or Reardons are an old Irish family descending from a *Righchordan* or Royal Bard. The word is derived from the Gaelic *righ*, a king and *chordan*, a bard or minstrel. The muted consonants in Irish are so many that Riordan was practically the ancient sound.[4] The family became armorial and their descendants were fine sailors, taking an active part in beating off the piratical raids of the French and Dutch off Lundy Island. The name 'Smith' was adopted by Daniel O'Riordan who visited Appledore in HMS *Weazle* in 1796[5] and he was ultimately transferred to HMS *Romulus* which was sent to the Nile during those troubled times.[6] He married the daughter of Captain Edward Gay of Bideford and both went to the Nile; they eventually had three sons and two daughters. Their eldest son born on board HMS *Romulus* was appropriately christened Owen Nile Reardon, and having been born under the flag on His Majesty's ship was duly accorded those traditional rights and distinctions which followed such an interesting event, namely the Master's Certificate of Servitude.[7]

Sir William's father was born at Appledore in 1809 and his mother, who came of well-known Devonshire stock, in 1813. His maternal grandfather was Captain Phillip Green of Appledore who was lost at sea in 1829, leaving a son and two daughters. Sir William's mother was born a cripple, and under such circumstances was taught the art of tailoring, which she plied with vigour after the loss of her husband in 1859. Employing women and battling against odds, she succeeded in bringing up a family of eight – three sons and five daughters.[8] The three sons took to the sea, and Captain John R. Smith commanded the first steamer of the Reardon Smith fleet, the *City of Cardiff*; he died in 1926 at the age of seventy-three. He lived to see the rapid growth of a modern fleet under the fostering care of his brother, Sir William Reardon Smith, and the organising abilities of his sons, Mr Willie and Mr Douglas Smith, and Mr A. J. Popham, who in 1914 married Sir William's second daughter.

Sir William was brought up at Appledore in the days when free education was unknown. At the Wesleyan Day School, under an old time tutor named Maunder, he was initiated into the mysteries of the 'three Rs', but much of his education was due to the private education of his mother, a remarkable lady of erudition and forcefulness of character. The time came when William Reardon Smith had to contribute towards his own livelihood, and at the early age of fourteen it was incumbent upon him to commence his career. The options open to him at Appledore were limited. There was of course the sea which had claimed many of his forbears, and it was to the sea that he took. Sir William, in reminiscent mood and with clarity remarkable in one past the three score years and ten, describes his first essay into working life. With pardonable pride he recounts his early struggles, the chapters following being replete with exceptional interest.

Chapter 1
I GO TO SEA

STRANGE AS IT MIGHT SEEM to some, I never wanted to go to sea, but there was little else to do at Appledore. So I shouldered my burden, conscious of what others had done before me and started as cook on board the smack *Unity*.[9] Appledore bar was crossed on 6 September 1870 and sails were set, with the wind being south and fresh, and with a nasty ground swell. I felt none too well on the commencement of my first voyage, but was not really seasick. I was put to peel potatoes, and having

Appledore quay as Reardon Smith would have known it in his youth. (National Maritime Museum, Greenwich, London)

A cartoon of Reardon Smith, wearing an 'Appledore frock' (the village's traditional knitted pullover) and peeling potatoes on board the Unity, *produced at the time of the firm's 'coming of age' celebratory dinner held at the Angel Hotel, Cardiff, on* 18 *December,* 1926. (Sir Antony and Lady Susan Reardon Smith)

no knowledge of this work, I peeled them too thick. The captain's idea of economy did not concur with mine and he peeled the potatoes himself. Ever after, this experience has stood me in good stead all my life, for it taught me the successful division of labour and never to do any work which could be more adequately accomplished by others. It was also indelibly impressed upon my mind that it is necessary to know how to do things myself, and so began my seafaring education.

After rounding Baggy Point and Morte Point, the wind freshened and became strong off the land. We got through at last, but instead of going to Newport where we were bound, we anchored at Cardiff East and during the night threw the ballast out. Now the reason for this is that it is a time-honoured practice that still prevails today in the management of coasting ships owned at Appledore. The owner gets one-third of the freight and keeps his vessel in trading condition, the captain gets two-thirds and out of this has to pay for the handling of the ballast taken on board, wages, food, port charges and all items pertaining to the vessel and its cargoes. Naturally the captain did not want the ballast and food bill to be too heavy.[10]

Both the captain and the mate were fine Devonshire sailors. The captain was a noted character; he could chew and smoke tobacco at the same time. The mate was his brother-in-law, and, as in other families, they disagreed very much. Although a small boy at the time, I was often called upon to decide between them. The varied experience I derived in these small vessels was of great use in my later life. The sailors in those days were hardy; they would stand at the tiller for days and nights on end and could, with very little rest, keep awake for just as long. Bad weather, wet clothing, and other experiences did not affect them.

Seine netting for salmon on the estuary of the Torridge. (National Maritime Museum, Greenwich, London)

I left that vessel in the following spring to go salmon fishing and for quite a good reason, in as much as directly the vessel returned to Bideford, both food and wages were stopped.[11] Sometimes these vessels would be in port a full week or more, and I thought that by salmon fishing I would better myself. Shortly, however it became necessary to look for another berth and I eventually secured one as cook on the sailer *Seraphina*.[12]

The captain on this vessel was a very fine, sturdy, independent Devonian. By trade he was a blacksmith, and I believe did well at his business in Appledore for some years, but as in many others at Appledore the call of the sea was strong and insistent and he thought he would advance his interests by venturing into shipowning. My remembrance of this man is strong – he used to bake good cake! This qualification appealed to me forcibly as a boy, and every Sunday when he used to bake the cake was a day I looked forward to, eating as much as I could get. Leaving this vessel I joined the sailer, *Joe Abraham*,[13] a polacker schooner. This vessel was built at Prince Edward Island, and although only sixty tons, sailed across the Atlantic some years previously. It was always thought at that time that nothing but a polacker schooner could beat out over the Appledore bar.[14] A period spent salmon fishing after leaving the *Joe Abraham* in the following September found me desirous of venturing further afield.

The 'Bideford polacca brigantine' Swan *under tow out of the* West Bute Dock, Cardiff *in the 1870s; note the 'pole' fore-mast that was typical of these vessels. The position taken by the photographer is today just in front of the foyer of the Wales Millennium Centre!*

Chapter 2

THE AMERICAN TRADES

IT WAS MY DESIRE, as is undoubtedly in the breast of every boy associated with ships, to go to foreign lands. Fired by this ambition, in February of 1872 I joined a fine ship called the *Ocean Pearl*[15] of 965 tons, sailing from Newport with a cargo of railway iron for New Orleans. At that time nearly all the rails for the Southern Pacific Railway went from this country.[16] She was the only ship I ever sailed in that had two reefs in the upper topsails.[17] I worked very hard discharging rails in New Orleans, helping to roll them along to the main hatch and slinging them. From New Orleans, the ship went in ballast to Pensacola and loaded a cargo of pitch pine for Liverpool. After the logs were loaded, we had to go down into the holds and roll them up in the wings.[18] It was a great delight to me to hear the coloured folk – the stevedore's men – singing:

> The sun is down in the hold below,
> Sundown, sundown, below;
> Six o'clock we will work no more,
> Sundown, sundown, below!

I could sing it with great gusto!

From Pensacola we had a very fair passage to Liverpool. The ship's officers were instructed by the captain to place me at the wheel to steer. This helped me considerably and I took my duty seriously. We arrived back in the month of August and the owner of the vessel having died, we were paid off and I went on to Appledore. I soon wanted to get away again. There were not the comforts that exist today and food was at that time poor. There was nothing else for me to do but go to sea. I knew my forefathers were good sailors and knew the art of building ships and rigging them, and my ambition was to be as good a sailor as they were. I was determined to make good.

The town and anchorage of Coquimbo, Chile, to which Reardon Smith sailed from Swansea in the Scout *in* 1872. (National Maritime Museum, Greenwich, London)

My next ship was the *Scout*,[19] one of Bath's copper ore traders, which I joined at Swansea.[20] The captain was a West Countryman, and we sailed for Coquimbo with a full crew, two passengers and a cargo consisting of coal, coke and generals, making a very good passage. At Coquimbo we discharged most of the general cargo and then went to Caldera and discharged the coal and coke. We partly loaded up with copper ores and went up the coast towards Peru, finishing loading at Paposa in Chile. The vessel was loaded from lighters, the ores being brought from the mines on the backs of mules. The lighters drew alongside and the cargo was hove up by hand winch and dumped into the holds, all this heavy work being accomplished by the crew.

After the vessel was loaded we sailed for Lota and discharged down the coast, the cargo again being winched up and dumped into lighters. We were some time discharging as the *lancheros* had customs which prevented regularity of work.[21] They would not get their pay until Friday, and spent their money on the following Saturday. On Sunday, Monday and sometimes Tuesday, they would absent themselves from work and generally on Wednesday a start was made. Thus the winches were scarcely worked more than three days a week, a circumstance which gives food for thought when contemplating the wealth of nations and how communities prosper.

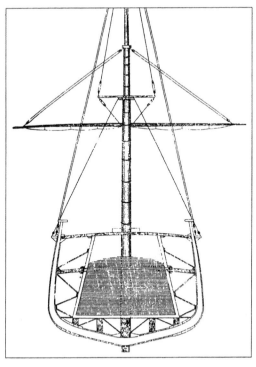

A cross-section of a 'Swansea-fitted' ship, showing the longitudinal trunk installed in the holds to raise the centre of gravity of the dense copper ore cargo.

From Lota we sailed to Loteria, between Lota and Coronel, and loaded a full cargo of coal;[22] we then set sail for Carrizal, discharged our cargo and loaded a full cargo of copper regulus for home.[23] The loading of copper regulus was interesting, for before operations commenced it was necessary to build a wood trunk.[24] These copper ore vessels were built with five high keelsons laid with flooring planks, and from the wing keelsons to the deck there were uprights of wood forming a trunk. Those we shored from the side, and every time during the homeward passage when bad weather was encountered, we ordinary seamen used to go below with the carpenter to see the keelsons and examine the trunk, to see whether it was weakened in any way. After a passage of ninety days we arrived at Swansea and from there I returned to Appledore by packet boat to Ilfracombe[25] and on a carriage to Barnstaple, where my mother had travelled, anxious to meet me after my venture to the Pacific.

It was not long, however, before I was again away, this time in the ship *Viscount Canning.*[26] She was an Indian teak-wood ship, in past days considered a very fine craft, and in my time was engaged in the timber trade. We left Bristol for the American trade, bound to a little-used port called Doboy, to approach which we had to cross Tybee bar. After levelling the ballast we commenced taking in pitch pine logs as cargo. The crew did the topping up and the coloured folk the stowing in the hold, and as was customary we had to go below to 'wing out', i.e. to roll the logs up in the wing. It was hard work, but to the crew of the young people of Appledore like myself, it was a delightful task as we could join in the songs sung by the coloured folk. Truly, a merry heart goes all day and a sad one tires in a mile.

The captain of this vessel was from Appledore, a great disciplinarian, and like his father before him, well-known in the American trade. During the homeward passage we met with a very severe gale, and had to heave to under main topsails. The vessel was strained so badly that the crew was kept at the pumps nearly all the night.[27] During the night she fell over on her side after a squall; the deck load on one side lifted and some of the running gear which was not securely fastened up got under the logs.[28] When daylight came and we set sail, we found a lot of this gear had to be cut.

Arriving back at Bristol I did not go to Appledore, but travelled to Cardiff and joined a barquentine belonging to Bowring,[29] called the *Jane*, of which my elder brother was second mate.[30] We loaded in Cardiff for Cadiz where we discharged a coal cargo and loaded salt on the owner's account for Newfoundland, the crew performing all the discharging and loading.

On arriving at Newfoundland we found that the *Jane* had been sold by Bowrings to the Tessier family.[31] This firm had had several vessels built for it previously by Cox and Son of Cleave Houses, between Appledore and Bideford.[32] Cox and Son were noted builders and the yard exists at the present time. After the salt was discharged, we loaded stockfish for the Brazils in white drums, every care being exercised that no stains got on the drums.[33] We made a very long passage down owing to the south-easterly wind. The captain was a West Countryman, several of whose family had served Bowrings for some years. His name was Walter Williams and shortly afterwards, whilst captain of the *Hamlet*, owned by Bowrings, [he] was lost at sea. On account of the heat the cargo was worked during the night and we had to take the lighters to the customs every morning. At that time the yellow fever was raging very badly, but fortunately we escaped sickness.

We then loaded sugar for New York and had a fair passage to this port. The American builders had considerable praise for our craft and thought she was a beautiful vessel. After discharging the sugar we loaded a cargo for [the] owner's account. We experienced a very bad passage from New York to Newfoundland, and as a consequence of the amount of sugar the crew had been eating and the very bad weather they were forced to put up with, they all more or less suffered from boils. At Newfoundland, my brother and I decided to leave and go home. We shipped in a brigantine loaded with seal oil, skins etc., for Bristol, from which port we went to Appledore.

Chapter 3

LEARNING SHIPBUILDING AND RIGGING

L ATER ON IN THE SPRING OF 1875, I joined a brig called the *Lucille*[34] belonging to an old family in Appledore and Prince Edward Island named Yeo.[35] We loaded at Bristol for Prince Edward Island with a full cargo of ship material, consisting of metal, wire rigging and materials for rigging and building of ships at ports on the island.

This was a great experience and one never to be forgotten. With youthful vigour and enthusiasm, I learnt how to construct wooden vessels and how to rig them. Picked men from the crew were consigned to work on the island and lived at a place called Port Hill, in bunks as on shipboard.[36] A cook was shipped at Bristol for our culinary requirements whilst on the island, and we were lucky to have a very good dining room with sleeping accommodation upstairs. Whilst we had plenty of work, we also had plenty of food. We fitted all the ships' rigging, constructed the blocks and did all the serving of the rigging and the brace pendants.[37] When a ship was ready to be launched, we would go to such places as Egmont Bay, Grand River, Alberton, and Cascumpec. We travelled to all these shipbuilding yards by horse and wagon, taking the rigging with us and assisting in the launching of the vessels. Sometimes we would fix the bowsprit and the masts before launching and other times, where the water was shallow, we would fix after the launching.

We went from port to port launching and rigging, an experience that I thoroughly enjoyed. We sang at our work and obviously it was a sailor's song, generally alphabetical as a rule, commencing on lines such as the following:

A stands for anchors that bring our ship to,
B stands for bowsprit shipped o'er the bow,
C stands for capstan that we walk around,
D stands for derrick that hoists in the rum

and similar alphabetical ditties!

So to the accompaniment of a rollicking old sea song the work went on. It was a wonderful experience. The food was good but it was nearly all salted, and a considerable number suffered from scurvy as a consequence.[38] After finishing the rigging of the last barque, the *Milo*,[39] we loaded this with birch, oats and stock fish for Bridgwater.

This was quite a hard passage since the vessel was leaky and needed continuous pumping.[40] We left late in November, got down to the bar at Malpeque and found that we could not get over.[41] Our anchor was frozen up for weeks and when the ice gave way we found we had no water but we decided to go to sea, saving all the snow and putting it in the water cask. The vessel's sides were several inches thick with ice, which we saved for water to take us to Bridgwater. On the night we left Malpeque it was blowing very hard and with the salt we had, an endeavour was made to thaw the ropes in the blocks. Unfortunately during the night the barrel capsized and the salt was lost. We had a very hard experience in getting out of the Gulf and more than once were very near the land, but after getting past St Paul's in the Gulf we had a reasonable passage home.[42] After being paid off at Bridgwater, I went home.

I then spent a few months trading on the coast with a dear old cousin of mine, visiting such ports as Lydney, Newport, Swansea and Neath, taking coals and culm in a coastwise schooner.[43] Afterwards I shipped as an AB in the barque *Souvenir*[44] that had capsized on the Scarweather Sands. This vessel, after drifting about the Channel for some time, was salved, taken to Appledore, re-masted and fitted and bought by a Bristol firm. I made a trip to the West Indies in that vessel and on account of bad weather in the Channel was given up as lost. We ultimately arrived at Barbados, however, and from there we had orders to go to Ponce on the island of Puerto Rico and load sugar for Leith. During this time I determined to improve my knowledge of navigation and took with me *Inman's Navigation Guide*.[45]

Chapter 4

SECOND MATE AT TWENTY YEARS OF AGE

I OWED MUCH TO *Inman's Navigation Guide*, which was a very fine book. I read, marked, learned and inwardly digested all that appertained to navigation. There were not such facilities in those days as exist at the present time. I learnt the semaphore and distance signals whilst on board the *Souvenir*.[46] A piece of wood fastened to the bulkhead was used for distance signals and I learnt by this contrivance with the aid of my AB friend who made the signals for me to interpret.[47] By this method I mastered the various signals, whilst every other spare moment was given to the study of navigation. I was not paid off with much at Leith and it was customary for me to give my mother half pay. I had therefore to husband my monetary resources very carefully. The result of my hard and continuous study at sea found me well equipped for the examination, and in a week or two I passed out as second mate. This was in the year 1876. I lost no time in going down to Appledore, and in the dry dock I found a large American ship being reclassed and reconditioned for transfer to Liverpool owners.

The captain was living with people I knew and with the confidence and enthusiasm of youth I arrived at midday, saw the captain and secured the position of second officer of this ship, the *Vermont* of Bath, Maine.[48] I was naturally very delighted to obtain, at the age of twenty, the position of second officer of such a fine ship through my own exertions and enterprise. I was at that period determined to make good, and was endowed with the feeling that I could command success. Such is the enthusiasm of youth and who would spoil it, for it lies at the root of our national greatness and prosperity. To those who have struggled and achieved, there is a kindly feeling towards the youths who today are coping with similar difficulties in their desire to secure success. After refitting, coppering,[49] etc., we left Appledore in October for Cardiff, there to load coals for Singapore. At this period south Wales coals had a good market east of Suez, but for some years past those markets have been lost owing to the exploitation of native coals.

A few months prior to my joining this ship, Cardiff and other shipping ports were agog with excitement owing to a very serious mutiny which broke out on board a barque called the *Caswell*.[50] The crew of that vessel were Greeks and had murdered the captain and the officers. As a consequence, Cardiff was full of Greek sailors. We had sailed from Appledore to Cardiff but upon reaching that port the captain, who was an American, decided to ship a Greek crew at low wages. They were very fine sailors but a hard-looking, sinister lot. I remember well the morning we got ready to go to sea. As we were going through the sea lock the berthing master and pier head man were much concerned about our Greek crew, and advised me to carry a revolver at all times. I thought of the people from whom I was descended, and I was always led to believe by my mother and elder brother that there was no fear in a good Devonshire sailor. The Greeks did not worry me. The captain was one of those who liked to make people believe that he was a hard case. Many a time, although very young, I thought how unreasonable he could be; for instance, when on deck at midnight, he would start doing things such as ordering the tightening up of the topsail halliards and sheets, and tightening braces, very often in a shower of rain.[51] We made a long passage through the Sunda Straits and from there through Bangka Straits to Singapore, a passage of forty-two days; we anchored on an average twice daily. During that period with an old-fashioned windlass, the pawls were not allowed to be used in order to keep the chain from running out when fleeting.[52] The work was very hard and my particular job was to keep the chain back as it was hove in and to pay out when anchoring.

During the passage from Java Head to Singapore one night during the eight to twelve watch there was a slight breeze off Bangka Island, and the captain, walking on the top of the deck house with me, asked what I thought of the sound we could hear. I replied that it put me in mind of the tide over the old walls and the Crow Rocks at Appledore. A few minutes afterwards we were hard and fast on the Timbiga Rocks in the Bangka Straits. Luckily it was a flood tide and we managed to get her off and came to anchor early next morning at Third Point. We lost an anchor and fifteen fathoms of chain, but we remained there until the tide and wind were in our favour when we got under weigh and as before stated, arrived at Singapore, the whole passage taking us forty-two days.

At Singapore we discharged our cargo of coals after which we went into Tanjong Priock dry dock where we lifted our mast. As I had experience in rigging at Prince Edward Island, I was put in charge of this undertaking. The mast was lifted, part of the main keel and all the false keel was renewed, and quite a lot of the bottom planking too, especially along the bilge. This took some time and we shifted out into the bay, awaiting orders. After receiving orders we set sail, and proceeded to Elephant Point whence we were sent to Moulmein for a cargo of rice. On the passage down it blew hard south-west monsoons with heavy squalls. This was the intimation to us what to expect, and we found on arrival that several of our old cotton sails were in poor condition. Arriving in Moulmein, we anchored in the usual berth with both anchors and commenced loading. There was continuous rain and we found that we could not unbend the sails. This was a very serious matter, as cotton sails made fast for so long in wet weather meant mildew, and mildewed sails meant rot.

To load a rice cargo required the use of good sails between the ship's rail and the lighter so as to keep the damp from the cargo. I was put in charge of the gig when no cargo was being taken alongside and when I was not employed in the hold, stowing the rice. The current was very strong and although having been brought up in boats, it required all my past experience to handle the gig in the strong current. One thing which used to amuse me, and which I used to watch with interest, was the large elephants going down to the water, picking up big logs, taking them to the saw mills and putting them on saw benches ready for sawing. They were just like human beings.

After loading and making ready for sea on the first high water, we got under weigh. The first day we made very little headway but afterwards got sufficient to windward to make long tacks and continue without anchoring. We found our sails very badly deteriorated as a result of the long days and nights of continuous rain. For nearly a month whilst loading at Moulmein it meant shifting all sails and repairing them, working continuously day and night, including Sundays. We got short of twine and as a substitute we took a length of cotton canvas, unravelled it and made twine from this. For sixty days we did not know one day from another, shifting and repairing sails and making the best of the ropes we had got.

On the fourteenth day out on the starboard tack, the wind started to increase during the night and we found by sounding that we were

The 'Merrifield School' at Plymouth, where Reardon Smith studied to obtain both his first mate's and master's certificates.
(Prof. Alston Kennerley)

getting near the land. We found ourselves in fifteen fathoms of water on the Tenasserim coast. I feel sure with such poor running gear and sails, we had made little progress and the captain must have become more or less nervous. He wrote a message 'Ship *Vermont* in sight of death' which was enclosed in a bottle and cast overboard. It was picked up shortly afterwards and taken to Moulmein, the signature recognised, and the message sent to London. As the vessel was much overdue, and having made such a very long passage, she was given up as lost, the premium paid against total loss being ninety guineas. From there to the Equator in the Indian Ocean we took over sixty days and thence to the Cape a hundred days in all, anchoring at St. Helena where we reached twenty days later. By this time we were getting short of the ordinary food and we had to have recourse to the rice cargo. Sailors were put on at each watch to pick out the paddy from the rice. This rice, with pieces of salt pork, made a good meal, and I was in very good condition. We made the passage to Falmouth in 180 days, and, on arrival there, the captain ordered some good English food – vegetables and fresh meat – and after a few good meals of this food, we forgot our troubles.

Chapter 5

MASTER'S CERTIFICATE SECURED

FROM FALMOUTH WE DISCHARGED at Bremerhaven where we were paid off. After obtaining a reference from the captain and the owner, and a short stay at Appledore, I went to Plymouth. The navigation schoolmaster at Plymouth at that time was a noted mathematician.[53] In a short time, by diligent prosecution of my studies I passed as mate, and after a short holiday, I was sent for by a friend to join the *Mary Hogarth*[54] of the firm of Hugh Hogarth & Sons, the owners, later on, of some beautiful clippers.[55] This vessel was named after Mrs Hogarth, whose maiden name was Mary McFee. I joined the ship early in March 1878, taking a cargo of coal from Penarth Dock for Bahia in the Brazils. The captain was what was called a 'Blue Nose' and was a very hard case.[56]

The crew we took were all coloured men and a very motley crowd they were. I thought it would be possible to get these men into decent shape but the captain decided otherwise. At the end of the first week out the second mate's watch refused duty and they were put in irons. After being there for a few days without food they decided they would work. Carlyle in one of his few humorous moments once said that there were two moving forces – 'the stomach and a policeman'.[57] On arrival at Bahia after a rather uneventful voyage we found the port a very unhealthy one. We worked all the cargo out and I as a young man tipped 900 tons. After the holds were cleaned we next loaded sugar for New York, which was another hard task for the chief officer, and to make matters worse some of the crew deserted. As chief officer, I had to go on shore for different stores, see the sugar loaded in the lighters, take the lighters alongside the ship and put the crew to watch during the night. I am not sure whether the same thing prevails today, for the task is not a very pleasant one. We sailed for New York and discharged at Jersey City where all the sailors deserted, as no wages were due to them, the stevedore being left in charge. Having cleaned out the holds we shipped a cargo of wheat for St. Nazaire taking an ordinary New York crowd as crew who were signed off at St. Nazaire. After the wheat was discharged we shipped a French crew and sailed in ballast for New York again.

At this port we loaded wheat for Bordeaux, the captain's wife and two boys joining us in the trip, which made things very pleasant for me. One of these boys was lost at sea later on and the other was killed in Ireland during the rebellion. I believe the grandson of the captain is still in one of Messrs Hogarth's vessels. The captain's wife used to make nice doughnuts and I used to get my share, which I greatly appreciated. After discharging we sailed in ballast for Cardiff. The owner came to Cardiff to see the ship and spoke very encouragingly to me stating that if I remained I would never regret it. I remained with the ship until a new chief officer joined, when I packed up and left for Appledore. I then went on to Plymouth, joined the Merrifield school again[58] and subsequently passed for master in 1879. Thus I secured my master's certificate before I was twenty-three years old.

I then joined at Greenock as chief officer in the *Cyprus*,[59] a vessel built in Milford Haven, bought by Messrs Hogarth from the builders; we loaded a cargo of coal for Singapore. The captain of this vessel was a Scotchman and took his wife and two daughters with him to sea. On the Equator, we

A *corner of Hamburg's busy dockland in the* 1870s. (National Maritime Museum, Greenwich, London)

The iron ship Macrihanish, *commanded by Reardon Smith in* 1883–84. (National
Maritime Museum, Greenwich, London)

spoke a fine ship called the *Endymion* from Australia, homeward bound. We
gave them papers and the latest news and in return we got two suckling pigs
which we looked after very carefully.[60]

On arrival at Singapore, after a fair passage, we discharged the coals and
were chartered for home with a general cargo that included gambier.[61] This
was a difficult cargo to handle and had to be stowed with sawdust and mats
to keep it from adhering. We also had sago, black and white pepper, and
copra. After loading, we sailed for Falmouth for orders and then proceeded
to Hamburg, and from that port to the Tyne, where I left to go to Appledore
to get married.[62]

After getting married, I joined the *Drumadoon*,[63] a very fine ship built in
Nova Scotia of which I was given command. We loaded shortly afterwards
at Ardrossan for Rangoon, and from Rangoon to London. From London we
sailed for Cardiff, and then to Diamond Harbour for orders, being sent to
Bassein where we loaded rice for Bremerhaven. From there we sailed again
for Newport and thence to Rio de Janeiro, where we discharged our cargo
and sailed in ballast for Galveston. From Galveston we sailed to New Orleans
and thence to Falmouth, where we were ordered to Glasgow.

I had a fine crew and I should like to have remained with this vessel.
I was, however, relieved of the command and was sent to the Port Glasgow
superintendent, who gave me command of the *Macrihanish*.[64] This was a beautiful vessel built by Robert Duncan of Port Glasgow, and was the clipper of

Messrs Hogarth's fleet. This vessel, which was a double topgallant and a main skysail yarder,[65] had attracted considerable attention, not only for her beauty of appearance but also for the number of very fast passages she had made, the best record being her famous run home from Portland, Oregon, to the Fastnet in eighty-nine days in 1892. She saw considerable service, and a few years ago was sold to the Norwegians and renamed the *Avance*. Naturally, I was very proud of this command. After being fitted out, we loaded coals at Port Glasgow for Rangoon and after discharging and loading rice we proceeded to Falmouth and were ordered to Liverpool.

Chapter 6

MY FIRST FINANCIAL INTEREST

FROM LIVERPOOL, I WAS SENT TO HALIFAX, Nova Scotia, taking two engineers with me in order that a steamer, which had been ashore, could be taken across.[66] This steamer had been patched up, but the Captain and crew refused to bring her across, with the consequence that I was sent out in order to make arrangements and bring the vessel home. Arriving at Halifax, we found the whole crew were waiting for their case to come before the Admiralty Court. It was with difficulty that we were able to secure a crew on account of the old crew advising the seamen not to join, but after some trouble we finally mustered a crew of 'beachcombers'.[67] I shipped these men one by one, and they were a very mixed lot. On the Friday, after five days, we ultimately secured a full crew, and prepared to leave. During the heaving of the anchor, by an old fashioned windlass that was worked by a messenger from the forward winch,[68] the old crew rowed round the vessel in boats, exhorting the men on board not to sail in the vessel. After repairing the messenger from time to time, we finally got the anchor up, the chief engineer and the Mate looking after this, myself on the bridge, and the second officer below.

We finally got her out and found that the old fashioned compass was at least two points out. We corrected this and started on our run across to Penarth Roads for orders. We had no knowledge of what was in the bunkers when joining, but as a precaution, we took some cross cut saws so that in the event of shortage, we could cut the wood cargo to replenish our bunkers. But the bunkers we possessed proved sufficient to take us to Avonmouth, where we arrived after a passage of fifteen days, and discharged our cargo. This steamer did not belong to my firm, but Messrs Hogarth were asked by the mortgagees to bring her home, and directly she got into Avonmouth a writ was put on the mast. There was some trouble in obtaining the money to pay the crew and other expenses, but after two or three days' detention, the mortgagees advanced this. They were a very unruly crew as might have been imagined and during the time they were waiting for their money, they broke all the windows in the Avonmouth Board of Trade office. I was kept on by the Marshal of the Admiralty to make an inventory of all gear, after which the vessel was sold by auction to a Glasgow firm.

I was advised my services were no longer required, and was informed by my owners, Messrs Hogarth, that they were building a ship at Port Glasgow. I was to superintend the building of this ship, to be named the *Ochtertyre*.[69] This vessel was built of iron in 1885, by Robert Duncan of Port Glasgow, together with the sister ship *Corryvrechan*, which was one of the first ships to be built of steel.[70] The sails were made of cotton canvas, woven in Yarmouth, Nova Scotia, and most captains always held that in light winds, this cotton canvas was worth an extra knot an hour in speed. I was allowed two sixty-fourths in each vessel, and was given the benefit of paying for these sixty-fourths out of dividends and any wages I would save.[71] With such a good wife, it did not take me long to pay off these shares, in fact these ships earned their first cost in five years.

The *Ochtertyre*, for the first voyage under my command, was fixed to load salt from Liverpool to Rangoon, and from that port we loaded rice for Rotterdam. After discharging we loaded a general cargo for Java. We made a very good passage of ninety-six days and discharged the first part of the cargo at Surabaya. We then sailed for Samarang, where we completed discharging. This was a very strenuous passage during the north-west monsoons, but we proceeded to Pekalongan, then to Tegal, where we completed loading sugar.

When we dry-docked the vessel at Rotterdam, we had coated the bottom with white lead and tallow. This proved to be an unsatisfactory coating for protecting the plates against barnacles in a place like Java. On sailing from Tegal we found the vessel to be very slow and decided that the bottom must have been very foul. The first stoppage we had was in the Sunda Straits. The cargo consisted of sugar, and was wet. There could be a great loss by drainage, so we stopped and anchored in the Sunda Straits to pump the drainage of molasses out. The best apparatus we could get was the sounding pipe with the water pump attached; the main pump would not bring it up on account of the specific gravity. After getting outside Java Head, we pumped some water in her and with the rolling of the vessel and the water mixing with the molasses, we were enabled to pump it out by the main pumps.

We had a patent scrubber on board which we used to clean the growth off the bottom of the vessel, but this did little to increase the vessel's speed.[72] We made a long passage to Liverpool as a result – 140 days – where the vessel, after discharging was dry-docked. Examination showed her bottom to be in a fearful state. The owners decided to have her coated with McGuinness composition, which proved to be an admirable protective covering, both for the plates and for speed.

Above: *The Circular Quay, Sydney Harbour, c.*1890.
(National Maritime Museum, Greenwich, London)

Right: *Handsome chap! The young Captain Reardon Smith photographed in Sydney in* 1888, *aged thirty-two.* (Michael Tamlyn)

On the next trip, which was in the year 1887, my wife joined me, together with my baby son – his first sea voyage.[73] We had a very good passage of 104 days to Rangoon; after discharging we loaded for Hamburg. After discharging and drydocking, we loaded a general cargo for Sydney, Australia. Amongst this cargo was a considerable quantity of schnapps and Dutch gin, wire for sheep ranches, German toys, etc. We made a very good passage from Hamburg, being ninety days from the Channel, arriving three days before Christmas, which was the cancelling date of the next charter.[74] I cabled to the owners that I was trying to save the charter. Fortunately, I was assigned to very fine people, Messrs Hoffnung & Co. I informed them of the position, got a berth at the Circular Quay, got alongside at noon, made fast and finished discharging by Saturday morning. On Friday I had given notice of readiness, and although threatened by the shipper on Saturday, he sent alongside tallow in casks, and so the charter party was saved. We loaded wheat in

41

The No. 1 dock, Barry, c.1900.

very good time, and sailed for London doing the passage again in ninety days. The voyage was completed in seven months, and the dividend paid was 42½ per cent. This was probably the best trip I ever made in a 'sailer'. We then went to Cardiff and loaded for Algoa Bay and from thence, after discharging a cargo of coals, we sailed in ballast for New Zealand, calling at Port Chalmers for orders. We were ordered to Wellington, loading mostly with wood, tallow and hemp for London. From London we sailed for Barry shortly after the Barry Docks were opened.[75] The charter party read that the vessel had to be in Barry undamaged at a certain date. The reason for this was that a good many vessels encountered difficulty at the outset in entering, and sometimes sustained damage in so doing.

Chapter 7

FAREWELL TO SAILING VESSELS

AFTER LOADING AT BARRY, a new captain took command. I left sail for good, but it was with considerable regret. After being at Appledore for a short period, I was sent for to proceed to Amsterdam to join the SS *Baron Douglas*,[76] the largest steamer owned by Messrs Hogarth at that time. The captain who I relieved was promoted to Harbour Master at Ardrossan. I was not enamoured of steamers then, and it took me some time to get used to their ways. There was more dirt about, less to do, and I had to depend on others to get the steamer along instead of as in sailing vessels where speed depended in a great measure on the master, officers and crew, practice being the driving force.

We completed loading in Amsterdam with a miscellaneous cargo consisting of stonework for the buttresses of bridges, railway station material, telegraph poles, and engines and tenders. Some of the latter were landed at Port Elizabeth, Algoa Bay, but the greater part was for Delagoa Bay for the development of African railways. The heavy stonework of the bridges had the usual dove tails while the holes in the centres were for the placing of keys by which they could be hove up and discharged without the necessity of slinging. Whilst my own crew were on the winches, things proceeded well, but when the natives allowed one stone to touch the rail, the runner slackened and the stone dropped out of key, going through the lighter deck and causing great delay. The discharging facilities at Delagoa Bay at that time were very poor indeed. Immediately on arrival we started to make our own lighters from large softwood deals.[77] It did not take us long to make some very serviceable lighters and most of the cargo was landed on the deck of these pontoons.

From Delagoa Bay we were ordered to Point de Galle and from there to Calcutta where we loaded a cargo of jute for Dundee.[78] From Dundee after discharging, we loaded a full cargo for Tuticorin, southern India, and from there proceeded to Akyab and loaded a cargo of rice for Liverpool. From that port we loaded up with salt and general cargo for Calcutta, discharged, and took a mixed seed cargo for Antwerp. On crossing through the southwest monsoons, we had a very rough time. From Antwerp we took a cargo of cement and plate glass for New Orleans and after discharging at that port, loaded a full cargo of cotton for Havre and afterwards proceeded to Glasgow to load coals for Rangoon. From there we loaded rice for Bremerhaven, discharged at that port, and went on to London, where I left and went on to Appledore in order to see my new baby.[79]

I remained there some time, and was then sent for to take command of the SS *Baron Elibank* at Swansea.[80] We loaded a cargo of tin for Batum and after discharging took case oil to Point de Galle for orders.[81] After passing through the Suez Canal and the Red Sea, we arrived at Point de Galle, and received orders to go to Tjilatjap, on the southern side of Java. From there we took a cargo and proceeded to Tegal, Pekalongan, and Samarang. After taking in parcels from these ports we proceeded to Padang and Emmahaven on the south side of Sumatra, and completed loading for Marseilles. From there we were ordered to Batum again to load for Colombo and Madras. After discharging we left for Calcutta, where we loaded with rice and general cargo

Ships anchored in the River Hooghly, Calcutta. (National Maritime Museum, Greenwich, London)

The port of Aden, where Reardon Smith took on a cargo of salt whilst master of the Baron Elibank *in* 1894.

and took about two hundred pilgrims on board.[82] We called at Berbera, Aden, Hodeida and Jeddah where we landed the pilgrims and finished discharging the cargo. We were then ordered to Aden to load salt for Calcutta and from Calcutta we took a part cargo of wheat for Rangoon.

After discharging the wheat and loading rice, we sailed for Port Said, later discharging at Alexandria, Smyrna, Piraeus, Constantinople, Galatz and Braila. Upon completing the discharge at the latter port, we loaded a cargo of wheat for Rotterdam. From that port we were ordered to Ardrossan where the steamer was laid up to take the place of one of the firm's boats that ran to Huelva.[83] I was then sent to the SS *Baron Belhaven* and joined her at Glasgow.[84] She was chartered by the City Line[85] and was loaded for Bombay and Karachi.After discharging at Karachi we proceeded to Rangoon in ballast and loaded a full cargo of rice, calling at Point de Galle for bunkers. Then we proceeded to Durban, crossed over to Rio; here we discharged part cargo and completed at Santos. We bunkered at Rio de Janeiro and loaded at Rio Grande do Sul for Philadelphia.[86]

Notes to the text

(William Reardon Smith is referred to throughout as WRS)

[1] Though it cannot be proved conclusively, it seems likely that this introduction to WRS's autobiography was written by Vernon C. Boyle in the early to mid–1930s.

[2] This quote comes from Charles Kingsley's novel, *Westward Ho!* (1855).

[3] To combat the threat of the Spanish Armada in 1588, Sir Richard Grenville (who was a substantial landowner in the Bideford area) assembled a fleet of five vessels from the ports of the Taw and the Torridge, which sailed to join Sir Francis Drake at Plymouth.

[4] The surname Reardon comes from the Irish *riogh*, meaning royal, and *bardan*, a diminutive form of the word for a bard or poet. In his application form to be examined as second mate in 1876, WRS gives his second name as 'Rairdon', though he signed himself simply William Smith. It is not clear where the additional surname Smith originated; WRS's father Thomas appears to have been the first to adopt it, though not consistently, and WRS's elder sister Harriet was always referred to as Miss Harriet Reardon. The hyphenated version 'Reardon-Smith' was adopted by deed poll by WRS's son Willie on 20 December 1929.

[5] HMS *Weazle* was a fourteen-gun brig-sloop built at Sandwich in 1783. Vessels of this type were most commonly employed on coastal protection and anti-smuggling duties around the British Isles during the Napoleonic wars, and on 7 December 1796 HMS *Weazle* was stationed at Appledore to take up such duties along the north coasts of Somerset, Devon and Cornwall. Amongst her complement of eighty men was a young Irishman from Co. Cork, Daniel O'Riordan. HMS *Weazle* was later lost with all hands under Baggy Point on the north side of Barnstaple Bay on the night of 10–11 February 1799. Amongst those initially believed to have been drowned was Daniel, but fortunately for him he had left the vessel just six days previously, and would make Appledore his home.

[6] HMS *Romulus* was a fifth-rate vessel of thirty-six guns, built at Deptford in 1785. There is no evidence, however, to suggest that she was actually present at the Battle of the Nile, as vessels of this size would not have been deployed at major naval engagements. Converted into a troopship in 1799, she was eventually broken up in Bermuda in 1816.

[7] Owen Nile Reardon was probably born on board HMS *Romulus*, either late in 1801 or early in 1802, and was baptised at Northam on 27 June 1802, after his parents returned to north Devon (Appledore did not get its own church until 1838). He would later become the first coxswain of the Appledore lifeboat; *see* 'Appledore lifeboat's first coxswain' by John Whitlock in *North Devon Heritage*, 7 (1995). It has proved difficult to establish just what is meant by a 'master's certificate of servitude'. However, the most likely explanation is that the certificate confirmed the new-born infant in his immediate legal environment, i.e. on a British ship in foreign waters, subject to the master's authority, but also the object of his responsibility.

[8] WRS was the youngest of nine, not eight, children; see the family tree in the appendices. His father, Captain Thomas Smith, lost his life on 31 October 1859 during the

so-called 'Royal Charter Gale', when the schooner *Hazard*, of which he was master, was lost on Burry Port Bar whilst bound from Llanelli to Appledore with a cargo of coal. Also lost in this tragic incident was WRS's eldest brother, Philip. Captain Smith's body was washed ashore near Laugharne in Carmarthenshire and he was buried in the churchyard there.

[9] The *Unity* was a wooden sloop of thirty-one nett tons, built at Barnstaple in 1818 and owned by the Appledore boatbuilder and blockmaker Henry Hinks. WRS joined her on 18 August 1870, less than a fortnight after his fourteenth birthday. However, it is not clear whether this was actually his first voyage, as he recalled in letters written to Vernon Boyle in 1932 that he had had sixty-four years experience of ships and shipping, going back to 1868, in which year he further claimed to have sailed on the *Joe Abraham* (see n. 13). In a maritime community like Appledore, this might well have happened in an unofficial capacity. However, he obviously chose to commence his autobiography in 1870 when he joined the *Unity*, the first vessel on which he served in an officially recorded capacity as an ordinary seaman.

[10] The division of the freight, with a third going to the owner and two-thirds to the master, was known in Appledore as 'sailing by the thirds', whilst the practice of disposing of ballast at sea to save costs in port was common on small coastal sailing vessels.

[11] WRS actually left the *Unity* on New Year's Eve, 1870. The salmon fishing which he mentions was seine netting on the estuary of the Taw and the Torridge – apparently referred to by some local wags as 'sieving water'! In WRS's youth there were as many as forty nets in use in the area, each handled by three or four men fishing according to a seasonally pre-established rota at fifteen recognised 'drafts', locations at which a net could be 'shot' and landed, using locally built eighteen-foot clinker boats. Henry Williamson's short story, 'The Crake', provides a fascinating semi-fictional account of netting salmon on the estuary of the 'Two Rivers'. Declining fish stocks and indifferent water quality eventually led to a total ban on fishing from 1990 until 1995, but this ban was relaxed in 1996 and by 2003 there were three operational seine net licences on the estuary of the Taw and the Torridge, allowing fishing during a season that extended from 1 June (formerly 1 April) to 31 August each year.

With regard to pay and provisions, it was an old-established practice on board Appledore-owned vessels that crews were paid and fed only when those vessels were sailing outside Bideford bar. On inward-bound vessels, the master would call out to the cabin boy, 'Take the kettle off the stove boy, the bar buoy is in sight!'.

[12] The *Seraphina* was a wooden sloop of thirty-eight nett tons, built at Appledore in 1839 and owned by George Parkhouse of Appledore at that time. However, in his application form to be examined as a second mate in 1876, there is no record that he ever served on board this vessel.

[13] The *Joe Abraham* was a polacker (*sic*, polacca) brigantine of thirty-six nett tons, built to James Yeo's order on Prince Edward Island, Canada, in 1850 (see n. 34). WRS joined her on 1 July, 1871.

[14] Although WRS describes the *Joe Abraham* as a 'polacker schooner', these little vessels were in fact rigged as brigantines (i.e., square-rigged on the foremast and fore-and-aft rigged on the mainmast) but were distinguished by having a one-piece

'pole' foremast that was noticeably shorter than the mainmast. Due to the peculiarity of this rig, they were also known as 'hermaphrodites', often shortened to 'muffy', a term used by WRS himself. This pattern of rig was unique to the 'polackers' built on the estuary of the Taw and the Torridge.

[15] The *Ocean Pearl* was a wooden ship of 965 nett tons, built on Prince Edward Island in 1865, and owned by Rowlands & Thomas of Cardiff at the time. WRS joined her at Newport on 6 February 1872.

[16] Although actual production figures are unavailable, rail production predominated in the output of most Welsh ironworks from the early 1850s until the mid–1870s. Welsh-made rails played an integral role in the geographical and political consolidation of both the USA and imperial Russia in the nineteenth century.

[17] 'Reefs' were ties whereby the area of a sail could be reduced in response to the strength of the wind. Two reefs in the upper topsails were unusual; normally there would have been just one.

[18] The 'wing' is the outer extremity of the hold, away from the hatch.

[19] The *Scout* was a wooden barque of 460 nett tons, built at Bideford in 1862 and owned by Henry Bath & Co. of Swansea. WRS joined her at Swansea on 19 August 1872.

[20] Henry Bath (1766–1844), a native of Falmouth and a Quaker, had developed interests in the copper trade from Cornwall before moving to Swansea in 1820. His grandsons, Henry, Edward and Charles acquired extensive interests in Chilean copper mines and had a notable fleet of vessels engaged in the copper ore trade from the 1820s onwards.

[21] Dock facilities at most ports on the Pacific coast of South America were almost nonexistent at this time, and most ships were discharged and loaded to and from large lighters. The *lancheros* were the apparently indolent crewmen that manned these vessels.

[22] Chile has quite substantial reserves of low-grade coal throughout the country, with one of the most important mining areas being in the vicinity of Lota.

[23] Copper 'regulus' is partly refined copper.

[24] The 'trunk' was a wooden structure constructed longitudinally within the holds to contain the cargo; it was designed both to keep the copper ore or regulus from shifting and to raise the vessel's centre of gravity. This would help to prevent a 'snap roll', which could at worst dismast a vessel and would in any case make it difficult to work aloft. Vessels having the facility to construct such a trunk in their holds were said to be 'Swansea-fitted'.

[25] This passage from Swansea to Ilfracombe would very probably have been on board the paddle steamer *Velindra*, owned by Captain J. W. Pockett of Swansea and a regular on this cross-channel service. At that time Pockett operated three steamers, running on regular packet services from Swansea to Ilfracombe and Bristol, as well as summer excursions to a variety of popular destinations in the Bristol Channel.

[26] The *Viscount Canning* was a wooden ship of 746 nett tons, built at Sunderland in 1855 and owned at that time by R. Morris of Bristol. WRS joined her at Bristol on 17 January 1874. However, she was not actually WRS's next ship, as he spent some

three months in the schooner *Caroline* between leaving the *Scout* and joining the *Viscount Canning*, an interval that he misplaces in his narrative – see n. 43.

[27] Such were the stresses to which the hull of a laden wooden vessel was subjected in stormy weather that the hull or deck planking could open up, with resulting ingress of water.

[28] As pine is not a very dense wood, additional cargo would be loaded on deck to bring the vessel down to her marks. It was undoubtedly this deck cargo that became entangled in the vessel's rigging during the storm.

[29] Benjamin Bowring left his native Exeter in 1816 for St Johns, Newfoundland, where he established a clock- and watchmaking business; he later expanded his venture into general merchandise and the colony's seal fur trade. In 1834 he moved to Liverpool, where the company of C. T. Bowring & Co. was established in 1841 by his eldest son, Charles Tricks Bowring; the other sons remained in St John's where they established Bowring Brothers. In addition to sealing activities, this transatlantic enterprise acquired a substantial fleet of sailing vessels during the nineteenth century; the company would later concentrate on oil tankers, eventually ceasing shipowning in 1982.

[30] The *Jane* was a wooden barquentine of 216 nett tons, built at Bideford in 1874 and owned by C. T. Bowring & Co.; WRS joined her at Cardiff on 12 August 1874. His brother John, the *Jane*'s second mate, would later command the pioneer Reardon Smith steamship, the *City of Cardiff*.

[31] Peter and Lewis Tessier were natives of Newton Abbot in Devon who became prominent Canadian shipowners, operating a substantial fleet of sailing vessels from their home port of St. John's, Newfoundland.

[32] George Cox was a native of Bridport who came to the Appledore area in 1841 and went into partnership with a local shipbuilder, Thomas Evans. Evans left the partnership in about 1845 and Cox later took his son John into the partnership. The business ceased in 1877 with George Cox's death. However, shipbuilding continued intermittently on the site of this yard into the twentieth century, most notably the ten steam coasters built on the site in 1920–4 by the Hansen Shipbuilding & Ship Repairing Co. Ltd.

[33] 'Stockfish' is a name given to cod, formerly caught in vast numbers off the north-eastern seaboard of north America, which was beheaded, cleaned, boned, salted and then dried in the open air on wooden racks known as 'flakes'. It formed a staple part of the diet in many African, American and European countries prior to the advent of refrigeration and was widely eaten in Catholic countries on Fridays, when devout Catholics abstained from eating meat. Stockfish destined for Europe was normally loaded in bulk between layers of pine bark, whereas that destined for the heat of Africa, the West Indies and South America was packed into barrels and sometimes termed 'tub fish'.

[34] There is some confusion here as to the identity of the vessel that WRS next joined. The *Lucille* was a wooden brig of 273 nett tons, completed by John Yeo of Prince Edward Island in 1874 for his own account, which accords with WRS's description of the vessel. Confusingly, WRS's application form to be examined as second mate shows that he joined a vessel called the *Milo* on 9 April 1875. However, as is made clear in a passage later on in this chapter, the *Milo* was not completed at that time, being the last vessel on which WRS and his fellow riggers worked before sailing her

back to the UK in November 1875. Moreover, the Charlottetown newspaper the *Patriot* reported the arrival, early in June 1875, of the *Lucille* from Bristol 'with a general cargo of merchandise and crews for new vessels'.

[35] The high freight rates prevailing in the early 1870s led to what proved to be the final flourish of large-scale wooden shipbuilding on Prince Edward Island (PEI), in which the Yeo family had played a major part since the 1820s. Amongst the vessels being completed for the Yeos on PEI in that summer of 1875, upon which WRS and his fellow riggers would have worked, were the 436 nett ton barque *Milo*, the 279 nett ton barquentine *Nellie*, the 327 nett ton barque *Northern Star*, the 417 nett ton barquentine *Nushka*, the 281 nett ton barquentine *Rosamond*, the 479 nett ton barque *Kwasind* and the 950 nett ton barque *Transit*. By the autumn of 1874, however, freight rates had tumbled, and this also affected the prices obtainable for these vessels back in the UK. After 1880, wooden shipbuilding ceased to be an important export industry on PEI and it thereafter chiefly supplied a local market.

[36] Port Hill was also the location of James Yeo's home on Prince Edward Island.

[37] The object of 'serving' a rope is to protect it from chafing by binding it in a rope of smaller diameter, using a serving mallet.

[38] The main cause of scurvy – a lack of vitamin C in the diet – was well known by the late nineteenth century, and it was illegal for a British merchant vessel embarking on a voyage of more than ten days' estimated duration to sail without having a sufficient supply of lime juice on board. It can only be assumed that the cook mentioned by WRS persisted in giving the rigging crew salted provisions ashore, although as they were on the island during the summer and autumn months, it seems strange that apparently no attempt was made to procure fresh produce.

[39] The *Milo* was a wooden barque of 436 nett tons, built on Prince Edward Island in 1875 by the Yeo family for their own account.

[40] Many of the vessels built for the Yeos' account on Prince Edward Island were quite roughly finished and were completed later at their Richmond dry-dock at Appledore after a transatlantic passage. This probably accounts for the problems with leaking to which WRS refers here.

[41] The massive bar across the mouth of Malpeque Bay was a persistent hazard to shipping, with the sole navigable channel being located at the eastern end of the entry to the bay.

[42] WRS was referring here to St Paul's Island in the Gulf of St Lawrence.

[43] It would appear that WRS's memory had failed him here, for the certificate of service on his application form for examination as second mate shows that it was after he left the *Scout* in October 1873 that he spent some three months in the local trades of the Bristol Channel. This period was spent in the wooden schooner *Caroline*, a remarkable vessel of fifty nett tons that had been built at Plymouth in 1824 and was still trading, re-rigged as a ketch, in 1908! She was owned by P. K. Harris of Appledore. One of her regular cargoes, culm, is anthracite dust, which was either rolled with clay to form small rounded briquettes and burnt as a domestic fuel, or used in kilns (of which there were at least seven on the banks of the Torridge between Appledore and Bideford) to burn lime for use as an agricultural fertiliser, or in maltings.

[44] The *Souvenir* was a wooden barque of 482 nett tons, built in Norway in 1875 and owned by E. H. Cummins & R. H. Marten of Bristol. WRS joined her at Appledore on 25 February 1876.

[45] The Revd James Inman (1776–1859) was a celebrated mathematician and the first principal of the Naval School at Portsmouth. In 1821 he published his *Navigation and Nautical Astronomy for the Use of British Seamen*, which has since been used by generations of seamen. This is the volume to which WRS is referring here, though he gives it a colloquial title.

[46] Most readers will be aware of the erstwhile importance of semaphore signalling, using flags, as a means of communication at sea. Distance (or geometrical) signals were made-up combinations of hexagons and triangles of differing colours and were intended to replace the flag code during light winds and calms, or when the various flags could not be made out at great distances.

[47] 'AB': an able-bodied seaman, defined as having at least three years' sea-going experience and competent at the helm.

[48] The *Vermont* was a wooden ship of 1,236 gross tons, built at Bath, Maine, in 1866 and owned by Henry T. Ropes of Liverpool. WRS joined her at Appledore sometime in mid-October 1876.

[49] 'Coppering' was the practice of covering the hull of a wooden vessel below the waterline with thin sheets of copper, chiefly to prevent the predations of wood-boring marine worms. It also imparted improved manoeuvrability and greater speed to ships so fitted.

[50] The mutiny on board the Swansea barque *Caswell* was something of a *cause célèbre* at the time. In May 1876, on the return leg of her maiden voyage, she arrived at Queenstown (Cobh), Ireland with a cargo of nitrates from Antofagasta, Chile. It was discovered that the captain, the first and second mates and the steward had been murdered by five crew members – three Greeks and two Maltese. The two Maltese had escaped ashore in a boat off the mouth of the river Plate, whilst the rest of the crew had subsequently overpowered the three Greeks, killing two of them in the ensuing struggle. The surviving Greek seaman, Christo Baumbos, was tried for murder at the Cork Assizes. With the jury unable to agree a verdict, the judge ordered a retrial, at which Baumbos was found guilty and subsequently hanged.

[51] These were minor (and perhaps unnecessary) alterations, ordered by the officer of the watch, to the tack on which a ship might already be sailing perfectly satisfactorily.

[52] To 'fleet' a cable or hawser is to allow it to slip on the drum of a capstan or windlass from the larger part of its diameter to a smaller one, thus allowing it to be paid out.

[53] The Plymouth School of Navigation opened in 1863 and was generally known as the Merrifield School after its first principal, John Merrifield. WRS studied for his first mate's and master's certificates at this establishment, the foremost of its kind in the west of England.

[54] The *Mary Hogarth* was a wooden barque of 588 nett tons, built in 1875 by W. & R. Wallace of Gardiner's Creek, New Brunswick, Canada, for Goodwin & Hogarth of Ardrossan, Ayrshire. WRS joined her at Penarth on 5 April 1878.

[55] The partnership of Goodwin & Hogarth was formed at Ardrossan in 1862. Initially trading as chandlers and shipping agents at the port, they became shipowners in

1868. Their partnership was dissolved in 1878 and Hugh Hogarth moved to Glasgow in 1880, acquiring his first steamship a year later. The company eventually became one of the largest Scottish tramp shipping concerns and retained close links with the Reardon Smith Line in later years; Hogarth's acted as agents for Reardon Smith vessels in Clyde ports, whilst Reardon Smith reciprocated for Hogarth vessels docking in south Wales. In 1968, Hogarth's merged with another prominent Glasgow firm, Lyle Shipping, to form Scottish Ship Management Ltd, but financial difficulties forced this company into receivership in 1987.

[56] 'Bluenose' was the somewhat pejorative nickname given to a native of Nova Scotia.

[57] Despite the kind assistance of members of the Carlyle Society, it has not proved possible to identify the exact source of this quote. Any suggestions would be gratefully received!

[58] See n. 53.

[59] The *Cyprus* was a wooden barque of 500 nett tons, built by J. D. Warlow of Neyland, Pembs., in 1878, to the order of Hugh Hogarth. WRS joined her at Greenock on 23 June 1879.

[60] It was a common practice to take various domesticated animals on long ocean voyages in the nineteenth century. Hens provided eggs and goats provided milk, although it seems unlikely that the two suckling pigs referred to here by WRS would have survived to the end of that voyage!

[61] 'Gambier' is the astringent extract of a tropical Asiatic climbing plant, *Uncaria gambier*, and was used in tanning processes.

[62] WRS married Ellen Hamlyn of Appledore at Appledore parish church on 16 May 1880. A year younger than WRS, she was the daughter of Thomas Hamlyn, variously described as a coal merchant or a shipwright, and his wife Elizabeth, who kept a grocer's shop and bakery at 25 Market Street.

[63] The *Drumadoon* was a wooden barque of 866 nett tons, built in 1876 by Lawrence de Lap & Co., Annapolis, Nova Scotia, and was acquired a year later by Goodwin & Hogarth of Ardrossan. WRS joined her at Calais on 17 July 1880.

[64] The *Macrihanish* was an iron ship of 1,699 nett tons, built in 1883 by Robert Duncan & Co. of Port Glasgow for Hugh Hogarth. WRS joined her at Port Glasgow on 5 November 1883.

[65] As sailing ship rigs developed during the nineteenth century, the deep single topsails and topgallant sails typical of vessels built before about 1850 were replaced by smaller upper and lower topsails and topgallants. This made the sails easier to handle and gave greater control over the area of sail exposed to the wind. The skysail was the uppermost sail carried on the *Macrihanish*'s mainmast.

[66] This vessel was the 1132 gross ton iron steamer *Colonsay*, built in 1882 by William Hamilton & Co. of Port Glasgow for J. Allan & Co. of Glasgow. WRS joined her at Halifax, Nova Scotia, on 17 September 1884.

[67] A 'beachcomber' is a vagrant who scrapes a living looking for articles of value along the foreshore, but the term is used here by WRS to indicate the fact that he did not consider the crew that he had assembled to man the *Colonsay* to be particularly competent seamen.

⁶⁸ A 'messenger' was a loop of stout rope or chain that was passed around the barrel of a capstan or winch and, in this case, over the old-fashioned anchor windlass. As it ran parallel to the anchor chain, it was 'nipped' (temporarily attached) to the chain sequentially at a number of places: the 'nips' were released as they neared the winch drum, with fresh 'nips' being applied back along the chain as it came up through the hawse pipe. In this way a continuous pull was applied to the anchor chain so that the anchor could be weighed (raised). In Nelson's navy, deck boys did the 'nipping' – hence the term 'nipper'!

⁶⁹ The *Ochtertyre* was an iron barque of 1,263 nett tons, built in 1885 by Robert Duncan & Co. of Port Glasgow for Hugh Hogarth (see frontispiece). Hogarth had charged WRS with the supervision of the construction of this vessel and her steel-built sister *Corryvrechan*. He subsequently took command of the *Ochtertyre* and signed on her first crew at Liverpool on 19 September 1886.

⁷⁰ Steel, with its advantages of greater strength and flexibility for weight over iron, became the preferred material for shipbuilding purposes from the mid-1880s onwards.

⁷¹ Of much-debated antiquity, the practice of dividing ships into sixty-four shares was enshrined in the Mercantile Marine Act of 1824. It was a common practice at that time for masters of merchant vessels to take a few shares in the vessels that they commanded, often as a condition of being appointed to that command, although in this case it would appear that Hugh Hogarth had actually loaned money to Reardon Smith to enable him to buy two shares each in the *Ochtertyre* and the *Corryvrechan*.

⁷² The 'patent scrubber' was an abrasive device that could be passed around underneath the hull of the vessel to help keep the bottom free of marine growth.

⁷³ WRS's second son, Willie, was born on 26 May 1887. His first son, Thomas Hamlyn Smith, had died of acute hydrocephalus on 12 November 1883, aged just sixteen months. This tragic event goes unmentioned by WRS.

⁷⁴ A 'charter party' is a legally binding agreement between a shipowner and the shipper of a cargo. If a shipowner was unable to have his ship ready for loading at the place and time stipulated in the charter party, the charter could be 'thrown up' (cancelled) and the shipowner subjected to a financial penalty; this was WRS's worry on this occasion.

⁷⁵ Barry Dock was chiefly the brainchild of the noted Welsh entrepreneur, David Davies of Llandinam (1818–90). Tiring of congestion and delays on the Taff Vale Railway and the Bute monopoly at Cardiff docks, he and other Rhondda coalowners promoted the Barry Dock and Railway Bill to enable the construction of a new railway route from Trehafod in the lower Rhondda valley to a new dock at what was then the tiny hamlet of Barry. Despite fierce opposition from the Bute faction in the Lords and lengthy inquiries in both Houses of Parliament, the bill was passed in 1884, and the new dock eventually opened on 18 July 1889.

⁷⁶ The *Baron Douglas* was a steel steamship of 2,700 gross tons, built in 1888 by Blackwood & Gordon of Port Glasgow for Hugh Hogarth. WRS joined her at Amsterdam on 3 June 1890.

⁷⁷ 'Deal' was an ubiquitous term for unseasoned softwood timber sawn into baulks no less than nine inches (22.5 cm.) wide and two inches (5 cm.) thick, and between

five feet (152 cm.) and thirty feet (912 cm.) in length. Cargoes of sawn timber were often made up of pieces of varying dimensions, known in shipping terminology as a cargo of 'DBB' – deals, battens and boards.

[78] Jute is a vegetable fibre extracted from the bark of the jute tree (*corchorus capsularis* or *corchorus olitorious*), used to make sacks and matting. Dundee was for many years the main centre of the jute processing industry in the UK, being one of the 'three Js' – jam, jute and journalism – for which the city was famous.

[79] WRS is referring here to the birth of his daughter Elizabeth (Betty), born in 1892.

[80] The *Baron Elibank* was a steel steamship of 1,772 gross tons, built in 1889 by Murdoch & Murray of Port Glasgow for Hugh Hogarth. WRS joined her at Swansea on 3 October 1892.

[81] Prior to the widespread adoption of tankers for the bulk transport of oil and petroleum products by sea, such liquids were transported in five-gallon Welsh terneplate cans, generally packed in twos or fours and protected by a wooden crate or case, hence the term 'case oil'. Terneplate was thin steel sheet covered in an alloy of lead and tin, which was much cheaper to produce than the pure tin coating required for the canning of foodstuffs.

[82] The pilgrims referred to here by WRS would have been Moslems from the Indian subcontinent travelling to Mecca, Islam's holiest shrine, in present-day Saudi Arabia; Jeddah, on the Red Sea, was the nearest port to Mecca. The pilgrims generally made the entire passage on deck, and were largely independent of the ship on which they sailed, bringing their own bedding and shelter and making their own catering arrangements.

[83] Though predominantly a tramp shipping company, Hogarth's also had a regular line of steamers – their so-called 'berth service' – running to Huelva in southern Spain, where they loaded pyrites ore mined by the Tharsis Sulphur & Copper Co. Ltd for the UK.

[84] The *Baron Belhaven* was a steel steamship of 2,356 gross tons, built in 1887 by Robert Duncan & Sons of Port Glasgow for Hugh Hogarth. WRS joined her at Glasgow on 5 November 1894.

[85] The City Line was founded by George Smith in Glasgow in 1839. The company was later absorbed into the well-known Ellerman group, running passenger and cargo vessels, chiefly to India.

[86] The autobiography concludes here, one third of the way down a torn sheet of foolscap paper. The approximate period during which the text terminates is the late spring to early summer of 1895.

Master Mariner,
Shipowner and
Philanthropist,
1895-1935

THERE IS A SOMEWHAT MACABRE SYMMETRY in the fact that, when Sir William Reardon Smith died in December 1935, he had left an uncompleted autobiography that covered the first half of his life almost exactly. Recounting as it does the career progression of an able and ambitious young seafarer in the latter half of the nineteenth century, the story that it tells, whilst very interesting, is not that unusual, for many hundreds of his contemporaries from coastal villages all around the British Isles also worked their way from the focsle to the master's saloon quite rapidly during those expansive years for the British mercantile service. Just a handful, however, took the momentous step of becoming shipowners themselves, and fewer still were as successful as was Reardon Smith. His second career as a shipowner would be the dominant story of the latter half of his life, whilst during his last twenty years he also became noted for his considerable philanthropy to a wide range of charities and institutions. This is a story which, unfortunately, he never set down in his own words. Notwithstanding the fact that the vast majority of the earlier records of the Reardon Smith venture were destroyed in a disastrous fire at their offices at Merthyr House in March 1946, there are, nevertheless, numerous documentary and printed sources relating to Sir William, his shipping ventures and his charitable activities, available in various different archives and repositories. By drawing upon these and some personal recollections, it is possible to re-create, in varying degrees of detail, the latter half of his life.

LAST YEARS IN COMMAND

The autobiography as left by Sir William finishes in the late spring or early summer of 1895, at which time he was still serving with Hogarth's as master of the *Baron Belhaven*. He would remain with the company on the same

Seen here perfectly framed by Brunel's Avon Gorge bridge, the Starcross *was owned by Anning Bros of Cardiff and commanded by Reardon Smith in 1896-97.* (York Collection, Bristol's Museums, Galleries & Archives)

ship for another fifteen months or so, eventually completing eighteen years' service with the Scottish company. However, sometime during 1896 he took the decision to leave the company with which he had gained so much valuable experience. His exact reasons for leaving Hogarth's will ever remain a mystery, but the fact that the company he joined in November 1896 had its roots in Devon may well have influenced his decision; indeed, various Devonian and West Country links were to have a crucial bearing on his career over the ensuing decades. In November 1896, he joined the steamer *Starcross* at Barry, where she was loading coal for the bunkering station on the Cape Verde Islands; she was one of three tramp steamers in the fleet of Anning Brothers of Cardiff.[1]

The Anning company was one of the most interesting of Cardiff's ship-owning concerns. John Henry Anning was born in the village of Kenton, a few miles south of Exeter, in about 1823, and by the early 1870s was established as a shipbroker and owner in Cardiff, owning two schooners and a barque. In 1877, he acquired his first iron steamship, the *Richard Anning*, thus placing him amongst Cardiff's earliest steamship owners. By 1892, his sons Richard and William would appear to have taken over the business from their father, forming the partnership of Anning Brothers and running three steamships.[2] The system of ship nomenclature that they initiated with the acquisition of the *Starcross* in 1894 reflected their Devonian origins; family names were gradually abandoned, and thereafter their ships bore the names of towns on the south Devon coast such as *Dartmouth*, *Dawlish*, *Exmouth* and *Sidmouth*.[3] Of greater significance, however, was the seminal influence of the Anning company in the growth of shipowning at Cardiff. Appointed master of the new *Richard Anning* in 1877 was Captain Evan Thomas from Aberporth in west Wales and in 1881 he and a clerk from Anning's office named Henry Radcliffe left the company to establish Evan Thomas, Radcliffe & Co., later to be Cardiff's largest shipping concern.[4] Five years later, a young lad from Appledore by the name of William James Tatem was taken on as a clerk by Annings, and in 1897 he too established himself as a shipowner on his own account in Cardiff, later becoming ennobled as Lord Glanely. And to complete a notable quartet of shipowners, another native of Appledore and future shipowner, Captain William Reardon Smith, joined the company in 1896, though he had already come into association with Anning's back in 1876 when they acted as agents for the barque *Vermont* (of which Reardon Smith was second mate) when she loaded coal at Cardiff.[5]

It was not only William Reardon Smith who became associated with Anning's at that time but his wife Ellen as well, for in 1896 six shares were purchased in her name in the Starcross Steamship Co. Ltd, the limited liability, single-ship company managed by Anning Bros that actually owned the *Starcross*. Whilst this was clearly a continuation of the practice initiated by the couple when they acquired two sixty-fourth shares each in the *Ochtertyre* and the *Corryvrechan* in 1885[6], there were nevertheless some important differences in the exact nature of their investment. Whereas their sixty-fourth shares in the Hogarth barques were shares in the actual ships, their shares in the *Starcross* were, rather, shares in the company that owned the vessel rather than the actual steamer herself. Numerous acts passed in the mid-nineteenth century enabled the creation of joint-stock, limited liability companies, and this was a development that was to be of particular significance with regard to investment in shipping during an age when the cost of building new ships – especially steamers – was generally rising. Sixty-fourth shares in a steamer costing, say, £25,000 would have cost nearly £400 each, beyond the pocket of many potential investors, but with a ship of the same value owned by a limited liability company, the shares could be broken down into far smaller denominations, thus reaching a far wider spectrum of potential investors. The Starcross Steamship Co. Ltd was capitalised at £26,000 (roughly the initial cost of the vessel), divided into 260 £100 shares,[7] so Ellen Smith's investment of £600 was quite substantial – a little over £34,000 in present-day (2010) values; this is a reflection of her skill at husbanding their financial resources to which Sir William referred in his the autobiography.[8] Moreover, it was through the formation of such a single-ship company that Reardon Smith would venture into shipping himself a decade or so later.

But in 1896 all this lay in the future, and the *Starcross* sailed from Barry under Reardon Smith's command on 20 November 1896. Having discharged at the Cape Verde Islands she headed across the Atlantic to New Orleans, where she loaded cotton for Dunkirk; by mid-February 1897 she was under the tips in Penarth dock loading coal once more. This coal was destined for Las Palmas, after which the *Starcross* crossed the Atlantic once more, bound this time for Santiago de Cuba, where she probably loaded copper ore for Baltimore. Another voyage from Baltimore to Cuba followed before the *Starcross* loaded grain from New York for home; she eventually arrived back at Barry on 5 July 1897. This, however, was to prove to be Reardon Smith's last voyage for the Annings, for during the eight months he had been master of the *Starcross* his fellow native of Appledore, William Tatem,

Left: *Shipowner William James Tatem; a fellow-native of Appledore, he was Reardon Smith's employer in 1897–1900.*

Below: *Under Reardon Smith's superintendence, Tatem's new steamer* Shandon *nears completion at Richardson, Duck's Stockton-on-Tees yard in 1899.*

had also left the Annings' employment to establish himself as a shipowner in his own right; moreover, he had also asked Reardon Smith to be master of his first ship, the *Lady Lewis*. Having been completed at Richardson, Duck & Co.'s Stockton-on-Tees yard, the *Lady Lewis* eventually steamed down the Tees under Reardon Smith's command on 24 July, bound for Cardiff where she would load coal for Venice. It is also worth noting that after her husband moved to a new employer, Ellen Smith similarly transferred her financial interest from Annings to Tatem, buying ten £100 shares in the Lady Lewis Steamship Co. Ltd.[9] Reardon Smith subsequently remained in command of the *Lady Lewis* until April 1899, undertaking seven typical tramping voyages to the Mediterranean, the Black Sea and the east coasts of both north and south America.[10]

Having left the *Lady Lewis* towards the end of April 1899, Reardon Smith was sent by Tatem to Stockton-on-Tees, again to the shipyard of Richardson, Duck & Co. where his third steamer, the *Shandon*, was nearing completion. At 3,850 gross tons, she was soon to become the largest ship owned and registered at Cardiff, and Reardon Smith stood by the vessel as she was fitted out on the Tees. By the beginning of July the new steamer was completed and on 7 July she sailed for Cardiff under Reardon Smith's command, to load coal for Ancona on Italy's Adriatic coast. He would undertake two voyages on the *Shandon*, the second ending at Manchester docks on 13 January 1900, discharging baled cotton from New Orleans. After a short break, he then rejoined the *Lady Lewis* at Cardiff on 23 February 1900 for what would prove to be his last voyage as master, a lengthy one visiting south and east Africa, Cuba, the USA and northern Europe before he eventually left the ship at Cardiff on 4 December 1900. His journey home would also have been considerably shorter at the end of this last voyage, for Ellen Smith and their family had by this date left their home in Appledore's Bude Street and moved to 52 Claude Road in the Cardiff suburb of Roath.[11]

'Tantalising' is perhaps the best way to describe the next few years of Reardon Smith's career. Whilst he was an active officer in the British merchant service, his activities and movements can be traced from crew lists and other sources such as the Lloyd's Captains' Registers; similarly, when he 'reappears' as a shipowner in his own right in 1905, his name is to be found in various Board of Trade records relating to the companies that he established and of which he was a director. But what exactly Reardon Smith was doing during the years 1900–4 is far from clear. A note in the chairman's archive, apparently based on information given years later by his youngest daughter, Grace, suggests that he and his family settled in Cardiff at that time because he had been offered the post of marine superintendent of Tatem's growing fleet, which comprised six new vessels by the end of 1900. Bearing in mind Reardon Smith's wide experience of seafaring and superintendence, it seems not unreasonable that Tatem might have offered his fellow native

A family portrait dating from about 1905; from left to right Gertrude (Gertie), William Reardon Smith, Lillian (Lily), with Grace at her feet, Ellen Smith, Douglas, Elizabeth (Betty) and Willie.

of Appledore such a post as his fleet expanded.[12] However, when Reardon Smith left Tatem, he was provided with the following testimonial;

> TO WHOM IT MAY CONCERN. We the undersigned have pleasure in certifying that Captain W. R. Smith has been in our employ as master of the steamers *Lady Lewis* and *Shandon* from July 22nd 1897 to December 9th 1900 during the whole of which time he gave us every satisfaction and we strongly recommend him as a most trustworthy, sober, industrious and capable shipmaster to anyone requiring his services, we understand he is leaving our employ with a view to obtaining a shore berth and may say we have known him for several years and would have pleasure in replying to any inquiries made respecting him [sic].[13]
>
> sgd. W. J. Tatem & Co.

This testimonial, whilst indeed confirming that Reardon Smith was looking for a 'shore berth', certainly does not suggest that he had been offered the post of marine superintendent by Tatem – had he been offered such a post, why should Tatem have written this testimonial? Or had Reardon Smith been offered the post by Tatem, only for some disagreement to arise between the two men that led to his never being appointed? It is impossible to know. However, further evidence that Reardon Smith appears never to have been appointed to the post, if indeed it was ever offered to him, can be found in the recollections of Captain William Hughes of Nefyn, who was appointed chief officer of Tatem's new steamer *Appledore* early in 1902. He recalled being in Cardiff on 6 February 1903, when,

> One day, while sitting in my room with the engineer and second mate . . . a big man passed and looked into my room, but said nothing . . . later the captain came out with him and called me . . . he said, 'This is Captain Wiseman, our new Marine Superintendent'. Previous to that we had only had an Engineering Superintendent . . . he was a very hard case, being Bluenose Irish, and he could fight too.[14]

Clearly not a man to cross (!), but from this evidence it seems clear that Captain Wiseman was Tatem's first marine superintendent and not Reardon Smith. What, therefore, was he doing during the first years of the new century? Miss Grace Smith's note further suggests that rather than looking for opportunities to invest in shipping at that time, her father was investing in property in Boverton Street and Morlais Street off Ninian Road in the Roath area of Cardiff, as well as in the Splott area of the town.[15] By 1903, however, it would appear that he was once again exploring the possibility of investing in the business that he knew best – shipping – and it is not surprising to find that he was exploring these possibilities with someone of West Country descent.

BECOMING A SHIPOWNER

William Henry Seager had been born in Cardiff in 1862 but his father, a builder by trade, came from Minehead, whilst his mother was a native of Ilfracombe; the family had moved across the Bristol Channel in the 1850s, attracted to the considerable opportunities offered by Cardiff's late nineteenth-century expansion.[16] Seager's initial hope was to train as an architect, but his father's subsequent lengthy illness meant that he had to put such ambitions aside and at the age of fourteen he started work in a chandlery in Cardiff docks. By 1892 he had established his own chandlery at 109 Bute Street, which he developed into a successful business over the following twelve years. When exactly he and Reardon Smith began to consider going into partnership as shipowners is not known, but there was sound reasoning behind their decision to embark upon their new venture in 1904. Coal exports from Cardiff totalled nearly 7½m. tons that year and would continue to rise steadily to a peak of 10½m. tons in 1913. And whilst freight

Sir William Seager, photographed in 1925 some twenty years after his short-lived partnership with Reardon Smith.

rates had undergone a considerable boom around the turn of the century, partly as a result of the Boer War, as the new century progressed they fell back rapidly, so much so that the years 1903–11 were characterised by consistently depressed rates. However, depressed freight rates also meant that ships could be obtained at considerably cheaper prices, and this was the opportunity that Reardon Smith and Seager seized upon. To quote their near-contemporary, the Newcastle-based shipowner Walter Runciman, recalling the purchase of his first ship, the *Dudley*, in 1885:

> I never doubted the wisdom of buying when prices were low, even if the vessel could not trade then at a profit. It is more than 99 per cent of a successful deal to buy when prices are low and sell when they are high. No one ever did or ever will make a mistake by carrying out a policy of this kind – if they can – and this is exactly what I laid myself out to do.[17]

On 4 March 1904, the partners jointly registered the Tempus Shipping Co. Ltd, with a capital of £31,600 divided into £10 shares.[18] The new company subsequently issued a prospectus on 23 April, explaining that it had been established to acquire and operate the steamer *Tempus*, a long bridge-decked vessel of 2,981 gross tons then under construction (under Reardon Smith's superintendence) at the yard of Craig, Taylor & Co. of Stockton-on-Tees. Having given details of the vessel, the prospectus was further keen to emphasise the combination of seafaring and commercial skills evident in the careers of both managing directors:

> As to the managers, it might be mentioned that Mr William Reardon Smith has had about 30 years' practical sea-going experience (of which some 24 as a master mariner), in the course of which he has been associated with some of the most successful managers

of shipping property in the United Kingdom. Mr William Henry Seager has had about 27 years' experience in Cardiff docks. With the experience these gentlemen possess, and bearing in mind the heavy holding they intend to take in the capital of the company, it is considered that the company's business will be efficiently and economically managed.[19]

Unfortunately, the initial shareholders' list of the Tempus Shipping Co. Ltd has not survived, so it is impossible to tell just how much of their own capital Reardon Smith and Seager invested in the new company. What is clear, however, is that far from being a mere investor in the company (as has sometimes been suggested hitherto), Reardon Smith was Seager's full business partner and joint manager of the venture. The *Tempus* was launched from Craig, Taylor's yard with Ellen Smith as sponsor on 30 July 1904[20] and was registered at the port of Cardiff on 2 September 1904; the vessel's registration document declares, 'William Henry Seager and William Reardon Smith, both of 109 Bute Street, Cardiff, designated the persons to whom the management of the ship is entrusted'.[21] Despite this clear declaration of their partnership, however, there was a clause in the prospectus that suggests that the partners wished to reserve the right to go their own way in the future should one or the other so wish: 'Each manager is to be at liberty to carry on any business, either in Cardiff or elsewhere, and whether this is to be identified in whole or in part with the business of the company'.[22]

The purpose of this statement may well have been to allow Seager to carry on running his chandlery business from the partners' office address on

The Tempus *leaves the River Tees on her maiden voyage in* 1904. (Michael Tamlyn)

Bute Street, but in a way it was to prove prophetic, for on 7 March 1905, just a year and three days after the initial registration of the Tempus Shipping Co. Ltd, Reardon Smith resigned from the partnership. Whilst there is no evidence available as to why their partnership was terminated at that time, a document dating from almost two decades later suggests that their parting might have been somewhat acrimonious. On 19 May and 5 June 1924, extraordinary general meetings of the Tempus Shipping Co. Ltd were called with the sole purpose of eradicating Reardon Smith's name from the company's records, as outlined in this resolution:

> THAT WILLIAM REARDON SMITH (now Sir William Reardon Smith, Bart), having on 7 March 1905 resigned his office as one of the Managers and Ship Brokers of the Company, the name of the said William Reardon Smith, wherever it occurs in the Articles of Association of the Company in relation to the Offices of a Manager and/or Ship Broker, shall be deleted and shall be deemed as not having appeared therein as on or at any time from 7 March 1905.[23]

This resolution has an almost Stalinist tone in its determination to extirpate Reardon Smith's name from the history of the Tempus company, and the events of 1904–5 apparently gave rise to a certain *froideur* that existed between the two families for some decades thereafter. Nevertheless, having parted company with Seager, he wasted no time in embarking upon the venture that was to dominate the rest of his life. Later in March 1905 he placed an order with Ropner & Co.'s shipyard at Stockton-on-Tees for the construction of a new steamship of 3,070 gross tons; built to the same long bridge-deck design as the *Tempus*, she was nevertheless built along severely functional lines, with king-posts to work the cargo holds aft rather than a mainmast. She was to be named *City of Cardiff*, in honour of the city status to be granted to Cardiff later that year. Then, on 19 May 1905, he registered the company that would eventually own and operate the *City of Cardiff*, the Instow Steamship Co. Ltd. Managed by W. R. Smith & Son (his elder son Willie), the company had a nominal capital of £32,800 in £10 shares and had its registered office at 124 Bute Street;[24] it took its name from the village that lies due east of Appledore, across the River Torridge. Why this particular name was chosen is not clear, although it may have had something to do with the fact that by 1905 his former employer W. J. Tatem managed sixteen single-ship companies and their vessels, twelve of which bore the names of north Devon towns and villages such as Appledore, Barnstaple, Bideford, Northam and Torrington – but not Instow!

Raising sufficient capital to float the company was the most daunting task facing Reardon Smith at the outset – £32,800 translates into a present-day (2010) sum of just over £1.8m. The construction costs were chiefly

An excellent portrait of Reardon Smith's first ship, City of Cardiff, *loading timber at Riga in August* 1908. (Kevin O'Donoghue collection)

covered by a mortgage of £24,000 from Sir Robert Ropner, with interest at 5 per cent per annum and secured on the vessel. The Smith family would appear to have staked much of the capital that they had built up through their shipping and property investments since 1885 in the company, with William Reardon Smith taking 400 shares and Ellen Smith 200; their son Willie took ten shares, as did their daughter Lillian. The fact that a fifth of the capital had been taken up by the family was mentioned in the prospectus as a sign of Reardon Smith's integrity, and it is also notable that he intended to take as his management remuneration a basic fee of £200 per annum and 5 per cent of the net trading profits earned, rather than the more usual practice of levying a commission on the gross earnings of the vessel. The latter system was open to criticism at the time as it meant that managing owners could make money on a vessel as long as the ship was at sea and carrying cargo, regardless of whether that particular voyage showed a profit or not. By depending partly for his own remuneration upon the ability of the new steamer to trade at a profit, however, Reardon Smith further demonstrated to potential shareholders his good faith in offering what he described as 'a secure and permanent investment where a steady, consistent and appreciable rate of dividend may reasonably be expected'.[25]

Unfortunately, the general public did not share his confidence. By the end of 1905, and with construction work on the *City of Cardiff* proceeding apace at Ropner's yard, only 1,429 shares – amounting to less than half the nominal capital – had been sold. Possibly in some desperation Reardon Smith had himself bought a further 250 shares in the company, whilst his wife had bought a further 200; Reardon Smith's elder brother John also bought 100 shares as a condition of being appointed master of the *City of Cardiff* when she was ready for the sea, a common arrangement at the time. Matters cannot have been helped by a critical and somewhat condescending article that appeared in the Cardiff shipping journal, the *Maritime Review*, on 16 February 1906.[26] In this, the relatively cheap £10 shares in the Instow company were derided as 'housemaid shares . . . for they enabled James, Mary, Annie and the rest of the "below-stairs crowd" to prattle of "my steamer shares"', whilst the article was also dubious of the long-term prospects of the company: 'if we were out for a little flutter, we shouldn't take much chance in this direction . . . people aren't falling over each other in a mad attempt to invest with more or less untried folk at the moment'. The article went on to concede somewhat grudgingly that the *City of Cardiff* was likely to be 'a good ship', though casting doubt on the claim in the prospectus that she was the cheapest vessel built for some time. It was hardly a vote of confidence in the infant venture – though the *Maritime Review*'s editor, Captain J. E. Ward, would soon find himself having to eat his words.

Then, in March 1906, the company received a considerable boost when John Holman & Sons of London bought 150 shares.[27] Once more, Devonian connections had manifested themselves, for this was a significant endorsement of Reardon Smith's nascent venture by an old-established firm whose roots were deep in the county, if on its southern coast. The Holman family came from Topsham on the Exe estuary and there is evidence of their involvement in shipowning and shipbuilding in the area as early as 1615. They developed these interests in the area over the succeeding centuries, moving into marine insurance in the 1830s, operating a substantial fleet of sailing vessels by the 1850s and acquiring their first steamer in 1870. By that date they had moved their registered office to London and in the early twentieth century they became increasingly involved in shipping finance, investing sums in a number of Cardiff-based shipping companies at that time.[28] The Holmans' backing of the Instow Steamship Co. Ltd appears to have been something of a turning point in the company's financial development, for thereafter a steady trickle of investors proved willing to invest in the venture. Over 200 shares were sold during the remaining months of 1906, whilst the first six months of 1907 saw almost 1,000 shares sold. It is also interesting to note that Reardon Smith would renew his ties with the Holman enterprise in 1920, when he was made a director of Holman's P and I club, the West of England Steamship Owners' Protection and Indemnity Association Ltd, a position he would hold until his death. His elder son, a grandson and a great-grandson would also serve on the association's board in ensuing years.

The *City of Cardiff* was launched from Ropner's yard on 8 February 1906 and Willie Smith was present for her sea trials on 17 March, when the new vessel achieved twelve knots at full steam in Tees Bay.[29] The steamer's funnel was painted red with a black top; a large black 'S' adorned the red section and this pattern was repeated in the new company's house flag, a black 'S' on a red background. There is also evidence from models, photographs and contemporary flag books to suggest that the funnels of Reardon Smith ships initially also had black bases, though this latter practice was later discontinued.[30] Contrary to a persisting yet erroneous popular belief which maintains that all Reardon Smith vessels were registered at Bideford to maintain an association with the founder's native area, the earliest Reardon Smith vessels were actually registered at Cardiff, with the *City of Cardiff* being registered at the port whose name she bore on 15 March 1906.[31] Shortly afterwards she sailed from Cardiff on her maiden voyage under the command of Captain John Smith, bound for La Plata in Argentina with a cargo of coal, subsequently returning to Genoa with a cargo of grain loaded at San Nicolas, up the Rio Parana; such 'coal-out, grain-home' voyages were typical of those undertaken by Cardiff tramp steamers in the years before 1914. The voyage showed a clear profit of almost £2,050, and Reardon Smith, probably recalling the old adage that 'revenge is a dish best served cold', sent a copy of the voyage accounts to the *Maritime Review*, which had been so disparaging of the vessel's prospects just months previously! Presented with such conclusive evidence of the *City of Cardiff*'s profitability and her manager's commercial skills, the editor had no choice but to publish the accounts and change his tune:

> The profit shown provides for a big dividend, and this appears to be the case in shipping companies which are under the control of those who have gained their experience of shipping matters in the same manner as applies with Capt. Smith – at sea.[32]

This result must have delighted those who had invested in the Instow Steamship Co. Ltd, and the performance of the *City of Cardiff* over subsequent voyages did not disappoint either. The steamer's profitability, especially if trading to the upriver Plate ports, was enhanced by her low nett tonnage (1,965 tons) set against her high deadweight capacity of 5,730 deadweight tons and her low laden draft. Her second voyage in the late summer of 1906 took her on from Genoa to load a part-cargo of grain for Rotterdam at Braila, an upriver port on the Danube, topping off at the Black Sea port of Sulina; it showed a clear profit of £660 7s.7d. Having returned to Cardiff in ballast, she sailed with coal for Rosario on 20 September 1906 and returned to Liverpool with grain on 25 January 1907; this voyage showed a profit of nearly £2,200, surpassing that of her first.[33] By the end of September 1907, in just eighteen months, the *City of Cardiff* had recouped just over a quarter of the initial cost of her construction. All this added

The first Leeds City *discharging a cargo of wheat and linseed from Rosario at Sharpness dock in June* 1912.

significantly to Reardon Smith's growing reputation as an astute and highly competent shipowner, and with the price of new tonnage still quite low, it is hardly surprising that he began to consider the acquisition of a second vessel around this time. In October 1907 he eventually announced that he had placed an order, again with Ropner's, for one of their 'improved-trunk type' vessels;[34] measuring 4,298 gross tons and costing £41,200, she was to be given the name *City of Leeds*. Her construction was to be funded in part by an issue of 2,220 new £10 shares in the Instow company and secured by a mortgage for £28,000 at 5 per cent per annum from Ropner's. Details of the new vessel and the new share issue were comprised in a prospectus issued on 19 October 1907.[35]

The prospectus was headed 'An Attractive Home Investment' and Reardon Smith quite justifiably went into some detail on the highly success-ful trading results of the *City of Cardiff*. Somewhat questionable, however, was his claim that he had, since 1885, played a major role in the financial suc-cess of no less than eleven vessels; significantly, perhaps, none of these was named, though their construction dates were given. It is possible to deduce from these dates that he had served as master of four of these vessels – the *Ochtertyre*, the *Starcross*, the *Lady Lewis* and the *Shandon* – and superintended the building of at least one other, the *Corryvrechan*. As for the other vessels listed, it can further be deduced that most of them were amongst the earliest vessels in W. J. Tatem's fleet, on whose operation and performance he can have had no influence whatsoever after he left Tatem in 1900, thus making this an extremely dubious claim to publish. Or does Reardon Smith's claim actually raise the intriguing possibility that he had indeed spent some time, however brief, as Tatem's marine superintendent? It is the only possible explanation of such a claim, however tenuous the evidence.

It was not long before experienced observers in shipping circles picked up on some of the apparent anomalies in the prospectus and a particularly vehement attack upon its contents appeared in the London shipping journal, the *Syren & Shipping Illustrated*, on 20 November 1907. From its opening phrase, the article was almost relentless in its critical and occasionally sarcastic tone:

> An 'Attractive Home Investment' might be a sewing machine, a potato peeler or a brass bedstead – in the case under notice, it is a few shares in the Instow Steamship Co. Ltd, for thus have Messrs W. R. Smith & Son headed their newest prospectus . . . We have no fault to find with the earnings of their first steamer and we hope that No.2 will do as well, but we do wish that Messrs Smith had exercised more care with their prospectus. It is too much of the 'Cardiff type'; there is a redundancy of superlatives which tend to give one indigestion, or bile, or something equally unpleasant . . . Of greater moment is the justification of a long reference to Mr Smith's experience. For nearly twenty years, we are told, 'he has been identified with the working of steamers with one of the most successful shipowners in the UK. As evidence of success, that comprised in the following brief list, with which Mr Smith has been connected, ought perhaps to suffice.' We have then ten instances given of more or less profitable vessels, but there is no indication whatsoever of what connection, if any, Mr Smith had to do with their management. Had he any more to do with them than command them according to the instructions of the managers? This is not the suggestion sought to be conveyed and it is not the impression which will be gained by the class of investor likely to be attracted by such a flamboyant invitation as this.[36]

To what degree Reardon Smith was stung by this criticism is impossible to tell – certainly he never repeated any claim to have been commercially associated with so many vessels in any subsequent prospectus that he published. However, the old saw about there being no such thing as bad publicity appears to have applied in this case, for even before the *Leeds City* (as she was eventually named) had undertaken her maiden voyage in March 1908, the new issue of shares had been oversubscribed. The naming of the new vessel was significant, for the consolidated shareholders' list of the Instow Steamship Co. Ltd, compiled after the new issue of capital,

shows a marked preponderance of investors from the woollen manufactur-
ing areas of the West Riding of Yorkshire.[37] Just over half the investors in
the Instow company were from Leeds, Bradford and nearby conurbations,
and they provided a little over a third of the company's capital. The interest shown by the people of both Lancashire and Yorkshire in investing
in Cardiff's shipping companies during the first decade of the twentieth
century was a phenomenon that had already been commented upon in the
Cardiff press at the time; in February 1904, the *Maritime Review* noted, 'some
towns "up North" could be painted red with their faith in the dividend-
paying capacity of Cardiff's leviathans'.[38]

Relatively little is known about the actual means whereby investors
living over 200 miles from Cardiff, and having no obvious maritime associations, were first induced to buy shares in Cardiff shipping companies.
It seems probable that the initial contact would have been made by agents
working on a commission who went from door to door distributing prospectuses and persuading people to buy perhaps just a single share. Until quite
recently, for instance, another Cardiff shipping company, Graig Shipping
plc, had a substantial number of shareholders in Wigan, the descendants of those who had been persuaded to buy shares by an agent acting
on Graig's behalf in the Lancashire town in 1919. Once acquired, if those
shares then proved successful, word would spread and more shares would
be acquired by old and new investors in the area as the opportunity arose.
This was reflected in a later circular issued to shareholders by Reardon
Smith in 1912, at the foundation of the St Just Steamship Co. Ltd: 'The
personal assistance given by many of our shareholders in bringing shares
before the notice of their friends has largely contributed to the success of
the previous issues, and we sincerely trust that the same assistance will be
forthcoming on this occasion.'[39]

In direct contrast to the enthusiasm of the Yorkshire investors, however,
the Instow company received very little support from the area after which
it was named. Just four investors came from Appledore (two of whom were
Reardon Smith's siblings, John and Harriet), whilst another four came from
Bideford. One possible reason for the lack of financial support forthcoming from maritime communities such as these may have been that their
inhabitants preferred to invest in the locally owned sailing vessels belonging to those communities. This was certainly the case in a similar maritime
community in Wales at that time – Porthmadog – where the local investors'
funds were tied up principally in the town's fine fleet of three-masted topsail
schooners; the names of those who invested in that local fleet were notably
absent from the lists of shareholders in the joint-stock shipping ventures
established by their kinsmen elsewhere in north Wales and in Liverpool
at that time, to own and operate large iron and steel sailing vessels in the
deep-sea trades.[40]

EXPANDING THE VENTURE

With Reardon Smith's reputation as a successful ship manager growing in Yorkshire, it was natural for him to continue soliciting financial support from that area to expand his venture. The practice of promoting further shipping companies to acquire new tonnage was common at that time in Cardiff and had the advantage of enabling owners to tap fresh sources of capital to expand their fleets. Reardon Smith would also have been aware of the fact that by setting up a series of separate shipping companies, he would also reduce the liability that might arise from claims for eventualities such as collision. Having moved to new offices at 1 Pierhead Chambers at the very bottom of Bute Street, he placed an order for the construction of a new steamer of 3,683 gross tons at Ropner's yard on 20 August 1909; she was to be named *Bradford City*, doubtless to further raise local interest in Yorkshire. To raise the capital required to finance this vessel, Reardon Smith issued a prospectus for a new company to be named the Bradford Steamship Co. Ltd, which had a nominal capital of £33,250, again divided into £10 shares. It is noticeable that amongst the list of fifteen initial subscribers to the company were ten Yorkshire professional and businessmen, including the Leeds architect Frederic Mason, land valuer Arthur Robinson, also from Leeds, Charles Booth, a Huddersfield ironmonger, Leeds shoddy manufacturer Frederick Vause and the wealthy draper brothers from Bradford, Frederick and Priestley Mitchell; the latter two would be prominent in their financial support of all of Reardon Smith's subsequent shipping firms.[41]

The first Bradford City, *completed by Ropner's in* 1906.

In February 1910, however, Reardon Smith once more found himself the subject of critical comment in the pages of the *Syren & Shipping Illustrated*.[42] Whilst acknowledging that his first two steamers had shown more than satisfactory trading results, the article questioned the financial arrangements into which Reardon Smith had entered to secure construction of the new steamer; was her construction secured upon a mortgage, or had he perhaps agreed to hand over the *Bradford City*'s freight for the homeward leg of her maiden voyage as security? The journal's speculation was, in fact, quite unfounded, as the *Bradford City*'s purchase (like all the ships Reardon Smith ordered from Ropner's before 1916) was secured by a mortgage from Ropner's, in this case for £23,450 with interest at 5 per cent per annum.[43] Further questions were raised about his management fees, which were thought difficult to justify, even though they were exactly the same as those of the Instow company and had not been criticised previously.

However severe the strictures voiced in the *Syren & Shipping Illustrated*, they had no effect whatsoever upon the readiness of Yorkshire folk to invest in the new company – the issue was oversubscribed and almost two-thirds of the company's investors came from the woollen towns and cities of the West Riding. The Reardon Smith family were also substantial investors once more, with Reardon Smith himself taking 200 shares, Ellen Smith 100 and Willie twenty-five; Leonard Ropner, Sir Robert's son, also took a token single share.[44] Family tradition has it that a close and mutually advantageous friendship developed between Reardon Smith and the Ropner family; as has been noted, the latter did all they could, by advancing affordable mortgages, to assist and encourage the new shipowner, who in turn placed orders for his first eight newbuildings with the Ropner shipyard.[45] The third of these, the *Bradford City*, was launched on 10 January 1910,[46] and left the Tees on her maiden voyage on 15 February; amongst her crew, signed-on as an ordinary seaman, was Reardon Smith's younger son, Douglas, on his first sea voyage.[47]

For the next two years, Reardon Smith's fleet consisted of just three ships, but all were trading very profitably. The *City of Cardiff* made an aggregate profit of £18,692 12s. 9d over her first twelve voyages, equal to 11.3 per cent per annum of her initial cost; over her first six voyages, the *Leeds City* made a profit of £12,899 15s.8d, equal to 11.2 per cent per annum of her original cost, whilst during her first three voyages the *Bradford City* made a profit of £5,018 10s. 4d, equal to 12 per cent per annum of her total cost. The vessels' profitability was reflected in healthy dividends for shareholders; over three years from March 1906, the Instow company paid an average dividend of 12 per cent per annum.[48] It should also be borne in mind that these results were obtained during a period of depressed freight rates, and therefore reflect Reardon Smith's good sense in ordering and operating large modern vessels capable of operating profitably at such times.

During 1911 the shipping market, which had been in the doldrums since 1903, began to show signs of revival again; freight rates began to improve and Reardon Smith obviously thought it prudent to order further new tonnage before building costs rose in response to the more buoyant market.[49] On 30 June that year, the capital of the Bradford company was more than doubled to £77,000, again in £10 shares, to cover the cost of the company's second steamer, a 4,707 gross ton vessel to be named *Atlantic City*. Another product of Ropner's yard, and again covered by a mortgage of £27,000 with interest at 5 per cent per annum, she was delivered in March 1912.[50] On the twelfth day of that same month, Reardon Smith suffered his first maritime casualty when the *City of Cardiff* was blown aground in hurricane-force winds at Nanjizal, just south of Land's End, whilst bound from Le Havre to Barry Roads in ballast.[51] On 2 May 1912, a replacement vessel was acquired with the purchase of the 4,017 gross ton steamer *Charlton*, built in 1906 for Williamson Lamplough of London; she was subsequently renamed *Cornish City*. Later that year, an order for two further identical new steamers of some 4,300 gross tons was placed with Ropner's. Both were built to the shelter-deck design which was proving increasingly popular with British shipowners at that time and were capable of carrying 8,000 deadweight tons on a maximum draft of twenty-four feet. The combined cost of both vessels was almost £105,000, reflecting the advances already made in the cost of new tonnage as freight rates had improved. They were to be named *Devon City* and *Eastern City* and were due for delivery in April and September 1913 respectively.[52]

To raise the capital necessary to acquire these two vessels, Reardon Smith decided to float a third shipping company called the St Just Steamship Co. Ltd. The prospectus of the new company was issued in August 1912, with a nominal capital of £90,000, once more in £10 shares.[53] The usual management fee of £200 per annum, plus 5 per cent of net trading profits, was to apply and Reardon Smith also undertook to send shareholders a monthly postcard giving details of the location and employment of all the steamers under his management; this was a thoughtful gesture that not only sustained the interest of the shareholders in his vessels, but doubtless helped to enhance his reputation as a conscientious and reputable shipowner. Bearing in mind the fact that, once again, over half the capital in the company came from the north of England (with 42 per cent coming from the West Riding of Yorkshire, and a further 13 per cent from Lancashire), the choice of the name St Just is initially somewhat intriguing. However, for the first time ever for one of Reardon Smith's companies, almost 25 per cent of the investors came from the West Country – neither from Appledore nor Bideford (which together produced just four investors), but chiefly from Cornwall, particularly the area in and around the town of St Just, a little to the north of Land's End. No fewer than seventy-nine Cornubians invested in the company, providing nearly

Using the breeches buoy to rescue crew members and their families from the City of Cardiff, *wrecked at Nanjizal near Land's End on 12 March 1912.*

10 per cent of the total capital. How was it, therefore, that one small town in the far west of Cornwall came to provide the name for Reardon Smith's new shipping venture?

Ironically, the answer is linked closely to the loss of the *City of Cardiff*. Reardon Smith went down to Cornwall in March 1912 to assess the wreck of the vessel at Nanjizal and during his visit he stayed at the Commercial Hotel in St Just. A 'snug' in the hotel was at that time the regular and exclusive retreat of the area's professional and business community (including local butcher John Angwin) and Reardon Smith was invited to join them on successive evenings during his stay. He was most interested to learn that there were still considerable reserves of capital in the area dating back to the zenith of Cornish metal mining in the late eighteenth and early nineteenth centuries, and that many of those who possessed such assets might well be persuaded to become potential investors in the Reardon Smith venture. Having returned to Cardiff and mulled over his conversations in St Just, Reardon Smith resolved to go back to Cornwall later that spring, armed with the annual reports and balance sheets of his existing shipping ventures, to offer his new Cornish acquaintances and their associates the opportunity to invest in a new shipping venture; to entice them further, he proposed that the new company be named the St Just Steamship Co. Ltd. This he did, his offer was taken up with enthusiasm and so the St Just company came into being. And had the *City of Cardiff* not been wrecked where she was, this opportunity might never have arisen; quite literally for Reardon Smith this was a case of 'it's an ill wind that blows nobody any good'.[54]

The *Devon City* was launched from Ropner's yard on 7 March 1913 and by 10 April she was steaming up the Bristol Channel, bound for Barry, where she was fixed to load coal for Rio de Janeiro. The *Eastern City* followed five months later, and by the end of September 1913 she was sailing for Punta Arenas in the Strait of Magellan, Chile, again with coal from Barry. The monthly postcards of steamer movements sent to shareholders provide a valuable indication of the trading pattern of the vessels under Reardon Smith's management. It soon becomes clear that he was not content with confining his vessels to the traditional 'coal out, grain home' tramping voyages to the Black Sea and the River Plate that were the 'bread and butter' of many Cardiff shipowners. As an experienced master mariner, he was more than familiar with the various bulk cargoes available at dozens of different ports throughout the world – knowledge gained chiefly during his days with Hogarth's – and this extensive knowledge was reflected in the numerous voyages made by his ships carrying cargoes between foreign ports before they returned to the UK. Having discharged her cargo of coal at Rio de Janeiro following her maiden voyage in May 1913, for instance, the *Devon City* was then ordered to proceed in ballast to Lourenço Marques in east Africa to load coal for Karachi. From there she sailed for Le Havre via the Suez Canal with a cargo of rice, before sailing in ballast to south Wales to load coal once more.

The first Devon City, *built in 1913. Judging by the dense black smoke pouring from her funnel in this view, her firemen are hard at work and she is unlikely to be burning Welsh coal!*

Similarly, the *Eastern City* left Cardiff with coal for Puerto Militar on 1 April 1914; having discharged, she then sailed in ballast for Pensacola, where she loaded sulphur for Fremantle early in July. Bunkering at Durban late in August, she proceeded to Australia, and having discharged her cargo, proceeded to Melbourne to load wheat for Europe early in October.[55]

TABLE 1: Positions of Reardon Smith ships, 1 September 1913

Name of ship	Position
Atlantic City	On passage, New York–Melbourne
Bradford City	Passed St Vincent for the River Plate
Cornish City	Leaving Ayr for Barry
Devon City	Passed Perim Island for UK/Continent
Eastern City	Fitting out, Stockton-on-Tees
Falls City	Under construction, Stockton-on-Tees
Leeds City	Bunkering at Durban, bound for Korea

Source: DoI, 86.231/1 (27).

It is most fortunate that a comprehensive file of accounts, balance sheets and shareholders' circulars for the St Just Steamship Co. Ltd for the period 1912–22 survived in the chairman's personal archive, and these documents give a valuable indication of the performance of at least one part of the Reardon Smith enterprise during those years. With freight rates having improved considerably since 1911, the accounts laid before shareholders at the first annual general meeting of the St Just company, held on 5 June, 1914, showed a most favourable situation.[56] A gross profit of £17,625 9s. 1d had been achieved, of which £8,100 had been passed on to shareholders in two dividend payments of 8 per cent and 5 per cent; a provision of nearly £6,000 was also made against depreciation.

In the meantime, Reardon Smith had also ordered two further shelter-decked steamers from Ropner's: the 4,729 gross ton *Falls City*, to be delivered in November 1913, and the 5,525 gross ton *Great City*, to be delivered in March 1914. The *Falls City* was allocated to the Bradford Steamship Co. Ltd, whose capital was further increased to £133,000, again in an issue of £10 shares, to take account of the cost of the new vessel. The *Great City*, however, was allocated her own new company, the Great City Steamship Co. Ltd, which had been floated in June 1913 with a capital of £60,000 divided into 6,000 £10 shares.[57] With Reardon Smith's reputation as a competent and successful shipowner now well established (the journal *Syren and Shipping*, once so critical, would feature him as their 'Maritime Mark Maker' in November

From master mariner to shipowner; William Reardon Smith aged fifty-eight, photographed on 9 November, 1914.

1914!), shares in the new company were taken up rapidly.[58] By October 1913 the issue was fully taken up and northern investors were once more predominant, with 23 per cent of the shareholders coming from Lancashire and 40 per cent from Yorkshire, again chiefly from the West Riding. No one from Reardon Smith's native area around the estuaries of the Taw and the Torridge invested in the company, though 23 per cent of the investors came from Devon and Cornwall, again comprising a strong representation from St Just and other nearby communities. It is also interesting to note that in comparison with their earliest ventures, where members of the Reardon Smith family had taken up large blocks of shares to achieve flotation, so established was the reputation of their companies by 1913 that Reardon Smith and his son Willie took just one share each as their initial investment in the both the St Just and the Great City companies.

OTHER ISSUES

The year 1913 also saw developments in the management structure of the overall venture. On 10 March, an agreement was drawn up between Reardon Smith and his sons Willie and Douglas to formally establish the partnership of William Reardon Smith & Sons.[59] The agreement, written in a style more reminiscent of an eighteenth-century apprentice's indenture than an agreement between partners, made it abundantly clear that Reardon Smith senior was the principal partner, with the power to dismiss either of his sons from the partnership at near-minimum notice and proscribing them from engaging in any other form of business. In return, Willie was to receive a salary of £250 per annum and Douglas £160, subject to an annual review. Later that year, in December 1913, a somewhat different company was established by Reardon Smith, namely the Devon Mutual Steamship Insurance Association. This was an unlimited company with no nominal share capital; its income came from a small annual premium on the earnings of each steamer, whilst its main objectives were to provide cover in cases of loss or damage to any steamer, liability arising from negligence, loss by non-payment of freight and compensation payments to injured parties. Reardon Smith and his sons were joined as directors of the Association by two prominent North Country share-holders, William Burton of Blackpool and Frederick Mitchell from Bradford.[60] The main reason for the establishment of this association was outlined by Reardon Smith in a circular issued on 10 September 1915: 'We found that Underwriters were continually demanding higher Insurance Premiums, and so decided that the time was ripe to form a Mutual Association for the ben-efit of all the steamers managed by us.'[61]

The demand for higher premiums that Reardon Smith mentions in his circular had its origins in one of the most disreputable episodes in the his-tory of shipowning in the UK, that particularly manifested itself at Cardiff in the first decade of the twentieth century. Reference has already been made to the slump in freight rates prevailing in tramp shipping between 1903 and 1911. Well-managed shipping companies owning larger and newer vessels (such as those overseen by Reardon Smith) had little cause for undue worry at such times, but owners operating older, smaller vessels with lower dead-weight capacity and higher repair bills soon began to realise that their chief assets were fast becoming considerable liabilities. And with low freight rates came depressed tonnage prices, so much so that many such vessels were worth considerably less than the sums for which they were insured. This discrepancy between actual and insured values would, with the benefit of hindsight, appear to have been too much of a temptation for some less scru-pulous Cardiff shipowners, so much so that from 1905 onwards there were a number of highly dubious losses involving Cardiff ships, whose insurance value as opposed to their actual value made them more attractive propo-sitions at the bottom of the sea rather than trading on its surface. Over-insurance was a recurrent theme in each of these losses; for instance, the *Powis*, lost in a gentle Aegean swell in June 1907, was insured for a total of £24,125, despite being valued at just £12,000.[62]

These dubious losses and the inquiries that followed them were widely reported in the local, national and maritime press, and repercussions soon began to make themselves felt on the London insurance market, where addi-tional premiums began to be demanded for insuring Cardiff-registered ships. So it was that a number of Cardiff's more reputable shipowners decided to reregister their vessels at other UK ports, usually at London; by the end of 1912, both the Radcliffe and Nicholl fleets, two of Cardiff's largest, aggregat-ing 144,000 gross tons, had 'flagged-out' to London registry. It was following these moves that Reardon Smith transferred his fleet to Bideford registry in 1913–14, with the *Bradford City* being the first to be reregistered at the north Devon port on 5 August 1913. It is often popularly supposed that this was done out of a sentimental attachment to his native area, but sentiment rarely figures highly in the business of shipowning. Feeling the pinch of rising premiums, and realizing the notoriety attached to Cardiff-registered vessels, it seems not unreasonable to surmise that this is what actually lay behind Reardon Smith's establishment of the Devon Mutual Steamship Insurance Association and the transfer of his vessels to Bideford registry at that time. By the mid–1920s, the legend 'Bideford' was carried on the sterns of some thirty-five Reardon Smith ships, and it is worthy of note that this would be a major factor in the restoration of Bideford to full custom-port status in 1928. This success owed much to the lobbying of Parliament by a delegation comprising Reardon Smith, local MP Sir Basil Peto and Bideford councillors Goaman and Huxham.[63]

Since 1875, the commercial interests of Cardiff shipowners had been represented by the Cardiff Incorporated Shipowners' Association, an organisation that had grown out of the Cardiff Chamber of Commerce.[64] Reardon Smith first joined the association with his then partner William Seager on 16 August 1904, but then had to resign in March 1905 after the dissolution of their partnership. He rejoined on 10 April 1906 following his acquisition of the *City of Cardiff*, but thereafter attended meetings only occasionally and appears never to have spoken.[65] However, between 1912 and 1914, he became embroiled in a bitter dispute which resulted in the split-up of the association and the creation of a rival shipowners' organisation at Cardiff, of which Reardon Smith was one of the founder members. The origin of the dispute lay in the rules of the association drawn up in 1884, which stipulated that voting rights at its meetings were not simply on the basis of 'one man, one vote'; each managing owner also had the right to cast a vote for each ship he managed, provided that he paid an annual levy of 10s. 6d per vessel to the association. This system of franchise obviously gave the larger, wealthier shipowners a clear advantage when it came to any vote, and during the 1890s a number of members operating smaller fleets began refusing to pay the vessel levy, as it brought them no electoral advantage whatsoever – they could always be outvoted by the larger shipowners. They, in turn, became very critical of the smaller owners because of what they perceived to be the deliberate flouting of the association's rules by their refusal to pay the vessel levy.

Having lain dormant for some years, the matter was raised again in November 1911 and a subcommittee of the association was convened to investigate the matter. The committee reported back on 1 December with a recommendation that vessel-related voting rights should be changed to one vote for every three vessels. The larger owners reacted with fury, putting forward a motion demanding that the franchise should remain unaltered, in response to which W. R. Corfield put forward a motion proposing 'one man, one vote', regardless of the number of vessels managed. A decision was deferred to a further meeting held on 11 December, at which the 'no change' party, with their vessel-weighted vote, won easily by 142 votes to 92. Then, at the association's AGM, held on 21 January 1912, sixteen shipowners announced their resignation from the association, further declaring their intention to establish an alternative body, the Bristol Channel Shipowners' Association, with a franchise based strictly upon 'one man, one vote', regardless of the number of vessels managed; amongst them, managing just three vessels at that time, was Reardon Smith.[66] The new association was formally constituted in July 1912; its chairman was Philip Turnbull of Turnbull Brothers, and Reardon Smith was appointed one of its directors.[67] This situation prevailed throughout 1913, though negotiations went on behind the scenes throughout the year to effect a reconciliation between the two bodies. This was eventually achieved in April 1914, when the principle of 'one man, one vote' won the day and the reunified association, under its new name of the Cardiff and Bristol Channel Incorporated Shipowners' Association, came into being. Thereafter, Reardon Smith participated only occasionally in the association's deliberations and it is interesting to note that, although he was elected to the council of the UK Chamber of Shipping in 1918, his attendance at this organisation's meetings would similarly be very sporadic.[68]

THE FIRST WORLD WAR

Coincidentally, returning to Reardon Smith's own enterprise, April 1914 also saw the delivery of the *Great City*, the first Reardon Smith vessel to be fitted with a wireless; just a month later the capital of the Great City Steamship Co. Ltd was increased to £114,000 with an issue of 5,400 new £10 shares. This was to enable the company to acquire a second vessel to be named *Homer City*; yet another product of Ropner's yard, she was due to be delivered in December 1914. In August that year, however, Britain declared war on Germany following the invasion of Belgium, a war that was to subject the British mercantile marine to the stiffest trial that it had yet faced. The First World War was to prove a period of mixed fortunes for British shipowners. Tremendous losses in tonnage and lives were to be experienced; indeed, the first Cardiff-owned vessel to be lost in the conflict was Reardon Smith's *Cornish City*, captured and sunk by the German light cruiser *Karlsruhe* on 21 September that year; no lives were lost.[69] Reardon Smith ordered a replacement vessel for the Instow company almost immediately from Doxford's yard, whilst early in 1915 the capital of the Great City company was further increased to £164,000 through the creation of 5,000 new £10 shares. This was to enable the company to conclude the purchase of the *Santeramo*, a 4,670 gross ton steamer completed for the Gulf Line Ltd (a subsidiary company within the Furness Withy group) in July 1914.[70] Handed over in London in

Atlantic City *in the Pacific! She is seen here loading railway sleepers via an aerial ropeway at Fort Bragg, north of San Francisco on 16 September 1916. Though not of the best quality, the view illustrates well the remote and minimally-equipped ports at which tramp steamers often discharged or loaded cargoes.*

January 1915, she was renamed *Jersey City*. Delivered in the same month from Doxford's was the ill-fated replacement for the *Cornish City*, which was given the name *Indian City*; in a little over two months she joined her predecessor on the seabed, torpedoed by U29 south of the Scilly Isles on 12 March 1915; again, no lives were lost.[71]

Even though the attrition rate achieved by the U-boats in the early months of the war was as nothing compared to the height of the campaign in 1917, nevertheless the slowly growing deficiency in carrying capacity gave added impetus to a steady advance in freight rates that exceeded anything within living memory at that time.[72] Any vessel at sea during the early years of the war was therefore a guaranteed source of profit, provided that she was not requisitioned for government service. An owner whose vessel was requisitioned, however, was paid the government's so-called 'Blue Book' rates, which were lower than those prevailing on the open market; moreover, he had no control over the employment of his vessel for the duration of the requisition. Some idea of the rapid advance in freight rates at that time can be gained from the results of the St Just company's second year; with its two vessels not requested for UK government service and on lucrative time charters to the French government bringing war supplies from the USA to Le Havre, the trading profit earned by the company during the twelve months up to 20 May 1915 was almost £30,000, close to double the previous year's results.[73] Of this sum, dividends absorbed £9,900, whilst a further £10,000 went towards depreciation reserves. Evidence of the continuing buoyant state of the freight market can be seen from the fact that the St Just company was able to pay further dividends of 6 per cent in July 1915 and another of 10 per cent in September that year. However, growing unease throughout the country at the excessive profits being made by many companies, on land and at sea, led to the imposition of an excess profits duty as part of the Finance Act of September 1915. This made provision for a duty of 50 per cent to be imposed upon any increase above pre-war profits; increased to 80 per cent in 1917, it was to prove a massive bone of contention between government and business during the war and for some years thereafter.[74]

The loss of the brand-new *Indian City* in March 1915 left the Instow company with just one vessel, the *Leeds City*, and in January 1916 Reardon Smith decided to transfer the vessel to the Bradford company and wind up the former company.[75] With berths at shipyards in very short supply due to wartime demands, it was becoming increasingly difficult to order a new vessel by this time, and a second-hand replacement was bought in the form of the *Coniston Water*, a 3,738 gross ton steamer dating from 1908, managed by a Cardiff company, McFarlane & Lander. Not only was the ship acquired, but the share capital of the single-ship company that owned the *Coniston Water* was also taken over by the St Just company at that time. Quite soon after she entered service, however, Reardon Smith heard of the loss of another of his vessels. On 9 April 1916, the *Eastern City* was captured by U66 eighteen miles north-west of Ushant, whilst bound from St Nazaire to Barry Roads in ballast; her crew members were allowed to escape in the lifeboats and the three-year-old vessel was then sunk by shelling.[76] Despite this loss, the accounts of the St Just company showed a gross profit in excess of £76,000 for the twelve months leading up to 20 May 1916, clearly reflecting the continuing high freight rates of the war years. However, the incidence of excess profits duty dramatically reduced this substantial fig-ure, with the Treasury taking £40,000 into its coffers, though this still left the company with £18,000 to distribute amongst its shareholders (a most handsome dividend of 21 per cent), with £9,000 being set aside for depre-ciation and £5,700 to carry forward. By this date the company had built up investments totalling some £66,000 in Treasury Bills and a 4½ per cent War Loan, whilst Reardon Smith had also been fortunate enough to obtain a berth at J. L. Thompson & Sons' Sunderland yard to build a new steamer in place of the lost *Eastern City*.[77]

In December 1916, the British shipping industry was brought even more closely under government control with the creation of the Ministry of Shipping, headed by the newly created post of shipping controller to which the Glasgow shipowner Sir Joseph Maclay was appointed. The system of requisitioning vessels as they were required was terminated and henceforth *all* British ships were taken under government control, and at the 'Blue Book' rates. It was a decision that met with great resentment amongst British ship-owners, especially as vessels belonging to neutral nations were still able to take advantage of a booming open market, but they had no choice in the matter; for the remainder of the war and for some time afterwards, the British merchant fleet, to all intents and purposes, was a nationalised fleet.[78] In response to this decision, Reardon Smith wrote to all the shareholders in the three shipping companies that he managed – Bradford, Great City and St Just – suggesting an amalgamation of all three companies into one, under the title of the St Just Steamship Co. Ltd. He further stated that this would impart numerous benefits, such as increased administrative efficiency that would place the whole venture on a firmer financial footing, but paramount in Reardon Smith's reasoning was the certainty (in his opinion),

> that it will be necessary for the government to retain a number of ships on requisition after the war, which on the present basis is bound to prejudice one company more than another. We think it is very necessary for this reason alone that the amalgamation should take place.[79]

TABLE 2: Restructuring the Reardon Smith companies, 1917

Vessel	Pre-1 July 1917	Post-1 July 1917
Leeds City, 1908 *Bradford City*, 1910 *Atlantic City*, 1912 *Falls City*, 1913	Owned by the Bradford SS Co. Ltd	All vessels owned by the 'new' St Just SS Co. Ltd from 1 July 1917.
Devon City, 1913 *Eastern City* (2) (delivery due 31 July 1917)	Owned by the St Just SS Co. Ltd	
Great City, 1914 *Jersey City*, 1914 *Homer City*, 1915	Owned by the Great City SS Co. Ltd	

Source: DoI, 86.231/1 (77).

It was proposed, therefore, that the capital of the St Just company should be increased from £90,000 to £387,000 (this being the aggregate capital of all three companies), and that a completely new issue of £1 St Just shares be distributed amongst the shareholders of the new amalgamated company, equal to their holdings in the three former companies; the new company would also take over all eight vessels then in Reardon Smith's fleet. The proposal was put before shareholders for their approval in a circular sent out on 24 April 1917 and within a few weeks over 90 per cent of them had replied affirmatively; the result was confirmed at an Extraordinary General Meeting of the three companies held on 17 May and amalgamation subsequently took place on 1 July 1917.

The last set of accounts published by the St Just company prior to amalgamation clearly demonstrated the combined adverse effects of excess profits duty and the absence through loss of one of the company's two vessels over half the financial year. Profits had fallen by almost a half from £76,000 to a little over £46,000, and of this sum £22,500 went to the Treasury. A total dividend of 15 per cent was paid, taking up almost £13,500, whilst the remainder of some £16,000 was carried over to the next accounts.[80]

Reardon Smith was also deeply concerned at this time about the proposed increase in excess profits duty, which the government eventually increased from 50 per cent to 80 per cent, back-dated to 1 January 1917. What most exercised him was not the actual increase, but the fact that a provision whereby companies could claw back any loss sustained within one accounting period from excess profits duty paid in another was specifically denied to shipping companies in the Finance Act of 1917. In a circular issued to all shareholders on 11 May 1917, he described this as 'a gross violation of all British sense of fairplay . . . deliberately intended to debar British shipowners recovering losses that the chancellor of the exchequer admitted would henceforth accrue'. He further encouraged all shareholders to raise the issue with their MPs and encourage them to vote against 'a proposal fraught with such serious consequences for the nation'.[81]

The spring of 1917 had seen a renewed campaign of considerably more ruthless submarine warfare by the Germans, causing the loss of over one million gross tons of Allied shipping at the time. Three Reardon Smith steamers – the *Jersey City*, the *Coniston Water* and the *Bradford City* – were lost between late May and mid-August that year. No crew members lost their lives in these incidents, but the master of the *Jersey City* and the gunners of the *Coniston Water* were taken prisoner. Since October 1915, the *Bradford City* had served as a 'Q-ship', one of the apparently innocent merchant ships bristling with armaments that played a significant part in First World War anti-submarine operations; she had operated chiefly out of Gibraltar under false names such as *Ballistan* and *Seros*.[82] These losses were offset to some degree by the delivery of the second *Eastern City* at the end of July 1917, but the fact that all British shipyards also came under the jurisdiction of the shipping controller made the ordering of further new vessels on the open market practically impossible.

Reardon Smith's solution was to turn again to the second-hand market, and early in November 1917 a circular to shareholders in the St Just

The Norwich City was one of the eight vessels bought from Pyman, Watson & Co. in 1917; like her sisters, she was easily identified by her distinctive 'tea-spout' bows. This highly embarrassing scene was the result of a collision with the 2nd Narrows Bridge near Vancouver in April 1928 – Sir William's reaction to the accident is not recorded!

company announced that he had acquired the eight steamers in the fleet of the London & Northern Steamship Co. Ltd, managed by Pyman, Watson & Co. of London, at a cost of £815,000. The inflated tonnage prices prevailing during the war were reflected in the fact that whereas the new *Devon City* had cost some £7 12s. 0d per deadweight ton when contracted for in 1912, the price paid for eight second-hand steamers in 1917 averaged some £15 per deadweight ton. Despite the high price paid for these vessels, Reardon Smith was keen to justify the purchase to his shareholders, declaring the importance of maintaining the strength of the fleet in preparation for the 'greatly improved trading conditions' which he felt sure would ensue after the war ended.[83] Three of these vessels would fall victim to torpedoes within the next few months, but the remaining vessels were all given -*City* suffix names by the end of 1918; however, they remained a distinctive group within the Reardon Smith fleet on account of their 'tea-spout' bows, that were a characteristic feature of many steamers built for Pyman, Watson & Co. over the years. The fleet was also augmented briefly in 1918–19 by four wartime standard merchant vessels which came under Reardon Smith management; the 'B class' dry cargo ships *War Camel* and *War Warbler* and, unusually for management by a dry-cargo tramping owner, the 'AO class' oil tankers *War Hunter* and *War Scot*.

The profit and loss account of the enlarged St Just company covering the period up to 31 March 1918 reflected the increased profits being earned by the enlarged fleet now trading in the company's name. A trading profit of over £99,000 was recorded, of which £38,700 was distributed to shareholders as a 10 per cent dividend, whilst over £40,000 went once more to excess profits duty. Plans were also outlined to increase the capital of the company to £½m. by creating a further 113,000 £1 shares, but the Treasury refused to sanction such an increase at that time.[84] Losses through wartime hostilities continued in 1918, with Reardon Smith's second steamer, the *Leeds City*, being lost on 6 May that year, along with the three Pyman, Watson vessels mentioned above. When hostilities eventually ceased in November 1918, the St Just company was left with eleven steamers, having an average age of some six years. Some Cardiff companies, however, were left with no vessels whatsoever and never again resumed shipowning.

BOOM AND BUST

The 'greatly improved trading conditions' that Reardon Smith had forecast after the end of the war did indeed transpire, though what began as an improvement was soon to transform itself into a heady shipping boom which lasted for some fifteen months until the late spring of 1920, and whose effects were particularly marked at Cardiff. It is often supposed that the main reason for this boom was a lack of tonnage as a result of wartime losses but in fact, thanks to the massive governmental programme of standard merchant ship construction commenced in 1917, the British merchant fleet in 1919 was only some 700,000 gross tons less than it had been in 1914, whilst the world-wide merchant fleet had actually grown over the same period from 42m. to over 50m. gross tons. And by 1921, this expanded fleet would be chasing a volume of world trade which had decreased by some 20 per cent since 1913.[85] There was nevertheless an apparent shortage of available tonnage on the market which was caused chiefly by severe congestion and delays at many ports as they gradually reverted to peacetime operation following the war, and this was exacerbated by the fact that many ships were still on wartime government charters, far away from their normal trading routes. However, ships were gradually released from government service from 1 March 1919 onwards, whilst in May 1919 came another welcome development when excess profits duty was halved from 80 per cent to 40 per cent. All these factors – the apparent shortage of tonnage available for charter, the post-war deregulation of shipping, the halving of excess profits duty and a growing post-war optimism – came together to fuel a classic cycle of boom and bust that would ultimately prove disastrous for some Cardiff shipowners, and from whose damaging effects Reardon Smith's enterprise would not be immune.

Merthyr House on James Street in Cardiff's dockland. The Reardon Smith head office was located on the second floor from 1919 until a disastrous fire struck the building in 1946.

The boom was relatively short-lived in its duration, but during that period it seemed as if Cardiff's shipping community was gripped by an almost all-pervading commercial mania. There was a headlong rush by many inexperienced newcomers to take advantage of the boom by floating shipping companies to acquire almost any available tonnage. During 1919, no fewer than eighty-eight prospectuses were issued, mostly by new companies, but also including a few existing enterprises (such as Reardon Smith's) seeking additional capital; the total sum sought was in excess of £7m. Tonnage prices also rocketed; a typical 7,500 dead-weight ton tramp steamer, which would have been valued at about £42,000 in 1914, could have been sold for almost £300,000 during the winter of 1919–20. Many of Cardiff's older-established and more sagacious shipowners distanced themselves from the boom, harbouring strong suspicions that it would not last long; some, such as Reardon Smith's former employer, William Tatem (recently ennobled as Lord Glanely), and the directors of the W. & C. T. Jones Steamship Co. Ltd, took advantage of it by selling off their entire fleets at the top of the market.[86] Despite the caution being displayed in certain quarters, however, Reardon Smith appears to have been swayed considerably by the general optimism of the time and, with the benefit of hindsight, the purchase of the Pyman, Watson fleet in 1917 can be seen to have marked the beginning of an expansive era in the history of Reardon Smith's shipping ventures that eventually led to some financial difficulties by the early 1920s.

This period of growth continued in the spring of 1919 with the opening of a London office in the Exchange Buildings adjacent to the Baltic Exchange – the world's foremost shipping market – in St Mary Axe; later that year, the company of W. R. Smith & Sons (London) Ltd, having a capital of £30,000 in £1 shares (all held by its directors), was established to oversee the London business. The new London office was headed by an experienced shipbroker, Thomas Davis, who had previously worked for Ropner's and for the Royal

An aerial view of the yard of the Monmouth Shipbuilding Co. Ltd at Chepstow, in which Reardon Smith (sensibly!) made a very short-lived investment in 1920.

Commission on Wheat Supplies; his assistant was Gordon Hall, who came from London shipowners and brokers Galbraith, Pembroke & Co.[87] New office premises were also established in Cardiff at that time, with the acquisition of the second floor of Merthyr House on James Street in the heart of Cardiff's docklands. Reardon Smith also took an interest in a number of other ventures; having ordered ten vessels from their yard since 1905, he was appointed a director of the Ropner Shipbuilding & Repair Co. (Stockton) Ltd in July 1919 and he also invested in a newly created chandlery company, Shipping Supply Ltd of Newport at the same time. Later, in March 1920, he made a considerable investment in the Monmouth Shipbuilding Co. Ltd, created to take over the government-promoted shipyard laid out on the River Wye at Chepstow in 1917 to produce standard First World War merchant vessels. However, rightly sensing that the future prospects for shipbuilding at Chepstow were far from bright, he sold these shares in December that year.[88]

The still buoyant trading conditions of that post-war boom were reflected in the profit of £181,642 made by the St Just company in the year ending on 31 March 1919. This enabled the payment of a substantial 17½ per cent dividend over the year and a further half-year dividend of 10 per cent was paid to delighted shareholders on 30 September that year. It was against this booming background during the late summer and autumn of 1919 that the expansion of Reardon Smith's enterprise reached its apogee, with the flotation of the Leeds Shipping Co. Ltd on 20 August (almost certainly so named to maintain the interest of the enthusiastic investors of the West Riding) and the Cornborough Shipping Line Ltd on 24 October (the company took its name from a tiny hamlet not far from Appledore). The Cornborough company came under the management of W. R. Smith & Sons but, probably in order to spread the administrative burden of expansion, a new management firm of W. R. Smith, Popham & Liley had been created on 31 August 1919 to oversee the Leeds company. The new directors, Arthur Popham and W. G. ('Bill') Liley, were Reardon Smith's sons-in-law, Arthur having married Gertrude ('Gertie') Smith and William having married Lillian ('Lily') Smith, in December and July 1914 respectively. By appointing his sons-in-law as directors, Sir William further consolidated family control over the shipping venture, and it was not until after his death that any non-family members became directors of the management company. It is also interesting to recount that Lillian's romance with Bill Liley apparently met with her parents' profound disapproval; at the time, Liley was an engineer on one of the Reardon Smith steamers. However, Captain and Mrs Smith had quite underestimated their daughter's determination to marry her sweetheart, for she left home and went into service as a maid in a house in Cathedral Road, Cardiff; only when her parents consented to the wedding did she return home![89]

The new companies each had a nominal capital of £400,000 in £1 shares; the Leeds company was created to acquire the two First World War standard 'B-type' steamers *War Panther* and *War Vulture* (respectively renamed *Bradboyne* and *Bradavon* under Reardon Smith ownership), whilst the Cornborough company was formed with the initial intention of acquiring three second-hand steamers (*Hurliness*, *Netherpark* and *Skegness*) bought from Letricheux & David of Swansea, and the First World War standard 'C-type' steamer *War Combe*, later renamed *Watsness*.[90] It is unfortunate that no initial shareholders' list of the Leeds Shipping Co. Ltd appears to have survived, although in a circular issued on 30 September 1919, Reardon Smith thanked the many shareholders in the St Just company who had also bought shares in the Leeds company. However, a shareholders' list for the Cornborough Shipping Line Ltd is available, and it reflects the all-pervading optimism of the shipping boom of the time. Having been launched on 24 October 1919, the entire Cornborough share issue was allotted by early January 1920. Once more the investors of the north of England showed their loyalty to Reardon Smith; 40 per cent of the investors came from Yorkshire (chiefly again from the West Riding) and 24 per cent from Lancashire; 14 per cent of the investors came from Wales, 15 per cent from Devon and Cornwall and the remainder were scattered all over the UK. Reardon Smith's fellow countrymen from around the Taw and the Torridge appear to have remained wary of investing in his new venture, though two well-known names amongst Appledore's sailing shipowner-masters, Richard Slade and William Quance, bought two hundred

An interesting view of the Bradclyde, *probably taken in 1919. Built in 1918 as* War Castle, *she is seen here still in her overall wartime grey, but evidence that peace has returned may be seen from the fact that her name has been painted on her bows — all merchant vessels sailed incognito during the war.* (Kevin O'Donoghue collection)

and three hundred shares respectively; they had never previously invested in any Reardon Smith venture and their acquisition of shares in 1919 quite possibly reflected the good freight rates that their coasting ketches and schooners were also earning at that time.[91]

In addition to the vessels mentioned in the prospectuses of both companies, further acquisitions were made in 1919–20. A further First World War standard cargo vessel, the F1-type *War Castle* of 1918, was bought by the Leeds company and renamed *Bradclyde*. The Cornborough company acquired four more vessels, three being further vessels offered for sale by Letricheux & David (*Dungeness*, *Stromness* and *Yarborough*) and one newbuilding, the *Alness* of 1920. The latter vessel was the last of three completed in that year for Reardon Smith by Ropner's, the first ships built to his order by the Stockton shipbuilders since the *Homer City* of 1915. The earlier pair, a second *Indian City* and a second *Atlantic City*, both also completed in 1920, were acquired by the St Just company. Also added to the St Just fleet in 1920 were two other new steamers, the *Jersey City* from the Thompson yard at Sunderland and the *Paris City* from Craig, Taylor & Co. of Stockton. This expansion of the St Just fleet was made possible by a capitalisation of the firm's considerable reserves, taking the form of a 300 per cent bonus issue of shares that increased the nominal capital of the company to £2,064,000; though never undertaken, a further increase in nominal capital to £3,096,000 was actually authorised at the time.[92]

The costs involved in the construction of these new vessels at that time were enormous. For instance, whereas the acquisition of the entire Pyman, Watson fleet, comprising eight second-hand vessels, had involved £815,000 in 1917, the new *Indian City* of 1920 cost £310,075 alone, making her the most expensive Reardon Smith vessel up to that time. The four nearly new steamers acquired for the Leeds company cost over £930,000.[93] This tremendous expansion and the creation of further shipping companies seemed to run

quite contrary to Reardon Smith's decision in 1917 to bring all his vessels under the umbrella of one company, though the release of vessels from government control from 1 March that year may have persuaded him to change his mind on this issue. Neither can there be much doubt that he had been swayed considerably by the boom;

Right: *Family firm: Sir William Reardon Smith and his sons Willie (left) and Douglas, c.1920.*

Below: *The* Indian City *of 1920 arriving at Avonmouth docks. Ordered and built at the height of the post-First World War boom, she cost a staggering £310,075.*

(Kevin O'Donoghue collection)

having himself predicted improved trading conditions after the end of the war, he would appear to have seen little reason to exercise the same degree of caution shown by others, such as William Tatem, in the unprecedented commercial euphoria of the time. Few foresaw potential disaster looming; a contemporary report captured perfectly the overwhelmingly optimistic mood of Cardiff's commercial community at that time; 'with this go-ahead spirit, added to the value of past experience, there is no fear that Cardiff will at any time fall away from the splendid position in the shipowning sphere which it is now privileged to hold'.[94]

Then, towards the end of May 1920, the boom suddenly collapsed. It had gradually dawned upon the market that far from there being a shortage of tonnage, there was in fact a considerable glut. Freight rates were soon tumbling; whereas it had cost 72s. per ton to ship coal from Cardiff to Genoa in February 1920, by December the 'going rate' was as low as 19s. Tonnage prices crashed too; the book value of the Cardiff-owned fleet tumbled from £14.5m. in early May 1920 to some £8.25m by December 1921, whilst by the summer of 1922 the price of a typical 7,500 deadweight ton steamer had fallen back from almost £300,000 at the height of the boom to about £60,000.

Moreover, the onset of the slump was compounded by adverse economic developments overseas. Coal exports from Cardiff, a vitally important outward cargo for UK tramp shipowners, fell from a peak of 10.5m. tons in 1913 to 6.6m. tons in 1925. Many markets for Welsh coal overseas had been lost during the First World War and this was particularly true of the lucrative South American market that had turned to cheaper coal imports from the USA since 1914. The punitive terms of the Treaty of Versailles meant that Europe was soon to be flooded with German reparations coal that undermined continental markets for Welsh coal in France and Italy, whilst the Royal Navy, having specified only Welsh coal for its use since 1851, was increasingly adopting oil-firing in many of its larger ships. Other important tramp trades were hit too; the Bolshevik revolution of October 1917 had led to the halting of grain exports from the Russian Black Sea ports, once a staple homeward cargo for Cardiff's tramp steamers. And as if to crown a lengthy list of adverse developments, in 1920 the government decided to raise the rate of excess profits duty once more (from 40 to 60 per cent), a move that was condemned by shipowners and other businessmen throughout the UK.[95]

In what was otherwise a gloomy year, Reardon Smith had reason to be particularly pleased on 1 July 1920 when he was elevated to a baronetcy as 'Sir William Reardon Smith of Appledore in the County of Devon' in the King's birthday honours list, for services to the country during the First World War; he took as his motto the Latin tag, *Quod facio, valde facio* (What I do, I do earnestly) – certainly an accurate reflection of his character! This was at a time when Cardiff was coming to be known as 'the city of dreadful knights', because many figures prominent in the public life of the city were being granted honours in return for substantial contributions to David Lloyd George's 'political fund' (a peerage could be obtained for £50,000 and a baronetcy for £15,000).[96] There is no conclusive evidence as to whether or not Reardon Smith paid for his honour, although two authorities on Welsh political history in the early twentieth century consulted by the author were able to confirm that his name was most definitely not linked to some of the more outrageous aspects of the honours scandal of the time. Perhaps it is not just coincidental, however, that at the time news of his elevation was announced, he donated to the National Museum of Wales a fine oil portrait of the prime minister by the Welsh artist, Christopher Williams. Together with the painting came a letter from the new Sir William to the museum's then director, W. Evans Hoyle, insisting that the painting be displayed at the National Eisteddfod, held that year in nearby Barry (where it would certainly be seen by Lloyd George, an inveterate Eisteddfod-goer), and thereafter, 'in a very prominent position, in fact in the best place in the museum'.[97]

Despite the increasingly grim economic outlook, expansion continued to be Sir William's keynote policy at this time. On 29 October 1920 a further new company, the Oakwin Steamship Co. Ltd, was established with a capital of £100,000 in £1 shares. Unlike other companies established by Sir William, however, the share capital was not offered for sale to the public; he and his

The Royal City, *formerly the* Erfrid, *was one of nine former German vessels surrendered to the British government after the war and bought by Sir William in* 1920-21.

(York Collection, Bristol's Museums, Galleries & Archives)

An unlucky vessel, and forever being sought out by treasure hunters, the Meropi *is seen here at Avonmouth docks in the mid-1920s.* (York Collection, Bristol's Museums, Galleries & Archives)

two sons held one share each, with the remainder being in the hands of the management company of W. R. Smith & Sons. Acquired for the company from Ashwin & Co. of London was the steamer *Oakwin*, originally built in 1919 as the First World War standard 'C-type' steamer *War Oasis*; she cost £95,000.[98] Further additions were made to the fleet in 1920 and 1921 as the British government began to offer for sale (under the 'Inchcape scheme', so named after P&O chairman Lord Inchcape, who oversaw the process) German merchant vessels which had been surrendered to the shipping controller after the war. Sir William went on to acquire no fewer than nine of these vessels, the eldest of which dated from 1907, though at £468,000 for the lot they were considerably cheaper than the newbuildings delivered in 1919–20. Six of them – *Erfrid*, *Haimon*, *Winfred*, *Wismar*, *Iserlohn* and *Answald* – were allocated to the St Just company, and one each to the Cornborough, Leeds and Oakwin companies, respectively *Schwaben*, *Riol* and *Berengar*; all but two were eventually given '-City' names.[99]

The expansion continued early in 1922 with the acquisition of the Unity Shipping & Trading Co. Ltd, which had been established in September 1921 with a capital of £30,000 in £1 shares to acquire the 1908-built Greek-owned steamer *Meropi*. Some mystery surrounds the origins of the company and its subsequent takeover. It had been promoted originally by the partnership of Smith & Fletcher, but with the partners apparently unable to raise the necessary capital, Sir William then stepped in to rescue the ailing venture. The circumstances surrounding the takeover of the company were outlined in the first annual report of March 1923, in which it was stated:

> This company, over which we assumed management after an attempt at flotation by the late firm of Messrs. Smith & Fletcher . . . owing to their inability to raise sufficient capital to take over the steamer bought, rather than those shareholders of ours who had subscribed losing their capital, Sir William Reardon Smith came to their assistance and found the necessary capital in order for the company to continue trading.

No reference is made as to who exactly the 'Smith' of Smith & Fletcher was, but the fact that numerous shareholders in various Reardon Smith ventures had also taken shares in the company suggests that there was perhaps a family connection, possibly Douglas Smith. The partnership agreement of 1913 between Sir William and his sons proscribed them from engaging in any other business; however, if there was no connection, then it is intriguing that Sir William should have bothered to extend a lifeline to this particular company at that time. It is also indicative of the degree to which tonnage prices had collapsed in so short a period that the *Meropi* could be acquired for a little over £30,000, but despite her bargain price she was never a lucky ship, casting propeller blades on her first voyage under Reardon Smith management and often involved in minor collisions and groundings. Moreover, one of Sir William's grandsons, Alan Reardon-Smith, recalled in 1969 that there had been a rumour that the *Meropi*, having been in a Russian Black Sea port at the time of the Bolshevik revolution of 1917, had had some of the Romanoff crown jewels brought aboard to be smuggled out of Russia. So widespread and persistent was this rumour that there were continual problems with treasure-hunting stowaways on the *Meropi* throughout her seven years in the Reardon Smith fleet![100]

The era of rapid expansion that had commenced with the purchase of the Pyman, Watson fleet in 1917 drew to a close in 1922 with the acquisition of two more newbuildings which were added to the St Just fleet: the *Welsh City* from Ropner's (a sister vessel to the *Indian City* of 1920) and the *York City* from Thompson's of Sunderland (a sister vessel to the *Jersey City* of 1920). At the end of 1922, therefore, Sir William controlled a fleet of thirty-nine steamers – twenty-four owned by the St Just company, eight by the Cornborough company, four by the Leeds company, two by the Oakwin company and one by Unity Shipping & Trading. Whilst these vessels may well have constituted, 'a truly fine fleet', many, nevertheless, had been contracted for at spectacularly high prices during the post-war boom; a grand total of £5.2m had been spent on tonnage since 1917, the equivalent of almost £156m. in current

(2010) values.[101] In the meantime, the boom continued to unravel in spectacular fashion during the early 1920s. In a survey of the state of Cardiff's shipping industry published at the time, the authors were careful to distinguish between, on one hand, 'newer shipowning concerns which are experiencing difficulties that may perhaps prove to be of an unsurmountable nature' and on the other, 'local owners . . . particularly those who have been long enough in the business to know that shipping is peculiarly susceptible to ups and downs of a more or less violent character'.[102]

Many of the newer shipowners in Cardiff soon found themselves unable to pay for vessels recently acquired at grossly inflated prices, and the local newspapers of the early 1920s were littered with reports of the demise of over-optimistic entrepreneurs who were left facing ruin as they were forced to sell ships for a fraction of the price for which they had acquired them only a few years before. Between 1921 and 1931, the number of shipping companies at Cardiff was to fall from almost one hundred and fifty to seventy-seven, including three of the four companies set up by Sir William in 1919–21. Indeed, it was almost inevitable that the adverse economic circumstances of the early 1920s would impact in some way upon the Reardon Smith enterprise, as a result of the expansionist policy pursued by Sir William at the time.

Nowhere would those circumstances impact more than upon the Cornborough Line Ltd. Having been established originally in October 1919 with a capital of £400,000 to acquire just four steamers, the buoyant trading conditions of the time had encouraged Sir William to borrow a further £400,000 to finance the purchase of five further vessels (though the oldest of the vessels purchased, the *Stromness* of 1902, was sold shortly after purchase in 1919). Initially, his optimism would appear to have been justified, for in its first annual report, covering the period from its inception in 1919 until 31 July 1921, a profit of £342,441 was reported by the company. However, as a company set up since the inception of the First World War, its entire profit was liable for excess profits duty, then set at 60 per cent. Presented soon afterwards with a tax demand for £228,793, Sir William protested bitterly that this was a totally disproportionate imposition in view of the fact that the value of the company's ships had slumped so dramatically, and he authorised a payment of just £40,000. Whilst the dispute with the Inland Revenue remained unresolved, however, it was deemed prudent to set aside a sum against future tax liability, and the Cornborough balance sheet of July 1922 shows that £145,000 had been nominated to this end. This remained an outstanding issue despite the announcement in the 1921 Finance Bill that excess profits duty was to be terminated, and in the annual reports for the Cornborough Line in the early 1920s, Sir William consistently returned to the issue of excessive taxation.[103]

Equally, if not more serious, however, was the issue of gearing the considerable debt that Sir William had incurred through the purchase of

'Sir William Reardon Smith' by Oswald Birley, RA, 1930.

Top left: *The barque*
Vermont, *which Reardon
Smith joined as second mate
in the Richmond dry-dock at
Appledore in* 1876. (National
Maritime Museum, Greenwich,
London)

Bottom left: *The barque*
Ochtertyre, *commanded by
Captain William Reardon
Smith in* 1885-90.

Above: *The funnel and flag
colours adopted by Reardon
Smith in* 1906. (Louis Loughran,
World Ship Society)

Right: '*David Lloyd George'
by Christopher Williams, RBA;
this painting was presented by
Sir William to the National
Museum of Wales in the
summer of* 1920, *shortly after
he had received his baronetcy.*

Above: The Reardon Smith family home, 'Cornborough', completed in 1916 and photographed in the spring of 2009.

Above: The wooden plaque recording the opening of Bideford's new hospital by Sir William on 23 September, 1925.

Left: 'The Reardon Smith family tomb in the Cathays cemetery, Cardiff.

additional steamers for the Cornborough company, many of which had been contracted for, or purchased, at the inflated prices prevailing in 1919–20. The balance sheets of 1922 and 1923 showed that sums of a little over £100,000 were 'due to bankers', and in the accompanying annual reports it was noted that the small trading profit being made by the ships was overwhelmed by interest charges on advances and loans. In 1923, for instance, the ships showed a trading profit of a mere £3,089 4s. 6d, whilst interest payments alone amounted to more than twice that sum at £6,877 11s.7d. The poor returns were exacerbated by the fact that it had been stated in the company's prospectus that its vessels would be fixed on individual voyage charters, rather than time charters.[104] Such a policy was very profitable whilst freight rates were buoyant, but led to a serious depletion in income after the crash in the spring of 1920. Had the vessels been fixed on time charters before rates collapsed, a better return could have been obtained in the early 1920s. In an attempt to alleviate an increasingly desperate financial situation, a loan of a little over £97,000 had also been made to the Cornborough Line by the St Just company, but with little prospect of an improvement in freight rates, Sir William faced a daunting prospect in his address to Cornborough shareholders whilst presenting the accounts for the year ending July 1923; with commendable honesty, he admitted,

> Turning to the balance sheet, it discloses an insolvent position. Liabilities are over £400,000, and the property, viz. eight steamers, have been valued at not more that £190,000 . . . sundry creditors will in due course be met, except the item 'Reserve for Taxation', which stands at £145,000 . . . the SS *Yarborough* has been laid up for a while and at present we also have the SS *Hurliness* laid up on the Tyne. The SS *Skegness*, now on passage to Japan, will be sold upon her arrival, and the proceeds utilised to reduce the bank overdraft, which is guaranteed by the Chairman. Continued low freights, long delays and general trade depression have been the cause of the poor results. We trust that under the circumstances the position will be accepted, and we are pleased that a larger loss has not been made.[105]

The tax issue remained only partially resolved – a successful claim for 'obsolescence' (a depreciation in the company's assets) led to a reduction of the tax demand by £63,000, but there remained an outstanding balance of over £85,000, which Sir William claimed there were no funds to pay. During 1924 the company's eight vessels were disposed of; two were sold outright, two were transferred to the Oakwin company and the remaining four were transferred to the St Just company. In December 1924, Sir William wrote to the registrar of companies,

The company has ceased trading and the mortgagees took posses-
sion of and sold the company's assets, the value of which was far
below the amount of the mortgage. Consequently, the company is
hopelessly insolvent and there are no funds available to pay the
claims of either the Inland Revenue, the creditors or the expense of
a voluntary winding-up. Under these circumstances we should be
glad if you could arrange to have the company struck off.[106]

The company was eventually dissolved on 7 July 1926. It had been without doubt Sir William's most disastrous venture in shipowning and he was
fortunate that its failure did not impact further upon his other companies.
Moreover, it seems clear that Sir William was touched personally by the
collapse of the Cornborough Line Ltd, for in July 1923 it was made known
by the company's board in a circular that also appeared in the *Western Mail*
that 'This position has given great concern to the chairman of the directors,
Sir William Reardon Smith'.[107]

Sir William subsequently made an offer whereby he proposed to give
every shareholder in the collapsed company one share from the personal
shareholding that he had built up in the well-established and financially
sound St Just company for every three Cornborough shares, further declaring that 'this offer is made in order that those shareholders who have supported me for so many years may still have an opportunity of saving some
part of their investment'.[108] The offer was accepted by the Cornborough
shareholders, and during December 1923 they became the recipients of
126,722 shares (which had a total value of a little over £48,000 at the time)
from Sir William's own portfolio. This share transfer was a remarkable
gesture, the like of which was not seen elsewhere in Cardiff's shipowning
community at that time, a period when shipping ventures were foundering
one after another, taking the entire savings of many modest investors with
them as they sank.

FACING THE DEPRESSION

The collapse of the Cornborough Line notwithstanding, Sir William still
found himself in the early 1920s in charge of a substantial fleet, but facing a
massive downturn in the global shipping industry. Nowhere was this downturn more evident than in the tramp trades, which were in fact destined to
suffer nearly two decades of largely unremunerative freight rates. Somewhat
more stable trading conditions could be obtained in the cargo liner trades,
but these trades tended to be dominated by well-established conferences,
effectively cartels of longstanding participant companies working together
to maintain cargo rates at a level that would provide regular and gainful

income. Breaking into such conferences was notoriously difficult, and those companies that tried to compete outside the conference system invariably found themselves facing stiff competition in the form of undercut freight rates and sustained legal challenges.

Despite these difficulties, however, it would appear that Sir William was considering an attempt to break into the liner trades in the early 1920s as a means of offsetting the deleterious effects of a flagging tramp market, and it is significant that eight of the nine ex-German vessels that he acquired in 1920–1 were originally built for cargo liner companies rather than tramping firms. The allocation of most former German vessels to shipowners in the Allied countries after the war had also effectively eliminated the German merchant fleet, leaving an obvious gap in some of the liner trades formerly operated world-wide by German shipping companies. During 1920, two of his sons-in-law went abroad at Sir William's behest to investigate possible sources of cargo for new Reardon Smith liner services; W. G. Liley went to New York, whilst D. A. Low (who had married Sir William's third daughter Elizabeth (Betty)) went back to his native Cape Town. Sir William himself left Southampton for a two-month working tour of the eastern seaboard of the USA on 8 January 1921, by which date W. G. Liley had opened an office in New York at 44 Beaver Street, just off Wall Street in the heart of the city's financial district.

The eventual outcome of these acquisitions, developments and exploratory visits was the establishment, on 27 October 1921, of a new company, the Reardon Smith Line Ltd. With a nominal capital of just £1,000 in £1 shares, it had three directors; Sir William held 998 shares, with Willie and Douglas holding one each.[109] Whilst it is not clear when exactly the service commenced, it comprised regular cargo liner services from certain US East Coast ports to destinations in the UK, Germany, South Africa and Australasia (see table 3); these services were established in association with the United States Navigation Company of New York, who were to act as general agents for the Reardon Smith Line in the USA.[110]

The inception of the new Reardon Smith liner service was noted in a contemporary account of the main shipping lines using of the port of New York:

It may not be amiss to give mention to the new blood, energy and brains that is ever being drawn from the four corners of the earth to partake of the wonderful opportunities here presented and to further enhance the fast-growing reputation of New York as the nerve center of world commerce. Such action on the part of men who have been leaders of maritime interests in other ports is their acknowledgement that this is the coming maritime capital of the world, as it is fast growing to be the financial capital. Of such men, there is none perhaps whose coming has had such significance in this direction as

Sir William Reardon Smith, Bart, of Cardiff, Wales. Sir William has achieved notable success in the maritime affairs of his native land and comes to the great port of the New World amply qualified by experience and ability to take the same commanding position in his new sphere of activity.[111]

TABLE 3: Summary of cargo liner services from the USA offered by the Reardon Smith Line, in association with the United States Navigation Company, January 1922.

From	To	Frequency
New York	Hamburg	Fortnightly
Philadelphia and Baltimore	Hamburg	Monthly
New York	London	Fortnightly
Philadelphia	London	Ditto
New York	Liverpool (and Manchester by inducement)	Ditto
Philadelphia	Liverpool (and Manchester by inducement)	Ditto
Norfolk, Virginia	Liverpool and London	Monthly
New York	South African ports (by inducement)	Ditto
New Orleans	South African ports (by inducement)	Ditto
New York	Australasian ports (by inducement)	Ditto

Source: DoI, 2007.86/13.

However, the new service had been in existence for just a few months when it became embroiled in controversy. Sir William had refused to join the North Atlantic/Continental Conference, believing the rates stipulated by the conference to be too high, and his views on this matter were supported by some American owners, such as United American Lines, which also left the conference. Other companies within the conference, however, such as the Royal Mail Steam Packet Company, were deeply critical of the Reardon Smith Line's tactics. Anxious to avert a damaging rates war, the vice-president of the United States Shipping Board, W. J. Love, went from Washington to New York on 6 March 1922 to enter into negotiations, though he pulled no punches in his references to the Reardon Smith Line; 'the situation has been aggravated by the ruthless competition of a British line to Hamburg which has declined to join the conference'.[112]

The eventual outcome of this meeting is not known, but it would appear that the liner services continued to operate. New trade was sought in South Africa through the creation of Reardon Smith (Union of South Africa) Ltd on 26 June 1923; with offices in Pretoria, it had a capital of £250,000 and its directors were Sir William, Willie Smith, Douglas Smith and Douglas Low. It was probably at this time too that Sir William became friendly with the Jersey-born master mariner Thomas Davis, who had established an extensive stevedoring business in a number of the dominion's ports.[113] Nevertheless, there are tantalising suggestions that these liner services seem to have been the source of considerable vexation arising from disputes over freight rates and certain consignments. On 7 April 1924, it was reported that Sir William had sailed from Southampton to New York on the *Aquitania* 'to figure in a certain law case in New York in connection with shipping contracts', whilst in June 1925 a case arose relating to a shipment of 150 casks of bourbon from Baltimore to London on the *Quebec City* in March 1923, which was allegedly thirty-five casks short upon discharge at London![114] It is not altogether clear when these liner services came to an end; they would appear to have lasted in some form until about 1927. In this context, it should also be noted that Sir William was not the sole British tramp owner to seek out new business in North America in an attempt to offset the years of the depression; Watts, Watts & Co. of London commenced a liner trade to the Gulf ports, with cotton the prize, whilst R. S. Dalgliesh Ltd of Newcastle upon Tyne pioneered the seasonal grain trade to Churchill in Hudson's Bay, following the completion of a rail link from the prairies to the port in 1930.[115]

Just before Sir William left to go on his business trip to the USA on 8 January 1921, he was asked by the editor of the Cardiff newspaper, the *Western Mail*, to give his impression of the general economic situation at the time and what cures, if any, might be found for the deepening commercial gloom. His response is worth quoting in its entirety, as it not only provides a clear reflection of his views on the economic situation prevailing at the time, but also shows that he envisaged a solution rooted solely in the principles of classic nineteenth-century *laissez-faire*:

> On the eve of my departure from Britain, you have asked me to express some cheery note on the prospects for shipping. Although all my financial interests are in shipping, my mind is not at the moment concerned as to the profits which may be made, but I am deeply anxious as to the necessity of the maintenance, extension and increased vigour of the industry which is of vital importance to the existence of our Empire. If, during the present period

of undoubted strain and heavy losses in trading, British shipping is to retire from the competitive field, and leave operations to other nations whose shipping is (in effect) subsidised, or free of excessive taxation, then (if the depression is of lengthy duration), we should probably entirely lose many of the trade routes upon which prior to the war, we were pre-eminent, and which were of such tremendous, though largely unappreciated value to our country before and during the war.

Every facility must be given to British steamers, every possible economy must be carried out to maintain the British flag on the seas; and to succeed in this, every person in industry, including dockers and miners, must realise the necessity of unity and personal sacrifice.

I do not hope for any improvement in the South Wales shipping ports until the export price of best Welsh coal is reduced to 40s. per ton, which is of course below the present price of production.

I remain, yours faithfully,

W. R. Smith.[116]

At that time, the 'going rate' for Admiralty Best Welsh coal was about 70s. a ton; it was also a period of considerable ferment in the coal industry. The Sankey Commission of Enquiry into the Coal Industry in 1919 had suggested that the industry should eventually be nationalised, whilst supporting the continuation of the wartime-imposed state control and improved wages and conditions for miners in the short term. Not surprisingly, Sir William's bold suggestion was condemned by the south Wales miners, and the *Western Mail* published a response by Mr Ted Williams, miners' agent for the Garw district of the south Wales coalfield:

If Sir William Reardon Smith implies that the miner should be prepared to forego part of his hard-earned wages in order that coal prices should be reduced to 40s. per ton, then his hope is a forlorn one indeed. In the light of the fabulous profits received by shipowners during the first two years of the war, his statement is very interesting, for during that period shipowners received not less than £300m. Since the war ships have been free from requisition in order that higher freights might be obtained. If Sir William had suggested that in shipping, as in all other matters of transport, that there should be co-ordination and unified control, which would necessarily make for economy and efficiency, there might be a probability of export prices coming down to the figure he mentions. We are now suffering from a manifestation of the virtues of competition, which have too often been lauded as conferring upon society the benefits of initiative, energy and industry.

I remain, yours faithfully,

Mr Ted Williams.[117]

This exchange resulted in a number of letters to the press, both supporting and decrying Sir William's stance. Amongst those who expressed their support were Mr Hubert Spence Thomas, managing director of Cardiff's Melingriffith tinplate works, and shipowners Sir James German and Sir William Seager. His comments were criticised by the Labour politician Vernon Hartshorn, MP for Ogmore and later to be president of the South Wales Miners' Federation. Hartshorn blamed German reparations coal as the main problem at that time, claiming that 24m. tons of cheap German coal had been sold to France since the conclusion of the Treaty of Versailles.[118]

On 21 February 1921 the *Western Mail* published another letter from Sir William, then still in the USA, on the economic prospects of the country as he viewed them. He was of the opinion that despite the fact that the production costs of US coal were less than half of those prevailing in south Wales, the inferior quality of the product meant that it posed little direct threat to Welsh steam coal in the home and European markets. Nevertheless, he emphasised the fact that US coal had gained a firm foothold in the important South American markets during the war, and stated bluntly 'the world is no longer dependent on Welsh coal'.[119] Such uncertainties as to the future of Welsh coal were made manifest back in south Wales when it was announced that month that the state control of the coal mines, in place since 1916, would terminate on 31 March that year. The coal owners immediately announced drastic wage cuts, which led in turn to an eleven-week strike by the miners. They were eventually forced back to work, having had to accept wage reductions of up to 40 per cent in some cases, an action that would play a crucial role in the origins of the far more serious dispute that broke out in 1926.

THE EMERGING PHILANTHROPIST

Despite the growing economic difficulties of the period and his apparent indifference to the plight of the miners in a period of recession, the 1920s saw Sir William emerging as a considerable philanthropist, both in his adopted south Wales and his native Devon. Prior to the establishment of the National Health Service in 1948, the provision of adequate health care facilities often depended in part on the munificence of wealthy philanthropists, and this was

The King Edward VII Hospital in Cardiff – later the Cardiff Royal Infirmary – to which Reardon Smith donated ten thousand guineas in 1916.

an area in which Sir William soon showed considerable generosity. In 1916 he had contributed ten thousand guineas to the King Edward VII Hospital in Cardiff (later renamed the Cardiff Royal Infirmary), a donation commemorated in a stained glass window in the hospital chapel. He was also a supporter of the Royal Hamadryad Seamen's Hospital in Cardiff. In the 1920s he became one of the main supporters of a fund to establish a new hospital at Bideford. Proposals for such a facility in the north Devon town were first mooted in the early 1920s, and by November 1924 plans had been finalised and an appeal for five thousand pounds was launched. Much of this sum was eventually donated by the two sons of Appledore who had 'made good' in Cardiff, Lord Glanely and Sir William; this was recognised when Lord Glanely was invited to lay the hospital's foundation stone on 10 December 1924, whilst the new hospital was opened by Sir William on 23 September 1925.[120]

Having received no more than a rudimentary schooling himself, education was another area in which Sir William was to show his generosity. In September 1917 he contributed the sum of £2,000 to the Cardiff Technical College (which had moved to a new site in Cathays Park the previous year) to initiate new classes for teenage boys in navigation and seamanship. Since the establishment, on 1 January 1851, of compulsory examinations for foreign-going officers in the British merchant fleet, a number of nautical academies or schools had opened in Cardiff, providing intensive 'cramming' targeted at getting candidates through the Board of Trade examinations. Sir William's ultimate intention, however, was to enable the college to provide longer-term training for boys whose ambitions were set upon a career at sea, whereby they could study navigation and seamanship alongside a core syllabus. To this end, he initiated a collection amongst his fellow shipowners at Cardiff, and by March 1921 he had gathered the considerable sum of £18,000, in addition to his initial donation.

This sum enabled the establishment, within Cardiff Technical College, of what was initially known as the Smith Junior Nautical School, later the Reardon Smith Nautical School, which provided an appropriate education for boys between the ages of thirteen and sixteen whose sights were set upon a sea-going career. The formal syllabus was to include geography, mathematics, science, navigation, nautical astronomy and elementary business practice, whilst practical courses such as boat-handling, first aid, rope and wire work, signalling and swimming were also to be taught as an integral part of the boys' training. The school opened on 3 October 1921 and on 1 August 1922, the Board of Trade recognised the Reardon Smith Nautical School as an approved school of nautical training; during the academic year that followed, some sixty boys were on the register. Moreover, the Board of Trade also sanctioned a remission of six months on the period of sea service required prior to sitting the second mate's examination for those who had successfully completed their three-year study period at the school.[121]

The facilities available to the boys attending the Reardon Smith Nautical School were enhanced considerably in February 1925 when Sir William Reardon Smith & Sons Ltd purchased the schooner-rigged steel yacht *Margherita*.[122] This handsome racing schooner had been the toast of the yachting world when completed by Camper & Nicholson of Gosport for Major Cecil Whitaker in 1913, but she had afterwards spent lengthy periods of time laid up. After the war, she appears to have been owned for some time by the noted diamond tycoon, Solomon Barnato ('Solly') Joel, but having been purchased by Sir William, a thorough refit of the yacht was undertaken to equip her both as a sail training vessel for the Nautical School and as the Reardon Smith family yacht. Her lofty racing rig was cut down and replaced with a more practical, though somewhat unattractive three-masted staysail schooner rig, and two 28hp Gardner diesel engines were installed, driving twin screws.[123] In a lengthy interview which appeared in *Lloyd's List*, Sir William outlined his ambitious intentions for the *Margherita*,

> No one deplores more than I do that the development of the steamer and the disappearance of the sailing vessel mean lack of opportunity for sailing ship experience for those who desire to take up the sea as a profession. Nothing can be a substitute for this. The knowledge of seamanship gained on a sailing vessel cannot be acquired as thoroughly any other way. I want them to experience the delights as well as the duties and hard work of sailing ship training, to train on to become first class officers.[124]

Above: *The yacht* Margherita, *which served both as a training vessel for cadets from the Reardon Smith Nautical School and the family's yacht, from 1925 until 1932.*

Left: *Clad in a substantial overcoat, Sir William surveys the deck of the* Margherita.

In another interview with the *Western Mail* he stated, 'My ambition is to give these boys a training similar to that I got myself in boating, navigating and in fact an all-round knowledge of all that pertains to sea life. The *Margherita* should help towards this end'.[125] Whilst the *Margherita* was primarily a training vessel, it should not be forgotten that she was also Sir William's yacht, bringing him much pleasure and doubtless reminding him of his days as a master under sail. He was a member of four prominent British yacht clubs – the Royal Torbay, the Royal London (based at Cowes), the Royal Temple (Ramsgate) and the Royal Thames (London);

amusingly, family tradition has it that he was considered too *nouveau riche* to be a member of the exclusive Royal Yacht Squadron! However, it was through his association with the Royal Thames club that Sir William became one of the founder members of the Honourable Company of Master Mariners, being present at the first meeting of the Company's Court in Lloyd's Committee Room at the Royal Exchange in London on 9 September 1926.[126]

It would appear that the *Margherita*'s main summer voyage each year, as both training vessel and family yacht, took her down the west coast of the UK and then up the English Channel to Cowes. Having finished his three-year course at the Reardon Smith Nautical School in the summer of 1925, for instance, the seventeen-year-old cadet Elfed Lewis from Aberystwyth joined the newly converted *Margherita* on the Clyde on 16 July 1925 for her first season in service as a training vessel. Having sailed down from the Clyde to the Bristol Channel, opportunities were taken by the Reardon Smith family to visit relatives in both north Devon and south Wales and the *Margherita* would also visit various regattas in the area; in June 1926, for instance, she was in Swansea's South Dock (from where the young William had sailed for Chile in 1872), participating in the Swansea Bay regatta and moored next to Thomas Davis's *Westward*.[127] The *Margherita* would then round Land's End, sometimes heading for the Channel Islands, or calling at ports such as Falmouth, Plymouth and Torbay, before heading for the Solent in time for Cowes week in early August. Some flavour of this is provided in this fascinating extract from a letter written on board by Lady Ellen Smith, whilst the *Margherita* was moored at Falmouth in July 1928. She was writing to her niece and her husband, Hilda and John Tamlyn, to congratulate them on the birth of their son, Michael.

> We have been moving about a lot lately since we left the Clyde. We tried to get to Appledore, there was too much sea on the bar. We were due there last Wednesday to open a new organ at the Baptist chapel. We went to Ilfracombe and stopped outside for an hour or two, we saw your Uncle Edward and Auntie Alice, from there went on to Barry Roads for two or three days. We stayed with Lily at Penarth. Arrived here on yesterday morning [sic]. We have had some dreadful tossing about since we came on board nearly five weeks ago. We are sailing for Plymouth on Friday.[128]

Even if Sir William was not considered to be sufficiently 'grand' to be a member of the Royal Yacht Squadron, the presence of the *Margherita* at Cowes, with her crew of smartly uniformed young cadets, drew the attention of no less a person than the Squadron's Admiral, King George V, in August 1926. The King duly requested further information about the vessel,

With caps set at jaunty angles, the crew and cadets of the Margherita *crowd around Sir William and members of his family in this view from the late 1920s. On the left, smoking a pipe, is Douglas Smith; seated in the middle are Grace Smith, Lady Ellen and Sir William, whilst Lily Liley stands at her father's left shoulder.*

which Sir William was only too happy to provide, and on 5 August 1926, His Majesty's assistant private secretary, Col. Clive Wigram wrote back,

> The King noticed the *Margherita* lying near the Royal Yacht and was impressed with the generous spirit which prompted you to give these boys such a practical experience of the sea, before being apprenticed. I need hardly say how interested His Majesty was to hear of all that was being done to give these boys a chance of a sea career.[129]

Four years later, the *Margherita* was at Cowes in early June to witness an event that drew as many members of the yachting fraternity together as Cowes week – the trial sailing of Sir Thomas Lipton's famous new J-class yacht, *Shamrock* V, British challenger for the America's Cup. Moored near to the *Margherita* in the Cowes roadstead on this occasion was another famous yacht owned by a master mariner turned shipowner, namely the *Sunbeam*, owned by Sir William's near contemporary, Sir Walter Runciman. One feels sure that the two former captains would have got together on each others' vessels to reminisce about their days at sea under sail. And as for Elfed Lewis, he had left the *Margherita* on 13 October 1925 to commence a two-year cadetship on the *Bradburn* – a move that doubtless constituted a sharp reality shock for the young cadet![130]

Neither did Sir William ignore his native county in his educational philanthropy. In 1926 he and Lady Ellen gave £7,000 to endow a chair in the geography department at the University of Exeter, and there is still a Reardon Smith Chair of Geography in the Department of Geography at the university today. They also gave a further £4,500 to endow three scholarships at the university. Two of these scholarships, the Thomas and Elizabeth Reardon Smith of Appledore Scholarship and the Thomas and Elizabeth Hamlyn of Appledore Scholarship were named after Sir William and Lady Ellen's parents respectively, and were granted annually to two students from the Bideford and Northam Urban District (that comprised Appledore), whilst the third, the Sir Richard Grenville Scholarship, was available annually to a student from anywhere within the county of Devon.[131]

There were also myriad donations to other causes, both great and small, in both Wales and Devon: £1,000 for the National Library of Wales in 1930; donations to the University College of South Wales and Monmouthshire, Cardiff (whose president was Lord Glanely); part-funding of the new sea defences at Westward Ho! near Appledore; countless donations, in both cash and kind, to all of Appledore's benevolent and religious causes, regardless of denomination, and the Reardon Smith Perpetual Challenge Cup for the best pair of junior oarsmen at Appledore regatta! Lady Ellen was prominent in her support of many seamen's charities such as the British Sailors' Society, the Royal Alfred Aged Merchant Seamen's Society and the Harbour Lights Guild (for sailors' wives) of the Missions to Seamen. Like many of Cardiff's most prominent shipping families, the Reardon Smiths were non-conformist in religion and were members of the impressive neo-Gothic Roath Park Wesleyan Methodist church; they also supported the work of the Boys' Brigade, the YMCA and the YWCA in the city. And, like many master mariners of his era, Sir William was a Freemason.[132]

There can be little doubt, however, that the philanthropic cause with which Sir William was most closely associated, and to which he was most generous, was the National Museum of Wales. Despite being a proud Devonian, he would prove to be a loyal and indefatigable officer (as both treasurer and president) of this important Welsh national institution between 1925 and 1932; indeed, it could be argued that the museum might not exist in its present form today had it not been for his diligence and generosity. The National Museum of Wales had been incorporated by royal charter in 1907; building work on the Cathays Park site in Cardiff's city centre started briefly in 1912, but was suspended with the onset of the First World War. Sir William was appointed a member of the museum's council in 1921, by which date construction had recommenced, and he and Lady Ellen made contributions to the building fund totalling almost £13,000 prior to his appointment as the museum's treasurer in 1925. He was immediately faced with a daunting challenge. The museum's building fund was so depleted that construction work had had to be halted in 1922; £5,000 was owed to the building contractors, whilst there was a bank overdraft that exceeded £20,000 by the summer of 1925. On 24 November 1925, Sir William instantly cut this Gordian Knot by visiting the director, Mortimer Wheeler, and writing a personal cheque for £21,367 4s. 9d to clear the museum's overdraft. It was his wish that his donation remain anonymous, but the museum's council insisted that his generosity be properly acknowledged and a formal vote of thanks was duly passed at the annual meeting of the museum's court of governors held on 22 October 1926.[133] By that date, Wheeler had moved on to be keeper of the Museum of London, but years later he would recall Sir William with great affection in his autobiography, *Still Digging*: 'I have never encountered a character at the same time so rich in experience, so shrewd, and withal so simple, so unspoilt, and so generous as that of Reardon Smith . . . we became great friends'.[134]

As treasurer, Sir William started restoring the depleted reserves of the building fund, setting a target of £100,000. He initiated a vigorous fundraising campaign targeted at wealthy individuals and companies in south Wales and beyond – not an easy task in an age of growing recession. Nevertheless, his contacts in the shipping and shipbuilding industries proved particularly fruitful; in Cardiff, Daniel Radcliffe and Willie Smith each

The imposing neo-Gothic Roath Park Methodist church, at which the Reardon Smith family worshipped.

Mortimer Wheeler, director of the National
Museum of Wales, 1924-26; despite
their widely differing backgrounds, he and
Sir William became firm friends.

gave £1,000, the Cardiff Channel Dry
Docks & Pontoon Co. Ltd (of which he
was a director) gave 250 guineas, his
erstwhile business partner Sir William
Seager gave £100 and the chandlers E.
Hughes & Co. gave twenty-five guineas.
Further afield, two Newcastle shipping
companies – W.A. Souter & Co. Ltd and
the Medomsley Steam Shipping Co.
Ltd – gave ten and five guineas respectively, whilst the Doxford shipyard at
Sunderland and the Workman, Clark
& Co. shipyard in Belfast gave £1,000
and £25 respectively; it is surely no
accident that these were both yards at
which Sir William had had ships built,
and in the case of Doxford's, would do
so again! The manner in which Sir William successfully re-invigorated and
sustained the building fund, thus enabling the completion of the museum's
east wing by 1932, can be seen from the following table.

TABLE 4: The National Museum of Wales' Building Fund, 1926–34

Year	Balance	Expenditure on building work.
1926	£29,207	£57
1927	£39,163	£38,000
1928	£16,343	£2,210
1929	£28,593	£10,813
1930	£33,790	£24,650
1931	£40,899	£37,689
1932	£31,809	£28,231
1933	£29,633	£25,384
1934	£15,520	£903

Source: *National Museum of Wales, Annual Reports, 1927–35.*

The presentation of the freedom of the City of Cardiff to Sir William Reardon Smith (left) and Lord Glanely (W.J. Tatem) in the council chamber of the City Hall on 23 March, 1928.

Sir William was also insistent that, wherever possible, preference should be given to engaging unemployed workers from south Wales in the construction work at the museum. In recognition of his considerable achievement in reviving the National Museum's fortunes in the late 1920s, he was appointed president of the museum in February 1929, following the death in office of his predecessor, Lord Aberdare.

Sir William's philanthropy, and that of his fellow native of Appledore, Lord Glanely, was recognised by the city of Cardiff on 23 March 1928, when both were made freemen of their adopted city. The impressive ceremony, held at the City Hall, was attended by almost a hundred guests, including, appropriately, members of the Anning family whose business had played an important role in the careers of both men, and a civic delegation from north Devon led by the mayor of Bideford, Councillor W. T. Goaman. In his speech, the lord mayor of Cardiff, Alderman A. J. Howell, praised the contributions of both men to the city's commercial life and their support of worthy causes in south Wales and further afield, describing them as 'Welshmen by adoption, but also true sons of Devon'. Sir William's scroll of admission was presented to him in an oak casket made from the timbers of the former Cardiff Ragged School ship, HMS *Havannah*, which bore the

Welsh words, Â *wnêl dda, da a ddyly* (Who does well, deserves well), and in his response to the lord mayor said, 'It is a pleasure for me to receive this great honour at your hands this afternoon, and at the same time as Lord Glanely; it is indeed a Devonshire day – or to narrow it down still more, it is an Appledore day!'[135]

NEW SHIPS, NEW TRADES

In the midst of this time-consuming philanthropic and civic activity in the 1920s, one might indeed wonder how Sir William also found time to run a shipping enterprise, and that, moreover, during a period of pronounced economic downturn. Whilst he attended the office on most days when not otherwise engaged, by this period he did of course have the help of his sons and sons-in-law as his fellow directors. A surviving firsthand account of the company's senior personnel and office staff at the time suggests that whilst Sir William was still very much in overall control, his second son, Douglas, who had served with the Duke of Cornwall's Light Infantry and the Cheshire Regiment in France in 1916–18, increasingly became a driving force behind the Reardon Smith enterprise during the 1920s. His elder brother Willie unfortunately suffered from tuberculosis and he spent considerable periods in sanatoria in Switzerland seeking a cure. Amongst Sir William's sons-in-law, A. J. Popham was company secretary to Sir William Reardon Smith & Sons Ltd and all the various subsidiary companies, W. G. Liley oversaw technical matters and the deck and engineering superintendents, whilst D. A. Low (a director from 1927 onwards) had responsibility for crewing and stores. At the company's Cardiff headquarters, a staff of some thirty supported the various directors in the operation of the entire business, with the exception of chartering. It was a sad reflection upon the declining importance of outward cargoes of Welsh coal for British tramp shipping in general that this was undertaken increasingly by staff from Reardon Smith's London office operating on the Baltic Exchange, rather than on the Coal Exchange at Cardiff. It is also worthy of note that ten of those who worked in Merthyr House were women who had first been employed during the war; unlike many employers, however, Sir William did not dismiss them upon the cessation of hostilities, and some worked in the office for many years thereafter. Weekday office hours were strictly from 9 a.m. until 6 p.m., with an hour for lunch; on Saturdays, staff went home at midday, whilst during the week smoking was permitted in the offices from 5.30 p.m. onwards![136]

Whilst there were occasional signs of trade revival during the early 1920s, freight rates nevertheless remained quite low and the somewhat improved rates that prevailed during the latter half of the decade were once more dashed by the Wall Street Crash of 1929. Initially, further vessels were acquired, taking advantage of the low prices of tonnage prevailing at that time. The cargo liner section of the fleet was strengthened in 1923 with the acquisition of the 4,365 gross ton steamer *Phoebus* from Soc. Les Affréteurs Réunis of Rouen for a mere £16,000; dating from 1921 and renamed *General Smuts*, she was allocated to the Oakwin Steamship Co. Ltd.[137] Also allocated to the Oakwin company were three new tramp-type vessels, all completed by Workman, Clark & Co. Ltd of Belfast in 1924, the second *Buchanness*, the second *Cragness* and the second *Skegness*. But with no sign of an improvement in the markets it was clear that a period of retrenchment was appropriate, and no further vessels were added to the fleet until 1927.

A policy of retrenchment was also applied to the Reardon Smith ship-ping companies at this time, in the form of reductions of capital so that the companies' nominal capital more accurately reflected the depleted value of their assets in the depressed circumstances then prevailing. On 21 July 1924, an extraordinary general meeting of the Leeds Shipping Co. Ltd, chaired by Sir William, approved a reduction in the company's capital from £400,000 to £150,000, 'to be effected by cancelling capital which has been lost, or is unrep-resented by available assets, to the extent of 12s. 6d per share'. Five months later, in December 1924, the St Just Shipping Co. Ltd underwent a similar proc-ess, with a reduction in nominal capital from £2,064,000 to £1,032,000, so that shares previously worth £1 became 10s. shares.[138] The shipowning structure of the overall Reardon Smith enterprise was later streamlined on 15 November 1926, when the six vessels in the ownership of the Oakwin Steamship Co. Ltd were sold to the St Just Steamship Co. Ltd for the sum of £308,000. The settle-ment of this considerable sum was made by a payment of £108,000 in equal annual instalments over a ten-year period and the creation of 400,000 new 10s. shares in the St Just company. This made the Oakwin company, whose stock was held almost entirely by Sir William Reardon Smith & Sons Ltd, a major shareholder in the St Just company until the former was wound up in 1939. An additional director was appointed on 1 January 1927, when Douglas Low joined the board of Sir William Reardon Smith, Popham & Liley, which was then renamed Sir William Reardon Smith & Partners Ltd.[139]

The mid-1920s saw the various Reardon Smith companies performing only very modestly. The St Just company was the most profitable, with profits of £119,171 in 1924, £50,000 in 1925 and £58,500 in 1926, enabling dividends of 1¼ per cent, 2½ per cent and 1¼ per cent respectively in those years. The Leeds company's performance was more disappointing; a £17,590 profit in 1924 enabled the payment of a dividend of 1¼ per cent that year, but there were no dividends at all in the following two years. Worst of all were the results of Unity Shipping & Trading, which showed a profit of a mere £59 in 1925 and paid no dividends whatsoever during its seven-year existence. The General Strike of 1926, disastrous though it was for the miners, brought new employment opportunities for the UK tramp fleet, and a number of Reardon

Smith vessels were engaged upon the import of American coal from the Virginian coalfields, either into south Wales ports or for discharge over-side into coasters in the Thames estuary off Sheerness. The last three years of the decade, however, showed considerably improved results, with the St Just company recording a profit of over £215,000 in 1927 and paying a dividend of 6¼ per cent from 1927 until 1929, whilst the Leeds company paid dividends of 5 per cent over the same period. Anticipating improving trade prospects towards the end of the decade and with shipyards crying out for business, no fewer than six new steamers were ordered in 1926 for delivery in 1927–8, four from William Gray's West Hartlepool yard and two from Napier & Miller of Glasgow. Three of these vessels – *Braddovey*, *Bradesk* and *Bradfyne* – were allocated to the Leeds Shipping Co. Ltd, with the remaining vessels – the third *Leeds City*, the second *Quebec City* and the second *King City* – being allocated to the St Just company, which was renamed the Reardon Smith Line Ltd in May 1928. The purchase of these new vessels was funded in part by the sale of most of the ex-German vessels bought in 1920–1.[140]

The years 1927–8 also saw a decisive change in the shipbuilding policy of the Reardon Smith enterprise, when orders were placed for its first two motor vessels. This could be viewed as something of a bold step, for Cardiff's shipowners at that time were only too aware of the utter commercial disaster that had befallen Owen Williams, the first of their number to acquire such vessels, the *Margretian* and the *Silurian*, in 1923 and 1924.[141] Since the early 1920s, with his steamers sailing further afield where it was not always possible to guarantee good quality Welsh or Durham coal for bunkering, Sir William had been interested in the potential of burning oil as an alternative fuel.

The third Leeds City, *built by Grays of West Hartlepool, was a long-lived vessel, serving the company from 1927 until 1951.*

He had personally specified that all the new steamers ordered for the various companies from 1922 onwards should be capable of burning either coal or fuel oil in their boiler furnaces; in 1926, the Reardon Smith fleet burned just over 20,000 tons of oil and 164,000 tons of coal. Bunkering with fuel oil was an infinitely cleaner and more convenient process than taking on coal bunkers, whilst the Reardon Smith engineering superintendents, working in conjunction with the Central Marine Engineering Works of Hartlepool (a subsidiary of William Gray's shipyard), also devised a system of heating coils which ensured a steady flow of the viscous fuel oil from bunkers to burners.[142]

The economy of operation imparted by marine diesel engines was not in doubt: crewing costs were reduced as there was no need to carry firemen; the absence of boilers and the fact that bunkers were carried in the vessel's double bottoms freed up more space for cargo; and heavy diesel oil was at that time quite inexpensive, being an almost unwanted by-product of the refining process. The critical question was that of reliability, and it was the relatively early adoption of new and partly unproven technology in his motor vessels that had led to Owen Williams's demise as a shipowner in the mid-1920s. However, considerable advances had been made in the reliability of the marine diesel engine by the late 1920s, and W. G. Liley, as Reardon Smith's technical director, took an active interest in these developments. According to family tradition, Liley set out to persuade his fellow directors of the advantages of adopting motor propulsion; apparently, Sir William was won over by his son-in-law's arguments, as were Arthur Popham and Douglas Low, but Willie and Douglas Smith remained implacably opposed to the acquisition of motor vessels. The story then has it that Sir William agreed to pay for the construction of two motor vessels from his own private funds and that once they were in service, they soon demonstrated the ample savings that could be made. Faced with such incontrovertible evidence, Willie and Douglas supposedly pleaded with their father to sell the vessels on to the Reardon Smith Line Ltd, which he eventually did.[143]

Other sources which have come to light more recently suggest a slightly different interpretation of events. It seems that it was Sir William who had asked Liley and the engineering superintendents to conduct some thorough research into the relative merits of the marine diesel engines then available, and they came to the conclusion that on paper there was very little to choose between those built by Doxford's at Sunderland and those of the Danish shipbuilders Burmeister & Wain (B & W), built under licence by Harland & Wolff in Belfast. Accordingly, orders were placed for two near-identical motorships of some 4,700 gross tons, to be named *West Lynn* and *East Lynn* after the rivers that meet at Lynmouth on the north Devon coast. The former vessel, to be equipped with a B & W engine, was ordered from Napier & Miller of Glasgow on 29 November 1927; the latter vessel was ordered from Doxford's on 4 March 1928. Once the vessels were in service, it was intended that the

The East Lynn, *built by Doxfords of Sunderland in 1928, was one of the first two motor vessels ordered by the company in the late 1920s.*

relative economy and reliability of the different engines could be compared, thus informing a decision on the type of engine to be installed in future newbuildings.[144] The *East Lynn* was the first to be delivered in July 1928, followed by the *West Lynn* three months later, but contrary to the tale quoted above, neither vessel was ever owned directly by Sir William. The statutory shipping register of the port of Bideford shows that, upon completion, both immediately became the property of the Oakwin Steamship Co. Ltd, which had been without tonnage since 1926, and they were not transferred to the Reardon Smith Line (under their later names of *Willamette Valley* and *Santa Clara Valley*) until the spring of 1937.[145] The Doxford opposed-piston engine proved to be the better in service, and engines of this make were fitted in the seven motor vessels subsequently built for Reardon Smith prior to the outbreak of war in 1939.

Just as Owen Williams had intended his ill-fated motor vessel *Margretian* to operate his Golden Cross cargo liner service to the Mediterranean, so the two new Reardon Smith motor vessels were also intended to operate on a cargo liner service, though in this case a new service to the Pacific coast of North America. Sir William made a number of visits to the USA in the 1920s, many in connection with the cargo liner service from the East Coast; however, he also travelled widely over the rest of the country at different times and by the end of that decade his attention was focused upon the commercial possibilities offered by the continent's Pacific coast. The St Just company having been renamed the Reardon Smith Line in May 1928, it was announced on

An unusual stern view of the Vernon City, *manoeuvring offshore and dressed overall; perhaps it is her maiden voyage in 1929?*

20 September that year that the East Lynn was already outward bound on the inaugural sailing of a monthly (later fortnightly) service which would call at Vancouver, Seattle, Portland, San Francisco and Los Angeles; initially, only a homeward service was offered, and the cargoes envisaged included grain, lumber, canned food and dried fruit. UK discharge ports were to be London and Liverpool, with Manchester offered 'by inducement'. The East Lynn was to be followed by the recently completed steamer King City at the end of October and her sister motor vessel, West Lynn, at the end of November. It was also noted that as Sir William had nearly forty vessels under his control, it would be a simple matter to increase the number of sailings on the service, should the demand warrant it.[146]

Other British companies with cargo liner services to the US and Canadian Pacific coasts at the time included Glasgow's Donaldson Line and Furness Withy, via its Norfolk & North American Steam Shipping subsidiary. Bearing in mind the controversy that had followed in the wake of the commencement of Reardon Smith's East Coast service earlier in the decade, it was emphasised that 'the new line is working in harmony with the regular conference lines; there will be no question of antagonism, but a friendly rivalry in obtaining cargo for the homeward run'.[147]

It would appear that Sir William did not have to contend with any subsequent serious controversy regarding the new service; indeed, he was in California in the spring of 1929 exploring further business opportunities for the Reardon Smith Line. On 18 April, he sent a telegram to the office at Cardiff to order a change of name for first ship in the second batch of motor vessels under construction at Doxford's at the time; the vessel then under construction as *San Francisco City* was henceforth to be known as *Fresno City*. One can only guess at what led him to change his mind – a successful business deal struck in the latter city, or perhaps he simply liked the place, just as he would later name a ship after Houston, Texas, following a visit. Whatever the reason, naming new vessels was quite clearly the chairman's prerogative! Further testimony to the developing relationship between the Reardon Smith Line and the agencies that handled their vessels on the Pacific coast became evident on 20 November 1929 when the new motor vessel *Vancouver City* was launched from Doxford's Sunderland yard by Mrs W. R. Crawford, the wife of the general manager of the Empire Stevedoring Co. Ltd of Vancouver. At the UK end of the service, meanwhile, representations from chambers of commerce at various Bristol Channel ports led to Avonmouth and Cardiff being added to the discharging ports of call from September 1930 onwards.[148]

Still anticipating improved trading prospects into the coming new decade, orders were placed for a further nine new vessels in 1928–9 – two motor vessels from Doxford's (*Fresno City* and *Vancouver City*) and seven steamers (*New Westminster City, Prince Rupert City, Tacoma City, Vernon City, Victoria City, Bradglen* and *Bradburn*), all from Gray's of West Hartlepool. All but two were named after ports on the North American Pacific coast, reflecting Reardon

The 'organised confusion' of the pre-container age port is wonderfully captured in this view of the Fresno City *amongst the junks at Chin Kiang on the Yangtze delta in January 1932.*

Smith's new interests in that area. Once more, a number of older vessels were sold to assist in the funding of the new, including the ill-starred *Meropi*; the company that owned her, Unity Shipping & Trading, was wound up soon afterwards. It was further reported in November 1928 that Sir William was still in negotiation with Gray's because,

> he is not prepared to place the contract unless the terms are of a nature that will bring substantial work to south Wales. According to an informant, he will insist upon Welsh steel ship plates being used – these plates will probably be rolled at Cardiff.[149]

As the order was eventually confirmed and the ships built, it must be assumed that Welsh-made steel plating, probably from Guest, Keen & Nettlefold's East Moors works at Cardiff, was used in the construction of the ships – though the cost of transporting the steel from Cardiff to West Hartlepool must have added considerably to the cost of the ships. It can be seen from this stipulation, therefore, that he was concerned to support other businesses in south Wales where he could, and the employment of local labour by those companies.

Nevertheless, he could also be decisive if there were obvious savings to be made. In 1890, a rival ship registration society to Lloyd's Register, the British Corporation Register, was established in Glasgow, and its surveyors soon gained a reputation for their progressive expertise in technical matters and their flexible approach to problems. In 1929 one of the companies' vessels was dry-docked at Cardiff after a lengthy voyage which had taken her away from the UK for almost two years. Large areas of corrosion were revealed on her underside and, under Lloyd's Rules, the Lloyd's Register surveyor had insisted that eighteen steel hull plates needed to be completely replaced. Purely by chance, the Reardon Smith superintendent overseeing the dry-docking later happened to meet the local British Corporation surveyor, and their conversation eventually came around to the repairs required by the dry-docked vessel. The British Corporation surveyor suggested that under the rules of his classification society, it might be possible to weld some of the least corroded plates, and they soon returned to the ship; he agreed that a dozen of the plates certainly needed complete replacement, but that the other six were capable of being welded, meaning a considerable saving. The Reardon Smith superintendent then returned to Merthyr House and asked to see Sir William, who, after giving the matter a few moments' consideration, made a couple of phone calls and initiated the transfer of the entire Reardon Smith fleet from Lloyd's to British Corporation registry.[150]

Hopes that the somewhat improved freight market of the late 1920s would signal the way to a new decade of prosperity in the 1930s were utterly dashed during the five days that followed 24 October 1929, when the Wall

The stevedores pause for the camera whilst discharging Australian wheat from the Bradburn *at Milazzo, Sicily, in April 1933. Their makeshift gangways would not conform to present day health & safety standards!*

Street Crash ushered in an era of profound economic depression around the world. By the end of 1932, 1.6m. gross tons of British shipping were laid up and over 40,000 British seafarers were unemployed.[151] Although Sir William took delivery of all the vessels he had ordered in 1927–9, no more newbuildings were ordered for another three years and many of the older vessels in the fleet spent varying periods of time laid up on the River Fal in Cornwall, or the Pembroke River off Milford Haven, during the early 1930s. Ships were also laid up on the River Torridge between Instow and Bideford at this time, but there is no record of a Reardon Smith vessel having been laid up at this location. Whilst it may be thought that Sir William wished to avoid the potential embarrassment of having his ships laid up on the Torridge, within sight of his native village, it seems more likely that his intimate knowledge of the river had led him to the conclusion that it was not the best location at which to lay up substantial cargo steamers. One of the casualties reported in Lloyd's List early in 1930, for instance, was the 5,344 gross ton steamer *Haggersgate*, owned by Turnbull Scott of London, which had suffered a badly buckled hull as she settled into an inappropriate lay-up berth on the ebb tide on the Torridge on 26 February that year.[152] But even if the distinctive red and black funnels bearing a large black 'S' were not seen on the Torridge during the depression, as late as June 1933 almost a third of the Reardon Smith fleet was inactive.

TABLE 5: Positions of Reardon Smith ships, 22 June 1933

Name of ship	Date built	Position
Alness	1920	Milford Haven, laid up
Atlantic City	1920	Cardiff
Bradburn	1930	Montevideo
Bradclyde	1918	River Fal, laid up
Braddovey	1927	Left Cardiff, 2 June
Bradesk	1927	Pernambuco
Bradfyne	1928	In the Red Sea
Bradglen	1930	New Caledonia
Eastern City	1917	River Fal, laid up
Fresno City (m.v.)	1929	Passed Gibraltar, 21 June
General Smuts	1921	Milford Haven, laid-up
Great City	1914	Baltimore
Imperial Valley	1924	Left Falmouth, 15 June
Indian City	1920	River Fal, laid up
Jersey City	1920	River Fal, laid up
King City	1928	Left Dairen, 8 June
Leeds City	1927	Hull
Madras City	1911	River Fal, laid up
New Westminster City	1929	Left Cardiff, 9 June
Orient City	1911	River Fal, laid up
Paris City	1920	River Fal, laid up
Prince Rupert City	1929	Saigon
Quebec City	1927	In the Panama Canal
Queen City	1924	Left Cardiff, 12 June
Sacramento Valley	1924	Left Los Angeles, 19 June
Santa Clara Valley (m.v.)	1928	San Francisco
Tacoma City	1929	Cardiff
Vancouver City (m.v.)	1930	Shanghai
Vernon City	1929	Rio de Janeiro
Victoria City	1929	Alexandria
Vulcan City	1909	River Fal, laid up
Welsh City	1922	River Fal, laid up
Willamette Valley (m.v.)	1928	Hull
York City	1922	River Fal, laid up

Source: *Lloyd's Daily Shipping Index*, 22 June 1933.

The old certainties of the 'coal out, grain home' trade which had sustained Cardiff's shipowners prior to the First World War were long since shattered, and whilst grain from Argentina continued to be an important homeward cargo for UK tramp shipping during the inter-war years, Sir William and his fellow directors had to work hard to find remunerative employment in the world-wide tramping trades for their substantial fleet at that time. In this context, however, Sir William's seafaring experience and his intimate knowledge of world trade were of paramount importance, as he knew full well when and where different cargoes were ready for export, how long it would take vessels to load at those ports and what the likely steaming time was to the port of discharge.

Nevertheless, it was an enormous challenge to keep most of the fleet employed in those difficult times, and this was reflected in a letter written by Sir William to Vernon Boyle in June 1932, when Boyle was trying to persuade him to write his life story: 'I have more serious things to think about today – to keep our vessels running and people employed'.[153] With a fleet of between thirty and forty ships under his management from the early 1920s until his death, Sir William was indeed a major employer and it is interesting to note from this quote that he appeared to be as concerned about maintaining employment during the depression as he was with keeping as many ships as possible running profitably – a sentiment that has become increasingly rare over the intervening years. A comparative memorandum drawn up by the directors in 1925, twenty years after the *City of Cardiff* was ordered, notes that whilst just twenty-five seagoing staff were employed in 1906, the same figure in 1926 was 1,304; by this date too, the first cadets from the Reardon Smith Nautical School would have been joining ships' crews. Whilst the school was intended to provide training for boys who aspired to a seafaring career with any British shipping company, there was in practice a close association between the school and the Reardon Smith fleet, an association which brought Sir William much satisfaction. In 1934, whilst visiting Houston, Texas on board his new motor vessel *Houston City*, he gave an interview to a reporter for the local newspaper, the *Houston Press*: 'I founded my own nautical school where the future commanders of my ships are trained. Mostly they are selected from Devonshire families I have known for years.'[154]

Despite the fact that Sir William was proud of and maintained close links with north Devon, a detailed study of the crew lists of Reardon Smith vessels shows that seamen from the area were but a tiny minority of their crews. In this context, it should also be remembered that during the 1920s and 1930s, there was alternative employment available for some north Devon seamen on the considerable fleet of coastal sailing vessels still operating out of Appledore and nearby ports in the area at that time (though apparently there was often a notice in the post office window at Appledore advertising vacancies on Reardon Smith ships).[155] Crew lists for all the Reardon Smith vessels for the year 1925 are available at the National Maritime Museum in Greenwich, and they reveal the following statistics relating to the origins of ships' crews in that year:

TABLE 6: Origins of Reardon Smith crew members, 1925 (manning a fleet of 37 vessels)

Area of origin	Number	%
North Devon coast (Hartland Pt–Foreland Pt)	25	2
Rest of West Country (Gloucester–Scillies–Weymouth and Channel I.)	75	6
North-east England (Humber–Tweed)	260	20
North-west England (Dee–Eden)	52	5
Rest of England	73	5
Scotland	66	5
S.E. Wales (Glam. and Mon.)	189	14.5
Rest of Wales	94	7
Ireland	106	8
Northern Ireland	14	1
Scandinavian countries	39	3
Mediterranean countries	14	1
Yemen and Aden	209	15
West Africa and Cape Verde I.	46	3.5
West Indies	41	3
Rest of world	19	1
Total	**1322**	**100**

Source: 1925 crew lists, National Maritime Museum, Greenwich.

What is quite clear from this table is that the crews of Reardon Smith ships were drawn overwhelmingly from the Welsh coast and the north-east of England, two areas whose major ports were the home of many tramp shipping companies and whose seamen had already developed a strong tradition of manning those companies' ships. A substantial group also came from coastal communities in Ireland, from Kinsale in the south-west to Arklow on the east coast; the Rosslare–Fishguard ferry service gave them ready access to the ports of south Wales.[156] Another significant group was made up of

Commodore of the fleet: Captain Dan Davies of New Quay (centre) and his deck officers on board the Indian City *in the early* 1920s.

those natives of Yemen and Aden who had been serving on Cardiff's tramp steamers since the latter years of the First World War; their ability to withstand the high temperature of the stokehold and the fact that, as Muslims, they did not drink alcohol, made them highly regarded members of ships' crews. There is no reason to believe that conditions on board the Reardon Smith ships were any better or worse than on most British tramp steamers during the depression years, though the large 'S' on the ships' funnels was almost inevitably interpreted as meaning 'Starvation'.

From wherever his ships' crews came, however, Sir William was convinced of the paramount importance of attracting and keeping both deck and engineering officers of the highest calibre to man his vessels. This was reflected in his remarkable decision in 1928 to introduce a pension scheme, initially just for masters and chief engineers, though it was later extended to other officer ranks and to office staff too later in the 1930s. A graduated bonus scheme was also under consideration. Certainly, many of his masters and officers served the firm loyally for many years, men such as Captain Dan Davies from New Quay, commodore master in the 1920s and 30s, who commanded eleven Reardon Smith vessels over the years from 1914 until he retired in 1936; his preferred pastime at sea was composing poetry to send back to *eisteddfodau* in Wales. And from Sir William's native village came the diminutive Captain Lionel Ford, who had first gone to sea as a boy in

Above: Mrs Dan Davies (*holding the bouquet*) was the sponsor of the Tacoma City
*when she was launched from Gray's West Hartlepool shipyard on 4 September, 1929.
Sir William Gray is third from right and next to him stands Captain A. E. Tamlyn,
Reardon Smith's marine superintendent. Lady Gray (in a light cloche hat) stands next to
Mrs Davies, whilst W. G. Liley, Reardon Smith's technical director, is sixth from the left.*

Above: Sir William with the master and officers of the Houston City *whilst on passage
from Jamaica to Houston in February 1934; to his right stands Captain Lionel Ford,
a fellow-native of Appledore.*

the beautiful Appledore-built schooner *Katie* in 1904; he commanded five Reardon Smith vessels between 1924 and 1939 before being appointed one of the firm's marine superintendents. By all accounts, what he lacked in stature he more than made up for in sheer force of character![157]

MUSEUM PRESIDENT

Sir William was appointed fifth president of the National Museum of Wales in February 1929. At about that time, the museum decided to commission the artist Oswald Birley to paint, at a cost of 100 guineas each, portraits of its past presidents and during the late 1920s he painted Lords Pontypridd, Treowen, Aberdare and Kenyon. Birley intimated that he would be ready to paint the new president in the summer of 1929, and it was the museum's secretary, A. H. Lee, who first suggested to the artist that it might be appropriate to portray Sir William in the uniform of a master mariner. Matters were delayed, however, by Birley's reluctance to come to Cardiff to undertake the commission, claiming that he had not the time to spare to travel to south Wales, whilst Sir William was equally insistent that he had better things to do than spend a long time in London! Stalemate ensued, but a compromise was eventually reached in October 1929 when Sir William eventually agreed to sit for Birley in his studio in St John's Wood whilst he was in London on business during the first week of November. In the meantime, the museum's new director, Cyril Fox, was also keen that Sir William should be portrayed in the uniform of a captain in the merchant service, and he wrote to Birley,

> We are proud of Sir William as a sea captain, a man who sailed his clipper ship in the days when steam had not succeeded in driving sail off the seas; it is as a master mariner that we should like to permanently record him. Do you think that you could paint him in his blue serge dress with brass buttons? The decoration is mainly in the cap, but we do not want his fine head obscured by that, so perhaps he could hold his cap in his hand? I am sure that you will enjoy the characterisation of so interesting a type – I have the greatest affection for him.

Even then, however, the matter was not completely settled, for Sir William cancelled his business trip to London and Birley had no option but to come to Cardiff later that month. He eventually sat for him in the museum on the afternoon of 19 November 1929 and during the ensuing two days, and as Cyril Fox had suggested, Sir William did indeed sit for his portrait in a captain's uniform, bareheaded and holding his cap in his hand. The resulting portrait, finished in 1930, captures well the indomitable authority that is so typical of an experienced master mariner, and contrasts quite markedly with the other somewhat bland portraits (some of which were painted posthumously) of the other past presidents executed by Birley at that time.[158]

The year 1930 saw Sir William being chosen as a deputy lieutenant for the county of Glamorgan, but it was also the year in which he and Lady Ellen celebrated their golden wedding anniversary. On 16 May, having received congratulatory telegrams from, amongst others, the Prince of Wales, Sir William and Lady Ellen left their home for the company offices at Merthyr House where they were presented with an illuminated address and a bound album of staff members' congratulatory messages. The senior marine superintendent, Captain Compton, spoke on behalf of both office and seagoing staff, conveying their congratulations to the couple, and Lady Smith was presented with a bouquet of flowers by Esme Angier, the youngest member of the office staff. That afternoon, three generations of the Reardon Smith family celebrated at the couple's Cardiff home, Cornborough, in the suburb of Penylan. To mark the occasion, the couple made a donation of £1,000 to the Cardiff Royal Infirmary to endow two beds, the 'W. Reardon Smith Bed' and the 'Ellen Reardon Smith Bed'.[159]

In 1932, Sir William was made a member of the Worshipful Company of Shipwrights (which honour also brought with it the Freedom of the City of London), but the year undoubtedly culminated on 25 October when his term as president of the National Museum came to an end with the opening of the museum's east wing and lecture theatre by Prince George, later the Duke of Kent. The prince was welcomed outside the museum by Sir William, and escorted into the building through a guard of honour made up of cadets from the Reardon Smith Nautical School. During the formal proceedings, effusive thanks were paid to Sir William and Lady Ellen by both the prince and the president-elect, the earl of Plymouth, for their exceptional generosity to the National Museum. It was in honour of their generosity, amounting to almost £50,000 over the years since 1921 (some £1.6m. in current (2010) values), that Prince George announced that the museum's impressive new lecture theatre was to be named the 'Reardon Smith Lecture Theatre'. Later that day, during the AGM of the court of governors of the National Museum, the museum's newly elected treasurer, Sir William's son Willie, noted that there had been an outstanding deficit of some £6,000 in the final accounts of the building fund, but was able to announce that the sum had been covered that day by a cheque – from none other than his father – handed to him with the words, 'Break the news gently to Mother'(!).[160]

The inaugural lecture in the Reardon Smith Lecture Theatre, entitled 'Wales and the Past – Two Voices', was given on 2 November 1932, by the eminent Welsh medievalist and professor of history at the University College of North Wales, Bangor, John Edward Lloyd; Sir William was present at this event. He retained a seat on the museum's council in his capacity as immediate past president, and his continued activity on behalf of the museum was reflected in the opening, in February 1933, of an exhibition of ship models and paintings, rather prosaically entitled 'Cargo-carrying Steamers', staged in the circular gallery above the new lecture theatre. Sir William initiated the idea during the last year of his presidency, and had been successful in persuading shipowners from Newport, Cardiff, Swansea and Llanelli and a Milford Haven ship repair yard to loan models and ship portraits from their offices for the exhibition, which ran until May that year. In association with the exhibition, a lecture on 'The cargo-carrying steamer: its history and development' was given on 21 March 1933 by the distinguished naval architect, Professor T. B. Abell of Liverpool University. When the exhibition finished, Sir William decided to donate the largest of the four models he had loaned (that of the *York City*) to the museum, and he would seem to have persuaded his fellow shipowners to follow his example, thus creating the core of the National Museum's ship model collection. Most of the twenty-seven models donated after the exhibition were of Cardiff and Newport tramp steamers, but there were also models of Milford trawlers and a stunning large-scale model of the turbine passenger steamer *St David*, built in 1906 for the newly opened Fishguard–Rosslare ferry service.[161]

The Reardon Smith Lecture Theatre in the National Museum of Wales, inaugurated by Prince George in 1932.

A part of the exhibition of ship models and portraits at the National Museum organised
by Sir William Reardon Smith in the spring of 1933. On the left is the model of
the Reardon Smith steamer York City, *which he donated to the museum when the*
exhibition closed.

FINAL YEARS

Events such as these must have provided a welcome distraction for Sir
William from the prevailing economic difficulties of the early 1930s. Neither
the Reardon Smith Line nor the Leeds Shipping Co. Ltd paid dividends in
1931; the Reardon Smith Line managed to pay 2½ per cent in 1932 and thereafter neither company paid a dividend until 1935. One notable casualty of the
depression was the *Margherita*, which was sold for £4,400 on 15 September
1932 to a Jersey-based banker, D. Ernest Townsend; this was a blow, not only
to the facilities of the Reardon Smith Nautical School, but also personally
to Sir William. Somewhat better news was reported in the *Western Mail* the
following month when it published a list of numerous Cardiff-owned ships
that were trading once more after being laid up; they included the *Atlantic
City*, *Imperial Valley*, *Jersey City*, *Orient City*, *Paris City*, *Sacramento Valley* and *York
City*, but by the following summer, four of these vessels were once more laid
up on the Fal.[162] When times are hard, it is advantageous for a shipowner
to be running large modern vessels whose repair bills are low and whose

greater deadweight capacity enables considerable economies of scale to be achieved. With four 9,000 deadweight ton motor vessels already in service and proving their enhanced economy of operation, it is hardly surprising that the five newbuildings ordered for Reardon Smith in the 1930s should also have been similar diesel-powered ships. The new motor vessels came in two batches, two (*Devon City* and *Houston City*) in 1933–4, and the remaining three (*Bradford City*, *Dallas City* and *Cornish City*) in 1936–7, after Sir William's death; all were powered by Doxford engines, but were actually built by the Furness Shipbuilding Co. Ltd at Haverton Hill-on-Tees. In the meantime no fewer than ten of the older steamers, all built between 1914 and 1920, were disposed of between 1930 and 1935.[163]

The continuing depression eventually led to calls for government action to improve the lot of the British tramp shipowner and, in turn, the seamen who manned their ships. The Chamber of Shipping voiced concerns over the subsidies provided by some foreign countries for their tramping fleets, and the Shipowners' Association at Cardiff described such subsidies as, 'an artificial stimulant of great danger'; however, the efforts made by the British government delegates to the World Monetary and Economic Conference in June 1933 to persuade those countries that subsidised their fleets to cease such payments came to nought. Many prominent shipowners such as Sir John Latta, E. H. Watts and Sir William himself were also strongly opposed to the notion of subsidies and were not reticent about voicing their views in public. On 4 October 1933, Sir William was at the Furness yard on Tees-side for the launching ceremony of the new motor vessel *Devon City*, sponsored by Lady Ellen. Speaking at the function after the launch, not only did he once more affirm his belief in *laissez-faire* economic policies relating to shipping, but also chided shipowners for not acting together to devise a voluntarily agreed programme for the scrapping of obsolete tonnage:

> I do not approve of any government subsidy for British shipping. I have always held that ways and means could have been found to help British shipping if all British shipowners had been unanimous and worked more closely together with regard to such policies as scrapping, instead of selling tonnage to foreigners.[164]

(There was more than a slight element of hypocrisy evident in this speech, for no fewer than twenty-two Reardon Smith vessels were sold to foreign owners during the thirty years when Sir William was in charge of the business!)

Despite the opposition of Sir William and other shipowners to the notion of subsidies, the Tramp Shipowners' Committee of the Chamber of Shipping made an application to the government in November 1933 for a subsidy of 10s. per ton on ships that were trading and 5s. per ton on laid-up vessels,

Above: *The launch party for the second* Devon City, *sponsored by Lady Ellen Smith, at the Furness shipyard, Haverton Hill-on-Tees, on 4 October, 1933. It was at the lunch after this event that Sir William launched a scathing attack on the suggestion that British shipping should receive government subsidies.*

Left: *The new* Devon City *approaches the Queen Alexandra lock at Cardiff in 1934.*

and a Cabinet committee was established to investigate the issue during the following month. After much heated debate in Parliament, the British Shipping (Assistance) Act was eventually passed in 1935. This legislation made provision for a £2m. subsidy for tramp shipowners that year, as well as loans to enable shipowners to buy obsolete tonnage for scrapping and place orders for new vessels at an approximate ratio of two obsolete gross tons to each gross ton of newbuilding; it was as a result of this clause that the legislation came to be known as the 'Scrap and Build' Act.[165] It may have been this provision for the scrapping of older tonnage, linked to subsidies, that led Sir William to relent in his opposition, for in 1935 two of the three new motor vessels ordered for Reardon Smith from the Furness yard were constructed under 'Scrap and Build' terms. Government loans of £88,554 and

£105,000, with interest at 2.75 per cent, were granted for the construction of the *Bradford City* and the *Cornish City* respectively; scrapped against the construction of the *Bradford City* were two obsolete Reardon Smith steamers, the *Orient City* (1911) and the *Indian City* (1920), whilst Ellerman Wilson's *Francisco* (1910) and James Westoll's *Salient* (1905) were bought and scrapped against the construction of the *Cornish City*.[166]

On 24 January 1934, Sir William, Lady Ellen, their daughter Grace and their grandson Alan arrived in Jamaica in the Elders & Fyffes steamer *Patuca* for a short holiday.[167] There they awaited the arrival of the motor vessel *Houston City* on her maiden voyage, outward bound on the US West Coast liner service. Upon her arrival, the party joined the *Houston City*, under the command of Captain Lionel Ford, and sailed for the city of Houston, Texas, where they arrived on 10 February. Greeting the reception party that met the ship, Sir William recalled that he had first visited the nearby coastal port of Galveston in 1881 whilst master of the *Drumadoon*, but since his first visit to the area the completion of a ship canal in 1914, connecting the city to the Gulf of Mexico, meant that Houston was now a port. His first visit to Houston itself had been on a business trip in 1929, and he spoke of how

The Houston City *was launched on 29 November, 1933 by Mrs Henry Mercer, the wife of the managing director of the Houston Port Authority. Eighth from left is Sir William's grandson Alan Reardon-Smith, who would later chair the company, and to his left are his uncle and aunt, Arthur and Gertrude Popham.*

impressed he had been with what he saw and how it inspired him to name the newest vessel in his fleet after the city:

> I admired you for your spirit and courage. I saw the energy and vision that you had put into the building of the Ship Canal. It is really a very great achievement. It all left me with a desire to do something in appreciation, and I have done it in the best way I could. I named her for Houston because I love Houston and the people that live here. I had a million other names I could choose from, but I picked this one because I like what it implies – there was no other reason in the world![168]

Sir William also stated his confident belief that the economic depression was lifting and, directly contradicting his often-proclaimed belief in *laissez-faire* economics, went on to praise the decidedly interventionist policies of President Franklin Roosevelt's 'New Deal':

> I've travelled all over the world a great deal and I've seen trouble like this before. Here in America you have a wonderful president who is trying to ease your burden. I don't see any reason to be pessimistic over the future of England or America – they have the stuff that is necessary to pull through.[169]

Members of the public were invited to tour the *Houston City* during the following three days, with a small admission charge being levied for the benefit of local charities in Houston; the visit culminated with the presentation of a fine boardroom model of the ship to the Houston Port Authority.

Sir William entered his eightieth year in August 1935; contemporary photographs show that age had by then started to take its toll, yet he remained quite hale and hearty and still attended the office regularly. He was seriously ill for just a few days before his death on 23 December 1935, which was recorded as having been caused by 'myocardial degeneration' and 'chronic interstitial nephritis'; in layman's terms, it may be said that simply he died of old age. His death was registered by his son Douglas on Christmas Eve. The funeral took place on Friday 27 December 1935; after a brief private service for the family at Cornborough, the funeral cortège then proceeded down Penylan hill to the public ceremony which commenced at 11.30 a.m. at Roath Park Methodist Church. Here, ten cadets from the Reardon Smith Nautical School acted as bearers for Sir William's coffin, escorted by four masters, two chief officers and two chief engineers drawn from Reardon Smith vessels. At the church, the hymns 'Abide with me' and 'Eternal Father, strong to save' were sung and the minister, the Revd C. A. Green, gave a valedictory address in which he described Sir William as 'a glorious son of Devon . . . who had devoted his whole life to making the world a better

The order of service for Sir William's funeral.

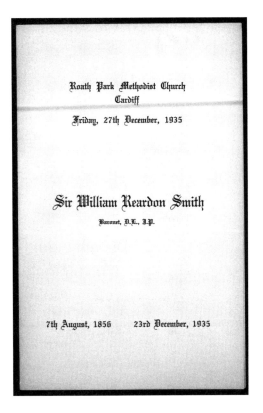

Roath Park Methodist Church
Cardiff

Friday, 27th December, 1935

Sir William Reardon Smith

Baronet, D.L., J.P.

7th August, 1856   23rd December, 1935

place than when he entered it'. The funeral was said to have been one of the largest seen in Cardiff for many years and comprised prominent figures from the local shipping community, together with representatives from the numerous organisations with which Sir William had been involved during his lifetime. Commencing at the same time as the funeral in Cardiff, a memorial service was held in Appledore parish church which was attended by many of Sir William's relatives in north Devon; the service concluded with the playing of Handel's 'Dead March' in *Saul* on the organ, whilst a muffled bell tolled out across the Torridge.[170]

Sir William's body was interred in Cardiff's Cathays Cemetery, in a vault above which a massive red granite memorial was later erected; it bears the inscription:

In loving memory of William Reardon Smith, First Baronet, JP, DL
Honorary Freeman of the City of Cardiff
The dearly loved husband of Ellen Smith
Born August 7th 1856
Died December 23rd 1935

'I hope to see my Pilot face to face,
when I have crossed the bar'.

Sir William left £209,751 14s. 5d gross, £116,465 14s. 9d net; almost all his obituaries noted that he had given away at least as much, if not more, than the gross sum during his lifetime. He appointed his two sons Willie (who succeeded him as the second baronet and as chairman of all the Reardon Smith companies) and Douglas and two of his sons-in-law, Arthur Popham and Bill Liley, as his executors; the four were also to be joined by the accountant J. Pearson Griffiths to create a trust to manage Cornborough free of charge as a home for Lady Ellen and Miss Grace Smith during their lifetimes. He bequeathed his shares in the various management companies to be divided equally between his three sons-in-law, whilst his shares in the shipping companies – the Reardon Smith Line, Leeds Shipping and Oakwin Steamship – were to be divided equally amongst his six children, with an additional £10,000 bequest for Miss Grace Smith. He also expressed a desire that when a favourable opportunity arose, the three shipping companies should be amalgamated to create a single company which would in turn be managed by a single management company, namely Sir William Reardon Smith & Sons Ltd. However, this latter aspiration would never be achieved in its entirety during the venture's subsequent fifty-year history. Another clause exhorted his children to 'help others, work and serve their country, as he has endeavoured to do'; more ominously, another clause stated that any beneficiaries disputing any of the will's terms automatically forfeited their interest.[171]

Lady Ellen outlived Sir William by almost four years, dying in her sleep at Cornborough on 9 August 1937, just six weeks short of her eighty-second birthday. Somewhat overshadowed during her life by her husband, she is nevertheless fondly recalled by those who actually knew her and was remembered as being,

'ever as gracious in spirit as she was unassuming in manner'.[172]

After her burial, the following inscription was added to the family memorial:

Also of his wife Ellen
Born September 29th 1857
Died August 9th 1939

'To live in the hearts of those we love,
Is not to die'.

A further inscription was also added in memory of their infant son, Thomas Hamlyn Smith, who had died aged just sixteen months on 12 November 1883 and who lay buried in the churchyard at Appledore.

THE MEASURE OF THE MAN

Angel penffordd a diawl pen pentan
(An angel abroad and a demon on the hearth)

In summing up the character of Sir William Reardon Smith, this Welsh proverb perhaps provides some useful pointers. He would appear to have been an archetypal Victorian patriarch, a martinet who believed firmly in such old adages as 'spare the rod and spoil the child' and 'children should be seen and not heard'. His great-nephew, Michael Tamlyn, still recalls Sir William with the same sense of awe that he felt when ushered into the great man's presence at Cornborough as a seven-year-old in the summer of 1935.[173] As he stood there nervously with his arms folded, Sir William barked at him, 'Don't stand like a washerwoman!', and he later taught him the following verse:

> A wise old owl sat in a tree,
> He did not speak, because you see
> The more he spoke, the less he heard –
> I wish there were more like that wise old bird!

He could be equally abrupt and overbearing with his own offspring. One of his grandchildren recalled that his relationship with his family, rather than that of a loving husband and doting father, perhaps had more in common with that of a ship's master towards his crew.[174] This is reflected in the recollections of the Cardiff accountant, J. Pearson Griffiths, who, whilst doing his articles from 1904 onwards, recalled being sent to Reardon Smith's first office at 127 Bute Street to audit the accounts of the Instow Steamship Company Ltd:

> their office was one room in a building in Bute Street, on the corner of West Bute Street, opposite the railway station. The only persons I saw there were Captain Smith and Mr Willie Smith. Mr Willie had evidently been well trained in the keeping of the books, and I always found them to be well kept. One thing quite often happened, and it was that Mr Willie and his father would have quite hot arguments about sundry matters in the books. Captain Smith tried to insist on certain matters being shown in the books against absolute refusals by Mr Willie, and often the latter would leave the room with tears in his eyes. Directly after he left the room, Captain Smith would come over to me to ask what Mr Willie had done about the matter of the argument, and when I told him, he would say that he (Mr Willie) was quite right, and that he (Capt. Smith) had only been arguing the opposite way in order that Mr Willie should not only know he was right, but know *why* he was right.[175]

A hard taskmaster indeed! However, as his daughter Lillian's determination to marry her sweetheart Bill Liley in 1914 demonstrated, it is clear that some of his children were very much 'chips off the old block'!

To junior staff in the office he was a distant and somewhat intimidating figure, and this was recalled in a story related to the author by the late Chris John, who started work as an office boy in Merthyr House in the early 1930s. Having arrived at work one morning he was about to step into the lift when, looking

A rarely-photographed smile from Lady Ellen is captured in this family group from the early 1930s. Clockwise from top left are: Mrs Elizabeth (Willie) Smith, Mrs Lillian Liley, Mr Willie Smith, Mrs Gertrude Popham, Lady Ellen Smith, Sir William Reardon Smith and Miss Grace Smith.

across to the entrance to Merthyr House, he saw Sir William stepping out of his chauffer-driven car. He therefore held the lift door open until Sir William had entered. No word of thanks was offered, and the following exchange ensued:

'Do you work for me boy?'
'Yes sir'.
A gesture with his walking stick was followed by one word 'Stairs!'[176]

Much of this apparently harsh attitude can doubtless be attributed to the fact that his own childhood had been spent in conditions of relative hardship after his mother was widowed, leaving her to bring up a family of eight whilst earning a living as a dressmaker, and resulting in the young William earning a living at sea by the time he reached his early teens. Before he left home to go to sea, he had received a basic education in the Wesleyan Methodist day school at Appledore, and his language, throughout his life, was not only characterised by a rich north Devon accent, but was also replete with biblical imagery and quotations. Recalling Sir William's visits to the Camper & Nicholson yard at Gosport when the *Margherita* was undergoing conversion to a training vessel, John Nicholson would later recall,

Margherita was purchased by Sir William Reardon Smith for conversion to a training ship for his shipping company; she was . . . given a three-masted rig and two diesel engines. Her new owner impressed us all with his Biblical quotations, at which he was the equal of the aircraft pioneer, Handley Page.[177]

Like many self-made men, there was a somewhat boastful element to his character and he seems never to have missed an opportunity of regaling people with his life story, with a particular emphasis upon the greater hardships of bye gone days! But it also appears that he could tell a tale with genuine verve, as is evidenced by the affable relationship that developed between him and Mortimer Wheeler during the latter's term as director of the National Museum of Wales. Wheeler himself said of Sir William, 'It was my joy to get him going on the saga of his travels, and to hear the names of the seaports of the world roll off his tongue with all the poetry of Homer's "Catalogue of Ships"',[178] whilst Wheeler's biographer, Jacquetta Hawkes, wrote in 1982:

> Between the Director and the self-made baronet there sprang up a warm personal relationship quite independent of the give-and-take of money. Rik [Wheeler's nickname] felt an immediate liking for the man who had first gone to sea as a cabin boy in a brig [sic] and had sailed the Seven Seas before becoming the owner of a shipping line. The fact that he loved to hear him tell of his adventures is proof, if one were needed, that the new Director had not lost the taste for heroic tales instilled in him by his father.[179]

Nevertheless, despite his stern demeanour, his partiality to quoting from the Scriptures and his tendency to sing his own praises, he did not lack a sense of humour. In the summer of 1931 the Cardiff shipping firm Williams & Mordey ceased trading when Barclays Bank foreclosed on the three steamers managed by the company, which were mortgaged to the bank. The management of these vessels was then entrusted by the bank to the Cardiff coal-exporting firm Evans & Reid, a decision which caused a good deal of surprised comment in Cardiff's shipowning circles, as the company had no prior experience in the running of ships. Not long afterwards, Sir William – who also banked with Barclays – met the then manager of Barclays Cardiff Docks branch, Samuel West, in Mountstuart Square and, with his tongue firmly in his cheek, suggested to Mr West that should he ever be in the position of needing to find someone to manage a colliery, to bear him in mind![180] Neither was he in any sense a dry Puritan. He enjoyed a smoke, being particularly fond of cigars and, like many seafarers, was not averse to a drink; moreover, when the occasion demanded, he could apparently turn the air blue with an extremely colourful turn of phrase!

The late expert on the history of tramp shipping, Robin Craig, once observed that in the late nineteenth and early twentieth centuries, there were two main paths to shipowning – either via the wheelhouse or via the counting house. Many of Cardiff's most successful shipowning concerns were commenced by a partnership of principals from these differing backgrounds, with Evan Thomas, Radcliffe & Co. perhaps being the outstanding example.[181] Sir William's initial venture into shipowning with William Seager also represented this conjunction of skills, but it did not last – one senses perhaps that he was determined to be the sole master of his own destiny. As a businessman, he founded a venture that may have been both paternalistic and nepotistic by present-day business standards, but as a dedicated, 'hands-on' principal, who knew most of his employees, he was ultimately successful, almost single-handedly creating a substantial enterprise that lasted for fifty years after his death. Nevertheless, it was not altogether a tale of progressive and unqualified success. His entry into shipowning on his own account was decidedly parlous, relying heavily on family resources that had been carefully husbanded by Ellen Smith since the 1880s, and although he would later claim that the *City of Cardiff* was, 'a family affair [with] no outside help', had it not been for the vital injection of capital into the Instow Steamship Co. Ltd provided by the Holmans, then the name Reardon Smith might never have been associated with the ownership of one of the UK's foremost tramp shipping fleets.[182] Ignoring early adverse comments (most of which were quite ill-founded) in the shipping press on his venture, he soon proved himself to be an exceptionally competent ship manager, with his thorough knowledge of world-wide trading patterns enabling him to employ his growing fleet with conspicuous commercial success in the years leading up to 1914.

However, having endured the vicissitudes of the First World War, he then hopelessly misjudged the short, sharp cycle of boom and bust that characterised the immediate post-war years. During the latter stages of the war he more than once expressed his firm belief that 'greatly improved trading conditions' would follow the cessation of hostilities, and as the brief boom of 1919–20 gathered pace, he must not only have felt himself vindicated, but was also overcome by the commercial euphoria prevailing at the time. Ignoring the prescient actions of some of his more far-sighted fellow shipowners (most notably his former employer, Lord Glanely), he floated new companies to acquire ships at greatly inflated prices, apparently convinced that any debt, however high, was worth taking on if it allowed him to participate in a game that apparently had no losers. Ultimately, however, he lost out himself; as the boom unravelled, he soon found himself with one insolvent company, and others dependent upon loans from the St Just company, which eventually proved to be the pillar of sound finance that carried Sir William's overall venture through the crisis. It must have been a chastening experience for him; nevertheless, it is to his eternal credit that he felt such an obligation to the disappointed Cornborough shareholders as to ensure that they were all compensated from his own personal shareholding in the St Just company. He may have misjudged the market, but Sir William was an honourable man.

The shipping market crash of 1920 ushered in a recession that was to affect the tramp shipping industry for almost two decades thereafter, but this was a period during which Sir William ceaselessly explored various options in order that he might maintain the overall viability of his venture. Despite the controversy that arose from the short-lived services from the US east coast offered by Reardon Smith vessels in the early 1920s, his entry into the liner trades showed considerable initiative, and the connections established with ports on the North American Pacific coast from 1928 onwards would endure in differing forms until the venture's eventual demise in 1985. And although his seagoing experience had been gained almost entirely in sailing vessels, he was not averse to new forms of maritime propulsion when he could be persuaded of their commercial viability; having been astute enough to wait until the late 1920s when the technology of the marine diesel engine was well proven, Sir William went on to become the first successful managing owner of motor vessels at Cardiff, reaping the rewards of the improved efficiency of his new ships.

Sir William's loyalty to his native north Devon was an enduring characteristic that never wavered in all the years after he left Appledore for Cardiff in 1900. In Cardiff, he and Lady Ellen looked forward each week to the arrival in the post of the *Bideford and North Devon Weekly Gazette*, which they perused with great interest, especially the 'Torridge Chat' column to which Sir William occasionally sent reminiscences. He was also a member and past president of the Cardiff Devonshire Society, whose annual dinner would always conclude with the rousing community singing of Devonian songs such as 'Widdecombe Fair' and 'Devonshire Cream and Cider'! Every Christmas, he and Lady Ellen would send a sum of money to be distributed amongst needy families in Appledore[183] and together with members of their family they would visit the village at least once a year. Sometimes, if sea conditions were favourable, this visit could be part of their summer cruise on the *Margherita*; more typically, they went by one of P. & A. Campbell's paddle steamers from Cardiff to Ilfracombe, where they would be met on the pier by their chauffeur, Huxley, who had set out a day or two earlier on the long drive via Gloucester! Sir William's granddaughter, Mrs Mary Davies, remembers as a child accompanying her grandparents from house to house in the village as they visited their seemingly countless Appledore kinsfolk, including Sir William's formidable spinster sister, Harriet.[184] His generosity to countless good causes in the area has already been noted, but it was not merely a sentimental attachment; up until the Second World War, for instance, all the lifeboats and working boats for Reardon Smith newbuildings were constructed by old-established Appledore boatbuilding families such as the Fords, the Hinks and the Waters. As Appledore was never on the national rail network, once completed, the boats would be rowed on the flood tide up the Torridge to Bideford, to the quayside sidings at East-the-Water; here they were lifted out and sheeted down on railway wagons in preparation for the long journey to the shipyards of the Tees, the Wear or the Clyde.[185]

There is one sense in which Sir William stood out amongst Cardiff's most prominent shipowners, and that was in the quite selfless application of his wealth, in ways hitherto outlined, for the benefit of others. Unlike many of his contemporaries, he did not spend a small fortune on the acquisition of a palatial villa with a sea view in Penarth, or a landed estate in the Vale of Glamorgan, or an ostentatious Regency pile in genteel Bath; neither were there packs of hounds in the Usk valley, nor stables of thoroughbred bloodstock in Newmarket. His Cardiff home, Cornborough, completed in 1916, though a large and comfortable house with many fine architectural details, is in no sense hugely extravagant; the family also had a bungalow of the same name at Porthcawl, with a prospect looking out over the Bristol Channel to Morte Point on the north Devon coast. When interviewed in the London office by a correspondent from *Lloyd's List* regarding his purchase of the *Margherita* in 1925, he made the following interesting comment which reveals his attitude to landed wealth:

> I have no use for land . . . I have a garden and in it are over 200 rose trees – and beautiful roses they are too – but if there were a ship in the midst of them, I am afraid that, notwithstanding all the charms with which bounteous nature has invested the blooms, the ship would claim all my attention.[186]

This indifference to the wealth and status which land was generally thought to confer was rooted to considerable degree in his Appledore upbringing and his seafaring background. As has been noted previously, it was a community whose outlook was totally orientated towards the sea; Sir William himself used the term 'landsman' in a slightly condescending manner for people who earned a living on land, rather than at sea, whilst Appledore folk gave farmers the even more derisory nickname of 'grasshoppers'![187]

Two other factors in his life doubtless also influenced his philanthropy. The first, already alluded to, was the fact that when he was three he lost his father and elder brother at sea, leaving his widowed mother with a family of eight to bring up alone. Sir William tells us nothing of this period in his autobiography, but they must have been difficult years during which the family doubtless suffered periods of hardship. Secondly, there was the elementary education that he received in the Wesleyan Methodist day school in Appledore. On one occasion, preaching upon what he perceived should be the proper attitude of a Christian towards material wealth, John Wesley – strongly reflecting the Protestant work ethic – declared 'gain as much as you can, save as much as you can, give as much as you can'.[188]

It is impossible to know whether or not Sir William was aware of this quote, but as has been shown above, he was well versed in the Bible; it follows therefore that he would also have been familiar with the numerous scriptural exhortations to the wealthy to be accountable to God for their wealth and above all, to be charitable to those less fortunate than themselves. This notion of assisting others may appear to be somewhat at odds with his firm belief in the benefits of *laissez-faire* economics (especially in the case of his apparent indifference to the miners' difficulties in his 1921 comments on the price of coal); conversely, there were also times, apparently, when other members of Sir William's family were somewhat exasperated by his constant generosity.[189] Nevertheless, Sir William was ultimately in accord with both John Wesley and the noted Scottish-American philanthropist, Andrew Carnegie; the latter believed that it was the sacred duty of those with excess wealth to distribute it in the way best calculated to produce the most beneficial results for the wider community, and this sentiment was echoed perfectly by Sir William in his speech as he opened the new hospital at Bideford in September 1925:

> To my mind, it is an act of religion and a public duty to support, in accordance with our means, the noble work carried on in our hospitals . . . if all those who are healthy could fully realise the sufferings of the sick, and those who are well-to-do the hardships and privations of the poor, it would go a long way towards solving many of the difficult problems that beset our country today.[190]

Concluding his lecture, 'Wales and the Past – Two Voices', the inaugural lecture in the Reardon Smith Lecture Theatre at the National Museum on 2 November 1932, Professor John Edward Lloyd stated:

> Cardiff is, indeed, fortunate in having at its doors this national institution, with its unlimited facilities for the study of the past and present of Wales. And it is good to know that you have among you those who realise the greatness of the existing opportunity and are ready, with whole-souled devotion, to respond to the call it brings with it. I refer especially to the generosity of your late President, Sir William Reardon Smith, which has made it possible to open this delightful auditorium free of debt. It will bear his name to all time and carry down to future generations the memory of a great benefaction. In spirit, if not in person, he will preside over many gatherings held within these walls, at which the experts of the Museum and others will discourse upon the treasures which find lodgement here, will show their significance in the history of Wales and their bearing upon the life of today.[191]

'He was a ragged-arsed urchin who left Appledore as a young boy and made good'; Sir William in ceremonial dress as a deputy lieutenant of Glamorganshire, 1930.

This glowing tribute from an obvious master of word-craft was also a perceptive prophecy of the many learned gatherings that have since been staged in the theatre. Less lyrical, but more concise and pithy perhaps, is an evaluation of Sir William by a former Appledore fisherman and seafarer, the late Richard Cann: 'a ragged-arsed urchin who left Appledore as a young boy and made good'.[192] Make good in shipping he most certainly did; he contributed his own incomparable seafaring knowledge to a remarkable conjunction of economic and social factors – the world-wide demand for Welsh steam coal, sources of capital from the West Riding of Yorkshire and industrial Cornwall, and the nautical skills of officers and seamen from Wales, the north-east of England, Ireland – and further afield – to create an esteemed shipping venture that, despite occasional vicissitudes, lasted for eight decades. And, loath to spend the proceeds of that venture on his own indulgence, he instead supported many worthy causes – hospitals, libraries, schools, universities, and above all the National Museum of Wales, which he almost single-handedly set upon a firm financial footing. Thanks to his munificence, therefore, many of us who live in Wales and the West Country today still benefit from the philanthropic legacy bequeathed by Sir William Reardon Smith to the generations that would follow him.

Notes to the text

[1] Guildhall Library, Lloyd's Captains' Registers 18567/70, 1896–1903.

[2] Lloyd's Register of Shipping, 1892–3.

[3] Ibid., 1913–14.

[4] J. Geraint Jenkins, Evan Thomas, Radcliffe & Co. – a Cardiff Shipowning Company (Cardiff: National Museum of Wales 1982), pp. 8–10.

[5] Paul M. Heaton, Tatems of Cardiff (Risca: Starling Press, 1987), pp. 12, 16; Western Mail, 30 March 1933

[6] See p. 40

[7] The National Archives, Kew (hereafter TNA), BT31/6012/42448.

[8] See n. 6. Ellen Smith was not an exception in the way in which she took charge of the family's maritime investments; see Helen Doe, Enterprising Women and Shipping in the Nineteenth Century (Woodbridge: Boydell Press, 2009).

[9] TNA, BT31/7121/50229.

[10] See n. 1.

[11] 1901 Census, civil parish of Roath, Cardiff. Confusingly, he was recorded by the enumerator as William Richardson Smith! I am grateful to Mr John Reardon-Smith for this information.

[12] Amgueddfa Cymru – National Museum Wales, Dept of Industry (hereafter DoI) 86.231/32; 82.

[13] Shipmates: Reardon Smith Seafarers' Newsletter, 27 (June 2003), 4.

[14] Captain William Hughes (1981), 'My fifty years of sea life' (part 1), Cymru a'r Môr/ Maritime Wales, 6, 109. 'Bluenose' is the somewhat pejorative nickname given to a native of Nova Scotia.

[15] See n. 12.

[16] Who was who, 1941–50 (London: Adam & Charles Black, 1952), p. 1036.

[17] Sir Walter Runciman, Before the Mast – and After: the Autobiography of a Sailor and Shipowner (London: Ernest Benn, 1924), p. 250.

[18] TNA, BT31/41319/80245.

[19] Ibid.

[20] World Ship Society (hereafter WSS), yard list 3B, Craig, Taylor & Co., Stockton-on-Tees; Maritime Review, II/.26 (10 August 1904), 239.

[21] Glamorgan Record Office (hereafter GRO), DRBS/1/8, statutory shipping register, port of Cardiff, 1901–6.

[22] See n. 18.

[23] See n. 18.

[24] TNA, BT31/17461/84645.

[25] Ibid.

[26] 'Maritime and other money matters', *Maritime Review*, IX/105, (16 February 1906), 16.

[27] For a history of the Holman company, see David B. Clement, *Holman's: a Family Business of Shipbuilders, Shipowners and Insurers from* 1832 (Topsham: Topsham Museum Society, 2005).

[28] Amongst the Cardiff shipping ventures that were beneficiaries of Holman finance in the first decade of the twentieth century were Jenkins Brothers and W. J. Tatem & Co.

[29] WSS yard list 13B, Ropner Shipbuilding & Engineering Co. Ltd; *Lloyd's Weekly Shipping Index*, 29 March 1906.

[30] See for instance the view of the *Leeds City* on p. 00 and *Lloyd's Book of Houseflags and Funnels* (London: Lloyd's of London, 1912), p. 72.

[31] See n. 21.

[32] *Maritime Review*, 11/140 (19 October, 1906), 165.

[33] Ibid., 13/157 (15 February 1907),16.

[34] For a comprehensive account of the Ropner trunk-deck steamers, see Harold Appleyard, 'Ropner trunk-deck steamers', *Ships in Focus Record*,1/2, 83–91 and 1/3, 154–9.

[35] See notes 21 and 24.

[36] *Syren & Shipping Illustrated* (20 November 1907), 184. I am grateful to the late Mr Robin Craig for this reference.

[37] See n. 24.

[38] *Maritime Review*,.1/2 (24 February 1904), 42.

[39] Desmond I. Williams, *Seventy Years in Shipping* (Cardiff: Graig Shipping plc, 1989), p. 13; DoI, 86.23I/1 (5).

[40] Aled Eames, *Ventures in Sail* (Caernarfon, Liverpool and London: Gwynedd Archives Service, Merseyside Maritime Museum and National Maritime Museum, 1987), p. 47; David Jenkins (June 2004), '*Llongau y Chwarelwyr?* Investments by Caernarfonshire slate quarrymen in local shipping companies in the late nineteenth century', *Welsh History Review*, 22/1.

[41] TNA, BT31/19011/105095.

[42] *Syren & Shipping Illustrated* (16 February 1910), 233. I am again grateful to the late Mr Robin Craig for this reference.

[43] GRO, DRBS/1/9, statutory shipping register, port of Cardiff, 1906–12.

[44] See n. 41.

[45] Information related by Sir Antony Reardon Smith, 23 February 2006.

[46] See n. 29.

[47] GRO, crew lists, *Bradford City*, 1910.

[48] See n. 41 and GRO, DBRS/1/10, statutory shipping register of the port of Cardiff, 1912–16.

[49] The ensuing pages rely heavily upon the author's article, (1986), 'Sir William Reardon Smith and the St Just Shipping Co. Ltd, 1912–22', *Cymru a'r Môr/Maritime*

Wales, 10, 45–62. I am grateful to my fellow editors of the journal for their permission to adapt sections of the article for use in this publication.

[50] See n. 41.

[51] For a full account of the loss of the *City of Cardiff*, see Richard Larn and Clive Carter, *Cornish Shipwrecks – the South Coast* (Newton Abbot: David and Charles, 1969).

[52] DoI, 86.23I/1,1.

[53] *Idem.*

[54] GRO, DRSL12/1, 2, shareholders' registers, St Just Steamship Co. Ltd, 1912–20 and 1917–21; information related by Mr Francis Angwin, St Just, 10 September 2007; Alec Osborne (June 1999), 'St Just Steamship Company Ltd', *Shipmates*, 11.

[55] DoI, 86.23I/1, 19, 20, 31–42, Reardon Smith shareholders' steamer movement postcards.

[56] See n. 55.

[57] TNA, BT31/21542/129693.

[58] *Syren & Shipping Illustrated* (8 November 1914), 1.

[59] GRO, DRSL/77/2.

[60] GRO, DRSL/5/21.

[61] DoI, 86.23I/1, 63.

[62] See Jess Bailie, 'Board of Trade Shipping Inquiries, 1875–1935', in *Annual Report of the Glamorgan Archivist*, 1989 and David Jenkins, *Jenkins Brothers of Cardiff: a Ceredigion Family's Shipping Ventures* (Cardiff: National Museum of Wales, 1985), p. 50.

[63] Robin Craig, 'The Ports and Shipping, *c.*1750–1914' in Glanmor Williams (ed.), *Glamorgan County History*, Vol. 5, *Industrial Glamorgan* (Cardiff: University of Wales Press, 1980), p. 502; Basil Greenhill and Michael Nix, 'North Devon Shipping, Trade and Ports, 1786–1939 in Michael Duffy et al. (eds), *The New Maritime History of Devon* , Vol. II: *from the Late Eighteenth Century to the Present Day* (London: Conway Maritime Press and the University of Exeter, 1994) p. 48; I am also grateful to Mr Peter Christie for information on the changing port status of Bideford.

[64] For a full account of the dispute, see David Jenkins, *Shipowners of Cardiff: A Class by Themselves. A History of the Cardiff and Bristol Channel Incorporated Shipowners' Association* (Cardiff: National Museum of Wales and University of Wales Press, 1997), pp. 29–33.

[65] GRO, D/D Com/C/3, Cardiff and Bristol Channel Incorporated Shipowners' Association, minute book, 1903–10.

[66] Ibid., minute book, 1910–15.

[67] TNA, BT31/13957/123706.

[68] Annual reports, UK Chamber of Shipping, 1918–35.

[69] *British Vessels Lost at Sea*, 1914–18 (HMSO, 1919), p. 2

[70] TNA, BT31/21542/129693.

[71] A. J. Tennent, *British Merchant Ships Sunk by U-Boats in the* 1914–1918 *War* (Newport: Starling Press, 1990), p. 210.

[72] D. E. Fayle, *The War and the Shipping Industry* (London: Humphrey Milford, 1927), pp. 151–3.

[73] DoI, 86.23I/1, 56.

[74] J. S. Boswell and B. R. Johns (1982), 'Patriots or Profiteers? British Businessmen and the First World War', *Journal of European Economic History*, 11/2, 426, 427.

[75] See n. 24.

[76] Fayle, *The War and the Shipping Industry*, pp. 151–3.

[77] DoI, 86.23I/1, 68.

[78] Fayle, *The War and the Shipping Industry*, p. 204.

[79] DoI, 86.23I/1, 77.

[80] DoI, 86.23/1, 82.

[81] DoI, 86.23I/1, 80.

[82] Carson Ritchie, *Q-ships* (Lavenham: Terence Dalton and Co. Ltd, 1985), pp. 86, 177.

[83] DoI, 86.23I/1, 85.

[84] DoI, 86.23I/1, 88

[85] D. Jeffrey Morgan (1989), 'Boom and Slump – shipowning at Cardiff, 1919–1921', *Cymru a r Môr/Maritime Wales*, 12, 138; Ronald Hope, *A New History of British Shipping* (London: John Murray, 1990), p. 358.

[86] J. Geraint Jenkins and David Jenkins, *Cardiff Shipowners* (Cardiff: National Museum of Wales, 1986), pp. 24, 36.

[87] DoI 86.23I/1, 113.

[88] TNA, BT31/24829/157095; GRO, DRSL 5/16; TNA BT31/25673/164932.

[89] DoI 86.23I/1, 107; information related by Sir Anthony and Lady Susan Reardon Smith, 23 February, 2006.

[90] GRO, DRSL/45/37.

[91] DoI 86.23I/1, 115; GRO, DRSL 5/7; TNA, BT31/25148/159924.

[92] DoI, 86.23I/1, 132.

[93] DoI, 86.23I/32, 49.

[94] Anon., *Cardiff: A Commercial and Industrial Centre* (Cardiff: Western Mail, 1919).

[95] Jenkins, *Shipowners of Cardiff*, pp. 41–2.

[96] John Davies, *A History of Wales* (London: Allen Lane, 1993), p. 528; *Burke's Peerage and Baronetage* (London: 2003), p. 3300.

[97] Amgueddfa Cymru – National Museum of Wales, Dept of Art (hereafter DoA), NMW A5145. The experts consulted were Dr J. Graham Jones, Head of the Welsh Political Archive at the National Library of Wales, Aberystwyth and Professor Kenneth O. Morgan (Lord Morgan of Aberdyfi), Fellow of the Queen's College, Oxford.

[98] TNA, BT31/32454/171126.

[99] DoI, 86.23I/32, 49.

[100] GRO, DRSL/67/4; DRBS/1/12, statutory shipping register, port of Cardiff, 1920–4; DoI 86.23/32, 49.

[101] Paul M. Heaton, *Reardon Smith Line: the History of a South Wales Shipping Venture* (Risca: Starling Press, 1984), p. 42.

[102] Anon., 'Cardiff – Shipping and Shipowning', in *Cardiff 1921* (London: The Syren & Shipping Illustrated, 1921), pp. 51–3.

[103] TNA, BT31/25418/159924; GRO, DRSL/67/5

[104] Ibid.

[105] GRO, DRSL/67/5

[106] TNA, BT31/25418/159924.

[107] GRO, DRSL/7/3; *Western Mail*, 20 July 1923.

[108] Ibid.

[109] *Western Mail*, 8 January 1921; GRO, DRSL/5/10.

[110] *Atlantic Reporter*, 129, 18 June–3 September 1925.

[111] Edward L. Allen, *Pilot Lore From Sail to Steam: and Historical Sketches of the Various Interests Identified with the Development of the World's Greatest Port* (New York: United New York and New Jersey Sandy Hook Pilots' Benevolent Association, 1922), p. 278.

[112] *New York Times*, 4, 7 March 1922.

[113] GRO, DRSL 5/27; I am also grateful to Mrs Mary Davies for recalling her grandfather's friendship with Thomas Davis and to Mr Doug Ford, curator of the Jersey Maritime Museum for further information on Davis.

[114] *Lloyd's List*, 7 April 1924; see also n. 110.

[115] I am grateful to Mr David Burrell for this information.

[116] *Western Mail*, 8 January 1921.

[117] Ibid., 11 January 1921.

[118] Ibid., 10, 15, 23 January 1921.

[119] Ibid., 12 February 1921.

[120] *Bideford and North Devon Weekly Gazette*, 25 November 1924; 24 September 1925.

[121] D. E. Jeffreys, *Maritime Memories of Cardiff* (Risca: Starling Press, 1978), pp. 6, 55, 56.

[122] North Devon Record Office (hereafter NDRO) 3319 add.3/2, statutory shipping register of the port of Bideford, 1923–62.

[123] John Nicholson, *Great Years in Yachting* (Lymington: Nautical Publishing Co. Ltd, 1970), pp. 74, 75; I am also grateful to Ms Hannah Cunliffe for information on the *Margherita*.

[124] *Lloyd's List*, 16 February 1925.

[125] *Western Mail*, 2 February, 1925.

[126] *Lloyd's Register of Yachts*, 1930; M. H. Disney, *The Honourable Company* (London: Honourable Company of Master Mariners, 1974), p. 31; information supplied by Mr John Reardon Smith.

[127] *Western Mail*, 25 June 1925; I am grateful to Mr Ronald Austin for this reference.

[128] I am grateful to Mr Michael Tamlyn for allowing me to quote from this letter.

[129] I am grateful to Sir Antony and Lady Susan Reardon Smith for making available a copy of this letter.

[130] *Times*, 5 June 1930; DoI, 86.231/33 (65).

[131] *Annual Report, University of Exeter*, 1926–27; correspondence from the late Mr Roderick Ross, Secretary, Exeter University, to Mr Michael Tamlyn, Topsham, 10 May 1972. I am grateful to Mr Michael Tamlyn for making this material available to me.

[132] I am grateful to Mr Huw Ceiriog, formerly of the National Library of Wales, for this information. See also *Bideford and North Devon Weekly Gazette*, 31 December 1935, *Western Morning News*, 27 May 1972 and *Western Mail*, 10 September 1939.

[133] D. A. Bassett (1983), 'The Making of a National Museum' (part 2), *Transactions of the Honourable Society of Cymmrodorion*, 202; *Annual Report, National Museum of Wales*, 1925–6, 10.

[134] Sir Mortimer Wheeler, *Still Digging: Interleaves from an Antiquary's Notebook* (London: Michael Joseph, 1955), p. 70.

[135] *Western Mail*, 24 March 1928.

[136] DoI, 2007.861/12; recollections by Tom Major, former technical director, Reardon Smith Line, in *Shipmates*, 10, February 1999; information supplied by Major W. H. White (retd) of the Duke of Cornwall's Light Infantry Regimental Museum, Bodmin.

[137] Heaton, *Reardon Smith Line*, p. 43.

[138] GRO, DRSL 5/7; DoI, 86.231/132.

[139] DoI, 86.231/132; *Shipbuilding and Shipping Record*, 2 December 1926. I am grateful to Andrew Bell for drawing my attention to the latter source. See also GRO, DRSL 45/12.

[140] *Western Mail*, 21 August 1924; 15 June 1925; 16 August 1926; 20 May 1927; 1 June 1928; 28 June 1929.

[141] For a full account of Owen Williams's venture into motor vessels, see David Jenkins, *Owen & Watkin Williams of Cardiff: the Golden Cross Line* (Kendal: World Ship Society, 1991).

[142] DoI, 86.231/34 (35); GRO, DRSL 40.

[143] Ibid. On this subject, see Max E. Fletcher (February 1975), 'From coal to oil in British shipping', *Journal of Transport History*, New Series, 3/1.

[144] See n. 136.

[145] See n. 122.

[146] *Journal of Commerce*, 21 September 1928.

[147] Ibid.

[148] GRO, DRSL 40; *Western Mail*, 20 November 1929; 23 September 1930.

[149] *Western Mail*, 19 November 1928.

[150] *Shipmates*, 11, June 1999; I am also grateful to Dr Roy Fenton for information on the British Corporation Registry.

[151] Hope, *A New History of British Shipping*, p. 375.

[152] *Lloyd's List*, 28 February 1930.

[153] DoI, 86.23/34 (8).

[154] *Houston Press*, 10 February 1934.

[155] Personal recollections, Messrs Philip and Sidney Ford in conversation with Mr Michael Tamlyn, Appledore, 4 June 2007.

[156] Captain Frank Forde, *Maritime Arklow* (Dun Laoghaire: Glendale Press, 1988), pp. 147–57.

[157] Lloyd's Captains' Registers; *Western Mail*, 1 June 1928; DoI 86.231/32 (30); see also n. 153.

[158] DoA, NMW A1702

[159] *South Wales Echo*, 16 May 1930.

[160] *Western Mail*, 26 October, 1932.

[161] J. E. Lloyd, *Wales and the Past – Two Voices* (Cardiff: National Museum of Wales, 1932); *Exhibition of Models of Cargo-carrying Steamers – Catalogue* (Cardiff: National Museum of Wales, 1933). The model of the *York City* is currently on display at the National Waterfront Museum, Swansea.

[162] See n. 122; *Western Mail*, 22 October 1932.

[163] Heaton, *Reardon Smith Line*, pp. 93–109.

[164] *Western Morning News*, 24 December 1935.

[165] David Burrell, *Scrap & Build* (Kendal: World Ship Society, 1983), pp. 8, 9.

[166] Ibid, p. 35.

[167] *Daily Gleaner* (Kingston, Jamaica), 25 January 1934.

[168] See n. 154.

[169] Ibid.

[170] *Western Mail* and *Western Morning News*, 28 December 1935.

[171] GRO, DRSL/77/1.

[172] *Bideford and North Devon Gazette*, 29 September 1925; *Times*, 10 August 1939.

[173] Recalled in a letter from Mr Michael Tamlyn to the author, 14 February 2005.

[174] Personal recollections, Mrs Mary Davies in conversation with the author, 6 March 2009.

[175] DoI, 86.231/34 (52).

[176] Related to the author and the late Dr J. Geraint Jenkins by the late Mr Chris John over lunch in the Exchange Restaurant, *c.*1984.

[177] Nicholson, *Great Years in Yachting*, p. 75.

[178] See n. 134. The 'Catalogue of Ships' is to be found in Book II of Homer's *Iliad*.

[179] Jacquetta Hawkes, *Mortimer Wheeler: Adventurer in Archaeology* (London: Weidenfeld and Nicolson, 1982), p. 96.

[180] Related to the author by Mr John Reardon-Smith, who heard it from his father, Mr Alan Reardon-Smith; see also Charles E. Evans, *Memoirs of Lieutenant-Commander Charles E. Evans* (Cardiff: Western Mail, 1946), p. 14 and also n. 175.

[181] Robin Craig, 'Trade and Shipping in South Wales – the Radcliffe Company, 1882–1921' in Colin Baber and L. J. Williams (eds), *Modern South Wales: Essays in Economic History* (Cardiff: University of Wales Press, 1986), p. 173.

[182] See n. 124.

[183] See n. 155.

[184] DoI, 86.231/34 (12); see also n. 174.

[185] Personal recollections, Mr and Mrs T. Waters, Appledore, in conversation with the author and Mr Michael Tamlyn, 13 August 2007.

[186] See n. 124.

[187] DoI, 86.231/34 (9).

[188] John Walsh, 'John Wesley and the community of goods', in Keith Robbins (ed.), *Protestant Evangelicalism: Britain, Ireland, Germany and America, c.1790–1860: Essays in Honour of* W. R. Ward (Oxford: Oxford University Press, 2001).

[189] See n. 160.

[190] *Bideford and North Devon Weekly Gazette*, 29 September 1925.

[191] See n. 161.

[192] See n. 185.

Appendices

Appendix 1

REARDON SMITH FAMILY TREE

(simplified)

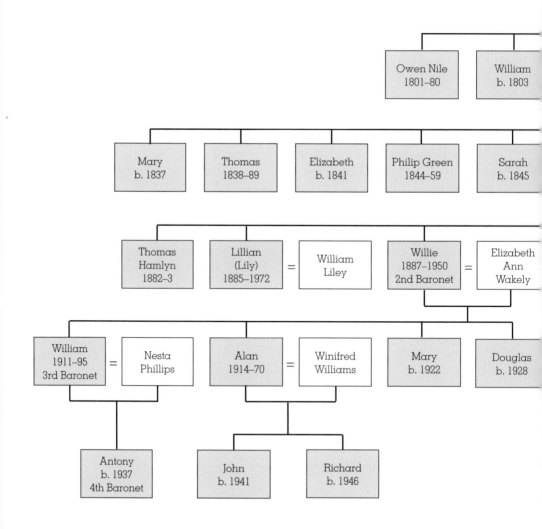

Owen Nile
1801–80

William
b. 1803

Mary
b. 1837

Thomas
1838–89

Elizabeth
b. 1841

Philip Green
1844–59

Sarah
b. 1845

Thomas
Hamlyn
1882–3

Lillian
(Lily)
1885–1972

=

William
Liley

Willie
1887–1950
2nd Baronet

=

Elizabeth
Ann
Wakely

William
1911–95
3rd Baronet

=

Nesta
Phillips

Alan
1914–70

=

Winifred
Williams

Mary
b. 1922

Douglas
b. 1928

Antony
b. 1937
4th Baronet

John
b. 1941

Richard
b. 1946

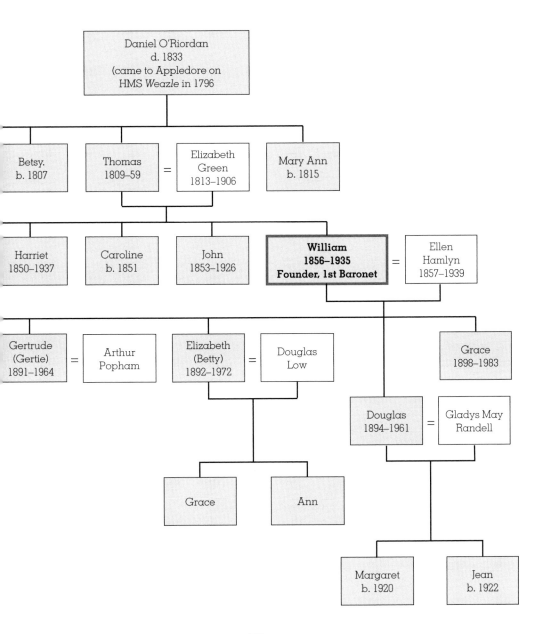

Daniel O'Riordan
d. 1833
(came to Appledore on
HMS *Weazle* in 1796

Betsy.
b. 1807

Thomas
1809–59
=
Elizabeth
Green
1813–1906

Mary Ann
b. 1815

Harriet
1850–1937

Caroline
b. 1851

John
1853–1926

**William
1856–1935
Founder, 1st Baronet**
=
Ellen
Hamlyn
1857–1939

Gertrude
(Gertie)
1891–1964
=
Arthur
Popham

Elizabeth
(Betty)
1892–1972
=
Douglas
Low

Grace
1898–1983

Douglas
1894–1961
=
Gladys May
Randell

Grace

Ann

Margaret
b. 1920

Jean
b. 1922

Appendix 2

WILLIAM REARDON SMITH'S SEAFARING
CAREER, 1870–1900

(Note: WRS recalled in letters written to Vernon Boyle in 1932 that he had had sixty-four years' experience of ships and shipping and also recalled a voyage that he undertook on the *Joe Abraham* (see below) in 1868. However, there is no record of his having gone to sea in an official capacity until he joined the *Unity* in 1870.)

Unity
Wooden sloop, 32 nett tons, built 1818, owned by Henry Hinks, Appledore.
Ordinary seaman (OS), August–December 1870.

Seraphina
Wooden sloop, 38 nett tons, built 1839, owned by George Parkhouse, Appledore.
OS, spring 1871.

Joe Abraham
Wooden polacca brigantine, 36 nett tons, built 1850, owned by William Yeo, Appledore.
OS, July–December 1871.

Ocean Pearl
Wooden ship, 965 nett tons, built 1865, owned by Rowlands & Thomas, Cardiff.
OS, February–July 1872.

Scout
Wooden ship, 460 nett tons, built 1862, owned by Henry Bath & Co., Swansea.
OS, August 1872–October 1873.

Caroline
Wooden schooner, 50 nett tons, built 1824, owned by P. K. Harris, Appledore.
Able-bodied seaman (AB), October 1873–January 1874.

Viscount Canning
Wooden ship, 746 nett tons, built 1855, owned by R. Morris, Bristol.
AB, January–May 1874.

Jane
Wooden barquentine, 201 nett tons, built 1874, owned by C. T. Bowring & Co., Liverpool.
AB, August–December 1874.

Lucille
Wooden brig, 273 nett tons, built 1874, owned by John Yeo, Prince Edward Island.
AB, April–June 1875.

June–November 1875: on Prince Edward Island with Yeo ship-rigging gang.

Milo
Wooden barque, 436 nett tons, built 1875, owned by John Yeo, Prince Edward Island.
AB, November–December 1875.

Souvenir
Wooden barque, 482 nett tons, built 1872, owned by E. H. Cummins & R. H. Marten, Bristol.
AB, February–July, 1876.

11 August 1876: passed examination for second mate's certificate at Leith.

Vermont
Wooden ship, 1236 nett tons, built 1866, owned by Henry T. Ropes of Liverpool.
2nd mate, October 1876–January 1878.

2 March 1878: passed examination for first mate's certificate at Plymouth.

Mary Hogarth
Wooden barque, 588 nett tons, built 1876, owned by Goodwin & Hogarth, Ardrossan.
1st mate, April 1878–May 1879.

6 June 1879: passed examination for master's certificate at Plymouth.

Cyprus
Wooden barque, 500 nett tons, built 1878, owned by Hugh Hogarth, Ardrossan.
1st mate, June 1879–March 1880.

Drumadoon
Wooden barque, 866 nett tons, built 1876, owned by Hugh Hogarth, Ardrossan.
1st mate, July 1880–September 1881.
Master, October 1881–October 1882.

Macrihanish
Iron ship (later re-rigged as a barque), 1699 nett tons, built 1883, owned by Hugh Hogarth, Ardrossan.
Superintended construction at Port Glasgow during 1883.
Master, November 1883–September 1884.

Colonsay
Iron steamer, 1132 gross tons, built 1882, owned by J. Allan & Co., Glasgow.
Master, September–October 1884.

Ochtertyre
Iron barque, 1263 nett tons, built 1885, owned by Hugh Hogarth, Ardrossan.
Superintended construction (and that of her sister-ship *Corryvrechan*) at Port Glasgow, 1884–5.
Master, September 1885–April 1890.

Baron Douglas
Steel steamship, 2700 gross tons, built 1888, owned by Hugh Hogarth, Ardrossan.
Master, June 1890 – April 1892.

Baron Elibank
Steel steamship, 1772 gross tons, built 1889, owned by Hugh Hogarth, Ardrossan.
Master, April 1892–November 1894.

Baron Belhaven
Steel steamship, 2356 gross tons, built 1887, owned by Hugh Hogarth, Ardrossan.
Master, November 1894–October 1896.

Starcross
Steel steamship, 2823 gross tons, built 1894, owned by Anning Brothers, Cardiff.
Master, November 1896–July 1897.

Lady Lewis
Steel steamship, 2950 gross tons, built 1897, owned by William J. Tatem, Cardiff.
Master, July 1897–April 1899.

Shandon
Steel steamship, 3850 gross tons, built 1899, owned by William J. Tatem, Cardiff.
Stood by vessel as she was completed at Stockton-on-Tees, April–June 1899.
Master, June 1899–February 1900.

Lady Lewis
(see above)
Master, February–December 1900.

Appendix 3

MANAGEMENT AND SHIPPING COMPANIES ESTABLISHED OR ACQUIRED BY SIR WILLIAM REARDON SMITH

W. R. Smith & Son, 1905–9.
W. R. Smith & Sons, 1909–22.
Sir W. R. Smith & Sons Ltd, 1923 onwards.

W. R. Smith & Sons (London) Ltd, 1919–23.

Sir W. R. Smith, Popham & Liley, 1919–27.
Sir W. R. Smith & Partners Ltd, 1927–38.

Instow Steamship Co. Ltd, 1905; original capital £32,800 @ £10.
Amalgamated with the St Just Steamship Co. Ltd in 1916 and wound up.

Bradford Steamship Co. Ltd, 1910; original capital £33,250 @ £10.
Amalgamated with the St Just Steamship Co. Ltd in 1917 and wound up.

St Just Steamship Co. Ltd, 1912; original capital £90,000 @ £10. Renamed the Reardon Smith Line Ltd in 1928.

Great City Steamship Co. Ltd, 1913; original capital £60,000 @ £10.
Amalgamated with the St Just Steamship Co. Ltd in 1917 and wound up.

Devon Mutual Steamship Insurance Association, 1913 onwards.
No nominal capital.

Coniston Water Steamship Co. Ltd, 1916; company and single ship bought in 1916; wound up in 1918 following the loss of the steamer *Coniston Water* by torpedo on 21 July 1917.

Leeds Shipping Co. Ltd, 1919 onwards, original capital £400,000 @ £1.

Cornborough Shipping Line Ltd, 1919; original capital £400,000 @ £1.

Wound up in 1923, shareholders given one St Just share (from Sir William's personal holding) for every three Cornborough shares and ships transferred to the St Just Steamship Co. Ltd

Oakwin Shipping Co. Ltd, 1920; original capital £100,000 @ £1. Initially, Sir William Reardon Smith & Sons Ltd held all but three of the shares in this company. Its ships were transferred to the St Just Steamship Co. Ltd in 1926, after which the Oakwin company was a major shareholder in the St Just company, later in the Reardon Smith Line. The first two motor vessels, *East Lynn* and *West Lynn*, were also owned by this company from 1928 until 1937. In 1931 the capital was raised to £250,000 and the shares redistributed amongst members of Sir William's immediate family. Wound up in 1939.

Unity Shipping & Trading Co. Ltd, 1921; original capital £30,000 @ £1. Company wound up on the sale of its sole ship, the *Meropi*, in 1929.

Reardon Smith Line Ltd, 1921; original capital £1000 @ £1. Company renamed Reardon Smith Navigation Co. Ltd in May 1928 when the St Just Steamship Co. Ltd was renamed the Reardon Smith Line Ltd.

Reardon Smith (Union of South Africa) Ltd, June 1923; original capital £250,000 @ £1.

Reardon Smith Line Ltd, 1928 onwards; 1928 capital £1,232,000 @ 10/-.

In addition to the above, Sir William also served at various times on the boards of the following maritime businesses and organizations:

Britannia Steamship Insurance Association Ltd, London.
British Corporation for the Registry of Shipping, Glasgow.
Cardiff Pilotage Authority.
Channel Dry Docks Ltd, Cardiff.
Council of the Chamber of Shipping, London.
Council of the Shipping Federation, London.
North of England Protection and Indemnity Association, Newcastle upon Tyne.
Ropner Shipbuilding & Repair Co. Ltd, Stockton-on-Tees.
Shipping Supply Ltd, Newport.
Tredegar Dry Dock & Wharf Co. Ltd, Newport.
United Kingdom Freight, Demurrage and Defence Association, London.
United Kingdom Mutual Steamship Assurance Association, London.
West of England Steam Shipowners' Protection and Indemnity Association Ltd, London.

$$\mathcal{A}ppendix\ 4$$

FLEET LISTS, 1905–35

(These lists are not intended to provide a comprehensive list of all Reardon Smith vessels, but rather to provide decennial 'snapshots' of the growth and development of the fleet during Sir William Reardon Smith's shipowning career.)

1905

City of Cardiff
(under construction)
Steel steamship.
In the fleet: 1906–12.
Official number: 123152.
Tonnage gross: 3089.
Tonnage nett: 1965.
Length: 330.5 x beam: 48.0 x depth: 21.7 feet.
Machinery: T. 3-cyl. by the North East Marine Engineering Co. Ltd, Sunderland.
History: 3.1906: completed by Ropner & Sons, Stockton-on-Tees for the Instow Steamship Co. Ltd (W. R. Smith & Son, managers), Cardiff. 12.3.1912: blown ashore in hurricane-force winds at Nanjizal, two miles SE of Land's End, whilst bound from Le Havre to Barry Roads in ballast. The entire crew, the wives of the captain and the chief engineer and the latter's son were rescued by breeches buoy from the adjacent cliff top.

1915

Leeds City
Steel trunk-decked steamship.
In the fleet: 1908–18.
Official number: 123198.
Tonnage gross: 4298.
Tonnage nett: 2630.
Length: 355.0 x beam: 51.0 x depth: 26.0 feet.
Machinery: T. 3-cyl. by Blair & Co., Stockton-on-Tees.
History: 7.1908: completed as *Leeds City* (having been laid down as *City of Leeds*)

by Ropner & Sons Ltd, Stockton-on-Tees for the Instow Steamship Co. Ltd (W. R. Smith & Son, managers), Cardiff. 1.1916: transferred to the Bradford Steamship Co. Ltd (W. R. Smith & Sons, managers), Cardiff. 1.7.1917: transferred to the St Just Steamship Co. Ltd (same managers), Cardiff. 6.5.1918: torpedoed and sunk by German submarine U86 five miles E by S½S from the Skulmartin light vessel, whilst bound from Portland, Maine, to Manchester with a cargo of flour and wheat. No lives were lost.

Bradford City
Steel steamship.
In the fleet: 1910–17.
Official number: 128503.
Tonnage gross: 3683.
Tonnage nett: 2257.
Length: 346.5 x beam 51.0 x draught: 23.2 feet
Machinery: T. 3-cyl. by the North East Marine Engineering Co. Ltd, Sunderland.
History: 2.1910: completed by Ropner & Sons Ltd, Stockton-on-Tees, for the Bradford Steamship Co. Ltd (W. R. Smith & Sons, managers), Cardiff. 16.10.1915: requisitioned by the Royal Navy for service as a 'Q-ship', operating chiefly from Gibraltar under the false names *Ballistan* and *Seros*. 1.7.1917: returned to original owners and transferred to the St Just Steamship Co. Ltd. 16.8.1917: torpedoed and sunk by Austro-Hungarian submarine U28 in the Straits of Messina. No lives were lost.

Atlantic City
Steel steamship.
In the fleet: 1912–29.
Official number: 132861.
Tonnage gross: 4707
Tonnage nett: 2934.
Length: 378.5 x beam: 51.5 x depth: 27.5 feet.
Machinery: T. 3-cyl. by Blair & Co., Stockton-on-Tees.
History: 3.1912: completed by Ropner & Sons, Stockton-on-Tees for the Bradford Steamship Co. Ltd (W. R. Smith & Sons, managers), Cardiff. 1917: transferred to the St Just Steamship Co. Ltd, Cardiff (same managers). 1920: transferred to the Leeds Shipping Co. Ltd, Cardiff (Sir W. R. Smith & Sons, managers), and renamed *Bradburn*. 1929: sold to the Anglo-Celtic Shipping Co. Ltd (Griffiths, Payne & Co., managers), Cardiff and renamed *Brynmêl*. 1935: sold to Costis E. Lemos, Chios, Greece and renamed *Maria L.* 4.11.1950: wrecked on Cape Villano in position 43.12N, 09.08W whilst bound from Antwerp to Cagliari with a cargo of coal.

Devon City
Steel steamship.
In the fleet: 1913–28.
Official number: 123210.
Tonnage gross: 4316.
Tonnage nett: 2686.
Length: 390.0 x beam: 52.5 x depth: 27.7 feet.
Machinery: T. 3-cyl. by Blair & Co., Stockton-on-Tees.
History: 4.1913 completed by Ropner & Sons Ltd, Stockton-on-Tees for the St Just Steamship Co. Ltd (W. R. Smith & Sons, managers), Cardiff. 1928: transferred to the Reardon Smith Line Ltd (Sir W. R. Smith & Sons Ltd, managers), Cardiff. 1928: sold to Pateras Bros, Chios, Greece and renamed *Kostanti*. 3.8.1933: beached on fire twenty miles NE of the Rio Doce, Brazil, whilst bound from Methil to Buenos Aires with coal, and became a constructive total loss.

Eastern City
Steel steamship
In the fleet: 1913–16.
Official number: 135956.
Tonnage gross: 4341.
Tonnage nett: 2707.
Length: 390.0 x beam: 52.5 x depth: 24.7 feet.
Machinery: T. 3-cyl. by Blair & Co., Stockton-on-Tees.
History: 9.1913: completed by Ropner & Son Ltd, Stockton-on-Tees for the St Just Steamship Co. Ltd (W. R. Smith & Sons, managers), Cardiff. 9.4.1916: sunk by gunfire from German submarine U66 eighteen miles NW of Ushant, whilst bound from voyage from St. Nazaire to Barry Roads in ballast. No lives were lost.

Falls City
Steel steamship.
In the fleet: 1913–29.
Official number: 135957.
Tonnage gross: 4729.
Tonnage nett: 2917.
Length: 378.5 x beam: 51.5 x depth: 27.5 feet.
Machinery: T. 3-cyl. by Blair & Co., Stockton-on-Tees.
History: 11.1913: completed by Ropner & Sons Ltd, Stockton-on-Tees for the Bradford Steamship Co. Ltd (W. R. Smith & Sons, managers), Cardiff. 1928: transferred to the Reardon Smith Line Ltd (Sir W. R. Smith & Sons Ltd,

managers), Cardiff. 1929: sold to the South Georgia Co. Ltd (C. Salvesen &
Co., managers), Leith and renamed *Seringa*. 1945: sold to the Basra Shipping
Co. Ltd (Galbraith, Pembroke & Co., managers), London. 1946: Sold to East
& West Steamship Co. Ltd, Bombay, and renamed *Firoza*. 10.1960: broken up
at Gadani Beach.

Great City
Steel steamship.
In the fleet: 1914–36.
Official number: 135958.
Tonnage gross: 5525.
Tonnage nett: 3359.
Length: 420.0 x beam: 56.7 x depth: 26.4 feet.
Machinery: T. 3-cyl. by Blair & Co., Stockton-on-Tees.
History: 4.1914: completed by Ropner & Sons Ltd, Stockton-on-Tees, for
the Great City Steamship Co. Ltd, (W. R. Smith & Sons, managers), Cardiff.
1917: transferred to the St Just Steamship Co. Ltd, Cardiff (same manag-
ers). 1928: transferred to the Reardon Smith Line Ltd (Sir W. R. Smith &
Sons Ltd, managers), Cardiff. 1936: sold to the Richmond Hill Steamship
Co. Ltd (Counties Ship Management Co. Ltd, managers), London, and
renamed *Richmond Hill*. 1937: sold to the Adamos Steamship Co. Ltd,
Chios, Greece. 1937: sold to Johs. Fritzen and Sohn vorm W. Kunstmann,
Stettin, and renamed *Dora Fritzen*. 21.1.1944: wrecked near the Flekkefjord,
Norway, but later salved. 6.1.1945: sunk by motor torpedo boats in the
Stavangerfjord.

Jersey City
Steel steamship.
In the fleet: 1914–17.
Official number: 135907.
Tonnage gross: 4670.
Tonnage nett: 2955.
Length: 385.0 x beam: 52.0 x depth: 26.9 feet.
Machinery: T. 3-cyl. by Richardson, Westgarth & Co., Hartlepool.
History: 7.1914: completed by Irvine's Shipbuilding & Dry Dock Co. Ltd,
Hartlepool, as *Santeramo* for the Gulf Line Ltd (Furness, Withy & Co., manag-
ers) West Hartlepool. 1914: sold to the Great City Steamship Co. Ltd (W. R.
Smith & Sons, managers), Cardiff and renamed *Jersey City*. 24.5.1917: torpe-
doed and sunk by German submarine U46 thirty-five miles NE of the Flannan
Isles, Outer Hebrides, whilst bound from Pensacola to Hull with a cargo of
wheat; the master was taken prisoner.

Indian City
Steel steamship.
In the fleet: 1915.
Official number: 135960.
Tonnage gross: 4645.
Tonnage nett: 2921.
Length: 380.0 x beam: 52.0 x depth: 27.0 feet.
Machinery: T. 3-cyl. by the builders.
History: 1.1915: completed by William Doxford & Sons Ltd, Sunderland, for the Instow Steamship Co. Ltd (W. R. Smith & Sons, managers), Cardiff. 12.3.1915: torpedoed and sunk by German submarine U29 ten miles S of St Mary's, Scilly Isles, whilst bound from Galveston and Newport News to Le Havre with a cargo of cotton and spelter. No lives were lost.

Homer City
Steel steamship.
In the fleet: 1915–29.
Official number: 135961.
Tonnage gross: 4914.
Tonnage nett: 3051.
Length: 384.9 x beam: 53.0 x depth: 27.0 feet.
Machinery: T. 3-cyl. by Blair & Co., Stockton-on-Tees.
History: 1.1915: completed by Ropner & Sons Ltd, Stockton-on-Tees for the Great City Steamship Co. Ltd (W. R. Smith & Sons, managers), Cardiff. 1917: transferred to the St Just Steamship Co. Ltd, Cardiff (same managers). 1928: transferred to the Reardon Smith Line Ltd (Sir W. R. Smith & Sons Ltd, managers), Cardiff. 1929: sold to the Wyn Shipping Co. Ltd (W. A. Young & Co., managers), London and renamed *Wyndyke*. 1932: sold to Ath. Coulouras, Athens, Greece, and renamed *Coulouras Zenos*. 2.4.1941: sunk in a bombing raid off Gavdos Island.

1925

Bradburn – see *Atlantic City* in 1915 fleet list.

Falls City – see 1915 fleet list.

Great City – see 1915 fleet list.

Homer City – see 1915 fleet list.

King City

Steel steamship.
In the fleet: 1917–27.
Official number: 120528.
Tonnage gross: 2883.
Tonnage nett: 1822.
Length: 331.0 x beam: 48.0 x depth: 21.5 feet.
Machinery: T. 3-cyl. by Blair & Co., Stockton-on-Tees.
History: 5.1905: completed by Bartram & Sons, Sunderland, as *Quarrydene* for the London & Northern Steamship Co. Ltd (Pyman Bros Ltd, managers), London. 20.11.1917: Sold to the St Just Steamship Co. Ltd (W. R. Smith & Sons, managers), Cardiff. 1918: renamed *King City*. 1927: Sold to J. Livanos, Chios, Greece. 1928: sold to Livanos Bros, (N.G. Livanos, manager), Chios, Greece, and renamed *Anastassia*. 1932: sold to Panos Protopapas, Athens. 1936: sold to C. Choremis (P. Protopapas, manager), Athens. 18.2.1940: torpedoed and sunk SW of Rockall.

Orient City

Steel steamship.
In the fleet: 1917–35.
Official number: 132622.
Tonnage gross: 5622.
Tonnage nett: 3547.
Length: 396.5 x beam: 53.5 x depth: 23.0 feet.
Machinery: T. 3-cyl. by Blair & Co., Stockton-on-Tees.
History: 10.1911: completed by Richardson, Duck & Co., Stockton-on-Tees as *Cloughton* for the London & Northern Steamship Co. Ltd (Pyman Bros, managers), London. 20.11.1917: sold to the St Just Steamship Co. Ltd (W. R. Smith & Co., managers), Cardiff. 1918: renamed *Orient City*. 1928: transferred to the Reardon Smith Line Ltd (Sir W. R. Smith & Sons Ltd, managers) Cardiff. 6.1935: sold to Italian shipbreakers under a 'Scrap and Build' contract to build the motor vessel *Bradford City*, completed in June 1936 for the Reardon Smith Line Ltd, Cardiff.

Norwich City

Steel steamship.
In the fleet: 1917–29.
Official number: 132596.
Tonnage gross: 5587.
Tonnage nett: 3513.
Length: 397.0 x beam: 53.5 x depth: 23.0 feet.

Machinery: T. 3-cyl. by the Central Marine Engineering Works Ltd, West Hartlepool.

History: 8.1911: completed by William Gray & Co. Ltd, West Hartlepool, as *Normanby* for the London & Northern Steamship Co. Ltd (Pyman Bros, managers), London. 20.11.1917: sold to the St Just Steamship Co. Ltd (W. R. Smith & Sons, managers), Cardiff. 1918: renamed *Norwich City*. 1928: transferred to the Reardon Smith Line Ltd (Sir W. R. Smith & Sons Ltd, managers), Cardiff. 30.11.1929: wrecked on Gardner Island in the south Pacific whilst bound from Melbourne to Honolulu in ballast. Eleven crew members were lost.

Leeds City (2)

Steel steamship.
In the fleet: 1917–25.
Official number: 135296.
Tonnage gross: 4809.
Tonnage nett: 2873.
Length: 411.2 x beam: 55.0 x depth: 24.3 feet.
Machinery: T. 3-cyl. by Blair & Co., Stockton-on-Tees.
History: 12.1913: completed by Richardson, Duck & Co., Stockton-on-Tees, as *Daleham* for the London & Northern Steamship Co. Ltd (Pyman Bros, managers), London. 20.11.1917: sold to the St Just Steamship Co. Ltd (W. R. Smith & Sons, managers), Cardiff. 1918: renamed *Leeds City*. 18.9.1925: struck a reef in the Java Sea and sank whilst bound from Java to Japan with a cargo of sugar. No lives were lost.

Madras City

Steel steamship.
In the fleet: 1917–33.
Official number: 129196.
Tonnage gross: 5461.
Tonnage nett: 3467.
Length: 383.9 x beam: 53.5 x depth: 29.0 feet.
Machinery: T. 3-cyl. by the Central Marine Engineering Works Ltd, West Hartlepool.
History: 5.1911: completed by William Gray & Co. Ltd, West Hartlepool as *Langholm* for the London & Northern Steamship Co. Ltd (Pyman Bros, managers), London. 20.11.1917: sold to the St Just Steamship Co. Ltd (W. R. Smith & Sons, managers), Cardiff. 1918: renamed *Madras City*. 1928: transferred to the Reardon Smith Line Ltd (Sir W. R. Smith & Sons Ltd, managers), Cardiff. 1933: sold to L. N. Embiricos, Andros, Greece and renamed *Epsilon*. 1938: sold to Frano Petrinovic, Split, Yugoslavia and renamed *Balkan*. 1941: sold to the Cavodore Steamship Co. Ltd, Panama and renamed *Armande*. 1941: sold to the Swiss

War Transport Office (Honnegger & Ascott, managers) Berne, and renamed
St. *Gotthard*. 1946: sold to Nautilus SA, Switzerland. 1955: sold to Cantieri Navali
di Golfo SA, Italy and renamed *San Gottardo*. 3.1959: broken up at La Spezia.

Eastern City (2)

Steel steamship.
In the fleet: 1917–33.
Official number: 136963.
Tonnage gross: 5992.
Tonnage nett: 3714.
Length: 400.0 x beam: 53.0 x depth: 32.7 feet.
Machinery: T. 3-cyl. by Blair & Co., Stockton-on-Tees.
History: 8.1917: completed by Joseph L. Thompson & Sons, Sunderland, for
the St Just Steamship Co. Ltd (W. R. Smith & Sons, managers), Cardiff. 1928:
transferred to the Reardon Smith Line Ltd (Sir W. R. Smith & Sons Ltd, man-
agers), Cardiff. 1933: sold to the Nereus Steamship Co. Ltd (E. E. Hadjilias,
manager), Athens, and renamed *Doris*. 9.1949: broken up at Antwerp.

Bradford City (2)

Steel steamship.
In the fleet: 1919–29.
Official number: 140587.
Tonnage gross: 5261.
Tonnage nett: 3178.
Length: 400.1 x beam: 52.3 x depth: 28.4 feet.
Machinery: T. 3-cyl. by Blair & Co., Stockton-on-Tees.
History: 8.1919: completed by Craig, Taylor & Co. Ltd, Stockton-on-Tees for
the St Just Steamship Co. Ltd (W. R. Smith & Sons, managers), Cardiff. 1928:
transferred to the Reardon Smith Line Ltd (Sir W. R. Smith & Sons Ltd, man-
agers), Cardiff. 1929: Sold to Charguers Reunis, Bordeaux, and renamed *Fort
Medine*. 25.7.1940: taken over by Ministry of War Transport (Sir W. R. Smith
& Sons Ltd, managers). 20.2.1941: struck a mine in the Bristol Channel and
sank in position 51.35N, 03.56W. The wreck was subsequently broken up.

Cornish City (2)

Steel steamship.
In the fleet: 1919–29.
Official number: 140858.
Tonnage gross: 5269.
Tonnage nett: 3239.

Length: 400.1 x beam: 52.3 x depth: 28.4 feet.

Machinery: T. 3-cyl. by Blair & Co., Stockton-on-Tees.

History: 6.1919: completed by Craig Taylor & Co., Stockton-on-Tees, for the St Just Steamship Co. Ltd (W. R. Smith & Sons, managers), Cardiff. 1928: transferred to the Reardon Smith Line Ltd (Sir W. R. Smith & Sons Ltd, managers), Cardiff. 1929: sold to Chargeurs Reunis, Bordeaux, and renamed *Fort Binger*. 8.9.1940: taken over by the Ministry of War Transport (Sir W. R. Smith & Sons Ltd, managers). 1944: returned to Chargeurs Reunis, under the management of Gellaty, Hankey & Co. Ltd, London. 1947: management reverted to Chargeurs Reunis. 10.1950: broken up at Briton Ferry by T. W. Ward Ltd.

Bradclyde

Steel steamship.

In the fleet: 1919–34.

Official number: 142667.

Tonnage gross: 5685.

Tonnage nett: 3558.

Length: 399.6 x beam: 53.0 x depth: 32.8 feet.

Machinery: T. 3-cyl. by North Eastern Marine Engineering Co. Ltd, Newcastle-upon-Tyne.

History: 10.1918: completed by the Northumberland Shipbuilding Co. Ltd, Newcastle-upon-Tyne, as *War Castle* for the shipping controller. 1919: sold to the Leeds Shipping Co. Ltd (W. R. Smith & Sons, managers), Cardiff, and renamed *Bradclyde*. 1934: sold to the New Era Steamship Co. Ltd (Frank S. Dawson Ltd, managers), Cardiff, and renamed *Alma Dawson*. 1935: sold to Avon Steamship Co. Ltd (Mark Whitwill & Co., managers), Bristol and renamed *Avon Bridge*. 1937: sold to M. N. & P. G. Lyras, Piraeus, and renamed *Lyras*. 1950: sold to M. N. Lyras and J. M. Pateras, Piraeus and renamed *Aeolos*. 13.3.1953: arrived at Briton Ferry for breaking up by T. W. Ward Ltd.

Bradavon

Steel steamship.

In the fleet: 1919–1933.

Official number: 142443.

Tonnage gross: 5204.

Tonnage nett: 3164.

Length: 400.1 x beam: 52.4 x depth: 28.5 feet.

Machinery: T. 3-cyl. by Blair & Co., Stockton-on-Tees.

History: 6.1918: completed by Richardson, Duck & Co. Ltd, Stockton-on-Tees, as *War Vulture* for the shipping controller. 1919: sold to the Leeds Shipping Co. Ltd (W. R. Smith & Sons, managers), Cardiff and renamed *Bradavon*. 1933:

sold to Darien Kisen KK, Darien, Japan and renamed *Shinkyo Maru*. 24.3.1944: torpedoed and sunk by American submarine USS *Bowfin* east of Mindanao, in a position 05.27N, 125.38E.

Watsness
Steel steamship.
In the fleet: 1919–27.
Official number: 142682.
Tonnage gross: 3090.
Tonnage nett: 1852.
Length: 331.3 x beam: 46.8 x depth: 23.1 feet.
Machinery: T. 3-cyl. by North East Marine Engineering Co. Ltd, Newcastle-upon-Tyne.
History: 10.1918: completed by the Tyne Iron Shipbuilding Co. Ltd, Newcastle-upon-Tyne as *War Combe* for the shipping controller, (R. Chapman & Son, Newcastle-upon-Tyne, managers). 1919: sold to Letricheux Lines Ltd (Letricheux & David Ltd, managers), Swansea and renamed *Watsness*. 1919: sold to the Cornborough Shipping Line Ltd (W. R. Smith & Sons, managers), Cardiff. 1924: transferred to the Oakwin Steamship Co. Ltd (Sir W. R. Smith & Sons Ltd managers), Cardiff. 1927: sold to the Mervyn Steam Shipping Co. Ltd (Martyn, Martyn & Co., managers), Newport and renamed *Marklyn*. 20.1.1942: stranded on the Mull of Galloway whilst bound from Pepel to Barrow. Subsequently refloated and towed to Glasgow for repairs. 1942: sold to the Ministry of War Transport (Martyn, Martyn & Co. managers), and renamed *Empire Usk*. 1945: sold to Constants (South Wales) Ltd (H. Constant, manager), Cardiff. 1946: renamed *Heminge*. 1948: sold to Crete Shipping Co. Ltd, London and renamed *Bluestone*. 1953: sold to Moller Line (UK) Ltd, London and renamed *Grosvenor Mariner*. 21.6.1955: arrived at Hong Kong to be broken up by Mollers Ltd.

Dungeness
Steel steamship.
In the fleet: 1919–27.
Official number: 118468.
Tonnage gross: 2748.
Tonnage nett: 1747:
Length: 331.0 x beam: 47.5 x depth: 20.0 feet.
Machinery: T. 3-cyl. by Blair & Co., Stockton-on-Tees.
History: 7.1904: completed by Richardson, Duck & Co. Ltd, Stockton-on-Tees for the Fargrove Steam Navigation Co. Ltd (Farrar, Groves & Co., managers), London. 1917: sold to the Letricheux Line Ltd (Letricheux

& David Ltd, managers), Swansea. 1919: sold to the Cornborough Line Ltd (W. R. Smith & Sons, managers), Cardiff. 1924: transferred to St Just Steamship Co. Ltd (Sir W. R. Smith & Sons Ltd, managers), Cardiff. 1927: sold to P. Dannebergs, Riga and renamed *Konsul P. Dannebergs*. 1941: seized by Germany and renamed *Brannau*. 1945: Seized by USSR *Braunau*. 17.10.1944: mined and sunk in the Oresund.

Indian City (2)

Steel steamship.
In the fleet: 1920–35.
Official number: 140680.
Tonnage gross: 6221.
Tonnage nett: 3889.
Length: 411.7 x beam: 54.5 x depth: 33.6 feet.
Machinery: T. 3-cyl. by Blair & Co., Stockton-on-Tees.
History: 4.1920: completed by the Ropner Shipbuilding & Repairing Co. Ltd, Stockton-on-Tees for the St Just Steamship Co. Ltd (W. R. Smith & Sons, managers), Cardiff. 1928: transferred to the Reardon Smith Line Ltd (Sir W. R. Smith & Sons Ltd, managers), Cardiff. 1935: broken up at Newport, Mon. by John Cashmore Ltd under a 'Scrap and Build' contract to build the motor vessel *Bradford City*, completed in June 1936 for the Reardon Smith Line Ltd, Cardiff.

Atlantic City (2)

Steel steamship.
In the fleet: 1920–36.
Official number: 140863.
Tonnage gross: 6236.
Tonnage nett: 3902.
Length: 411.7 x beam: 54.5: x depth: 33.6 feet.
Machinery: T. 3-cyl. by Blair & Co., Stockton-on-Tees.
History: 9.1920: completed by Ropner Shipbuilding & Repairing Co. Ltd, Stockton-on-Tees for the St Just Steamship Co. Ltd (W. R. Smith & Sons, managers), Cardiff. 1928: transferred to the Reardon Smith Line Ltd (Sir W. R. Smith & Sons Ltd, managers), Cardiff. 1936: sold to Brynymor Steamship Co. Ltd (Ambrose, Davies & Matthews Ltd, managers), Swansea and renamed *Penybryn*. 1937: sold to Ho Sien Ching, Tsingtao, China. 1939: sold to Matsuda Kisen KK, Japan and renamed *Matuyama Maru*. 1940: sold to Nissan Kisen KK Japan and renamed *Hiyama Maru*. 17.2.1942: torpedoed and sunk by American submarine USS *Seadragon* off the Caroline Islands, in a position 13.48N, 109.33E.

Jersey City (2)

Steel steamship.
In the fleet: 1920–40.
Official number: 140861.
Tonnage gross: 6322.
Tonnage nett: 3937.
Length: 411.8 x beam: 55.0 x depth: 33.6 feet.
Machinery: T. 3-cyl. by Blair & Co., Stockton-on-Tees.
History: 6.1920: completed by Joseph L. Thompson & Sons Ltd, Sunderland, for the St Just Steamship Co. Ltd (Sir W. R. Smith & Sons, managers), Cardiff. 1928: transferred to the Reardon Smith Line Ltd (Sir W. R. Smith & Sons Ltd, managers), Cardiff. 31.7.1940: torpedoed and sunk by German submarine U99 NW off Malin Head in a position 55.47N, 09.18W; two lives were lost.

Paris City

Steel steamship.
In the fleet: 1920–38.
Official number: 140862.
Tonnage gross: 6343.
Tonnage nett: 3959.
Length: 412.2 x beam: 55.0 x depth: 33.5 feet.
Machinery: T. 3-cyl. by Blair & Co., Stockton-on-Tees.
History: 8.1920: completed by Craig, Taylor & Co. Ltd, Stockton-on-Tees for the St Just Steamship Co. Ltd (Sir W. R. Smith & Sons, managers), Cardiff. 1928: transferred to the Reardon Smith Line Ltd (same managers) Cardiff. 1938: sold to Rokos Vergottis, Greece and renamed *Gerassimos Vergottis*. 1940: sold to Poseidon Steamship & Trading Co. Ltd, Athens. 1950: sold to World Wide Steamship Co. Inc., Monrovia and renamed *Greenville*. 21.9.1953: foundered and sank in a gale 600 miles N of the Azores; two lives were lost.

Alness

Steel steamship.
In the fleet: 1920–33.
Official number: 140864.
Tonnage gross: 3683.
Tonnage nett: 2225.
Length: 346.7 x beam: 51.0 x depth: 24.1 feet.
Machinery: T. 3-cyl. by Blair & Co., Stockton-on-Tees.
History: 10.1920: completed by Ropner Shipbuilding & Repairing Co. Ltd, Stockton-on- Tees, for the Cornborough Shipping Line Ltd (Sir W. R. Smith & Sons, managers), Cardiff. 1924: transferred to the Oakwin Steamship Co.

Ltd (same managers), Cardiff. 1926: transferred to the Reardon Smith Line Ltd (same managers), Cardiff. 1933: sold to the Alexandria Navigation Co. SA, Alexandria (Watts, Watts & Co., London, managers) and renamed *Star of Ramleh*. 1940: taken over by Ministry of War Transport (Glover Bros, managers), London and renamed *Empire Lotus*. 19.4.1942: foundered and sank in heavy weather in a position 44.06N, 62.70W whilst bound from New York to Belfast.

General Lukin

Steel steamship.
In the fleet: 1920–8.
Official number: 142770.
Tonnage gross: 3099.
Tonnage nett: 1866.
Length: 331.1 x beam: 46.8 x depth: 23.1 feet.
Machinery: T. 3-cyl. by the Central Marine Engineering Works Ltd, West Hartlepool.
History: 2.1919: completed by William Gray & Co. Ltd as *War Oasis* for the shipping controller (W. D. C. Balls & Son, North Shields, managers). 1919: sold to Ashwin & Co. Ltd, London and renamed *Oakwin*. 1920: sold to the Oakwin Steamship Co. Ltd (Sir W. R. Smith & Sons, managers), Cardiff. 1923: renamed *General Lukin*. 1926: transferred to the St Just Steamship Co. Ltd (same managers), Cardiff. 1928: sold to Shoyei Kisen KK, Kobe, Japan, and renamed *Shoyei Maru*. 22.6.1939: wrecked south of Gensan, Korea, but later salved. 20.12.1943: sunk by US naval aircraft off the Marshall Islands, in a position 08.42N, 167.44E.

Royal City

Steel steamship.
In the fleet: 1920–8.
Official number: 143099.
Tonnage gross: 5411.
Tonnage nett: 3481.
Length: 419.7 x beam: 53.8 x depth: 26.3 feet.
Machinery: T. 3-cyl. by the builders.
History: 4.1913: completed by Earle's Shipbuilding and Engineering Co. Ltd, Hull as *Federico Glavic* for Nav. A Vap. Unione, Dubrovnik. 1914: sold to Globus Rehederei AG, Bremen and renamed *Gerfrid*. 1919: surrendered to the UK shipping controller as a war prize, (C. T. Bowring & Co. Ltd, Liverpool, managers). 1920: sold to the St Just Steamship Co. Ltd (Sir W. R. Smith & Sons, managers), Cardiff and renamed *Royal City*. 1928: sold to D. C. & J. C. Mazaraki, Athens, and re-named *Anna Mazaraki*. 27.5.1942: wrecked on Sable Island, Nova Scotia.

Quebec City

Steel steamship.
In the fleet: 1920–7.
Official number: 143413.
Tonnage gross: 4936.
Tonnage nett: 3134.
Length: 402.3 x beam : 54.0 x depth: 26.7 feet.
Machinery: T. 3-cyl. by the builders.
History: 2.1911: completed by Flensburger Schiffsbau Gesellschaft, Flensburg, as *Haimon* for the Roland Linie AG, Bremen. 1919: surrendered to the UK shipping controller as a war prize, (T. L. Duff & Co., Glasgow, managers). 1920: sold to the St Just Steamship Co. Ltd (Sir W. R. Smith & Sons, managers) Cardiff and renamed *Quebec City*. 1927: sold to Norddeutscher Lloyd, Bremen, and renamed *Haimon*. 8.1935: broken up.

Siam City

Steel steamship.
In the fleet: 1921–7.
Official number: 143333.
Tonnage gross: 5271.
Tonnage nett: 3296.
Length: 409.0 x beam: 55.1 x depth: 28.4 feet.
Machinery: Q. 4-cyl. by the builders.
History: 4.1911: completed by J. Frerichs & Co. AG, Einswarden, Germany as *Winfried* for the Hamburg Bremer Africa Linie AG, Hamburg. 1919: surrendered to the UK shipping controller as a war prize (H. Hogarth & Sons, Glasgow, managers). 1921: sold to the St Just Steamship Co. Ltd (Sir W. R. Smith & Sons, managers), Cardiff and renamed *Siam City*. 1927: sold to Jugoslavenske-Americanska Plovidba, Dubrovnik and renamed *Gundulic*. 19.3.1934: wrecked at Puerto Bueno, Smyth Channel, Chile, whilst bound from Rosario to Coronel. 1944: wreck bought by the Chilean Navy, refloated, and towed to Talcahuano for repairs. 1945: entered service with the Chilean Navy as transport *Magallanes*. 1955: sold to Cia. Naviera Santa Barbara, Chile, and renamed *Sanbar*. 1957: sold to Solmar Cia. Nav., Panama, and renamed *Springwater*. 1958: broken up at Spezia by Cant. Navali del Golfo.

Truro City

Steel steamship.
In the fleet: 1921–7.
Official number: 144398.
Tonnage gross: 4641.

Tonnage nett: 2903.
Length: 400.0 x beam: 54.1 x depth: 25.6 feet.
Machinery: T. 3-cyl. by builders.
History: 11.1910: completed by AG Neptun, Rostock, Germany, as *Wismar* for Deutsch-Australische Dampfschiffs Gesellschaft, Hamburg. 1914: detained at Benjuwangi, Dutch East Indies. 1919: surrendered to the UK shipping controller as a prize (British India Steam Navigation Co. Ltd, London, managers). 1921: sold to the St Just Steamship Co. Ltd (Sir W. R. Smith & Sons, managers), Cardiff and renamed *Truro City*. 1927: sold to Reederei F. Laeisz Gmbh, Hamburg and renamed *Pilot*. 1933: broken up at Bremen.

Vulcan City

Steel steamship.
In the fleet: 1921–33.
Official number: 144303.
Tonnage gross: 5297.
Tonnage nett: 3324.
Length: 420.4 x beam: 54.5 x depth: 27.7 feet.
Machinery: C. 4-cyl. by the builders.
History: 12.1909: completed by Bremer Vulkan Schiffbau und Machinenfabrick, Lobbendorf, Germany as *Answald* for the Hamburg Bremer Afrika Linie AG. 1919: surrendered to the UK shipping controller as a prize (Cunard Steamship Co. Ltd, Liverpool, managers).1921: sold to the St Just Steamship Co. Ltd (Sir W. R. Smith & Sons, managers), Cardiff and renamed named *Vulcan City*. 1928: transferred to the Reardon Smith Line Ltd (Sir W. R. Smith & Sons Ltd, managers), Cardiff. 7.1933: broken up at Blyth by Hughes, Bolckow & Co. Ltd.

Union City

Steel steamship.
In the fleet: 1921–5.
Official number: 143916.
Tonnage gross: 4672.
Tonnage nett: 2921.
Length: 412.6 x beam: 53.8 x depth: 25.4 feet.
Machinery: T. 3-cyl. by the builders.
History: 9.1909: completed by Reiherstieg Schiffswerfte & Maschinenfabriek, Hamburg, as *Iserlohn* for the Deutsche-Australische Dampschiffs Geselschaft, Hamburg. 1914: interned at Batavia. 10.8.1919: surrendered to the UK shipping controller as a prize (British India Steam Navigation Co. Ltd, London, managers). 10.2.1921: sold to the St Just Steamship Co. Ltd (Sir W. R.

Smith & Sons, managers), Cardiff. 1925: sold to Shipping Co. Wasaborg
(J. A. Zachariassen & Co., managers), Nystad, Finland and renamed *Wasaborg*.
1935: sold to Achille Lauro, Naples and renamed *Erica*. 6.1940: seized as a
prize at Liverpool, taken over by the Ministry of Shipping (T. & J. Brocklebank
Ltd, Liverpool, managers) and renamed *Empire Defiance*. 1944: management
transferred to J. & J. Denholm, Greenock. 8.6.1944: sunk as a blockship in
Gooseberry 5 at Ouistreham, Normandy. 1951: raised and arrived at Antwerp
for scrapping on 15.9.1951.

Riol

Steel steamship.
In the fleet: 1921–7.
Official number: 146204.
Tonnage gross: 5431.
Tonnage nett: 3418.
Length: 420.5 x beam: 54.5 x depth: 27.9 feet.
Machinery: Q. 4-cyl. by the builders.
History: 5.1907: completed by Bremer Vulkan Schiffbau und Machinenfabrick,
Lobendorff, Germany for the Roland Line AG, Bremen. 8:1914: detained at
Valparaiso for the duration of the war. 9.1918: engines sabotaged by her crew.
1919: surrendered to the UK shipping controller as a prize. 8.1920: towed to
Bremerhaven for repairs. 1921: sold initially to Douglas Smith and then on
to the Leeds Shipping Co. Ltd (Sir W. R. Smith & Sons, managers), Cardiff.
1927: sold to Jugoslovenski-Amerikanska Plovidba, Dubrovnik and renamed
Preradovic. 1940: sold to Crest Shipping Co. Ltd, London and renamed *Fircrest*.
25.8.1940: torpedoed and sunk by a submarine in the north Atlantic, in a
position 58.52N, 06.34W.

General Botha

Steel steamship.
In the fleet: 1921–6.
Official number: 146583.
Tonnage gross: 4848.
Tonnage nett: 3026.
Length: 399.6 x beam: 53.7 x depth: 27.6 feet.
Machinery: T. 3-cyl. by the builders.
History: 4.1911: completed by Bremer Vulkan Schiffbau und Machinenfabrik,
Lobbendorf, Germany as *Berengar* for the Roland Linie AG, Bremen. 8.1914
detained at Talcahuano, Chile, for the duration of the war. 9.1918: engines
sabotaged by her crew. 1919: surrendered to the UK shipping control-
ler as a prize. 7.1920: towed back to Bremerhaven for repairs. 1921: sold

to the Oakwin Steamship Co. Ltd (Sir W. R. Smith & Sons, managers), Cardiff. 1923: renamed *General Botha*. 1926: sold to Norddeutscher Lloyd, Bremen and renamed *Berengar*. 1935: sold to Hamburg Sud-Amerikanische Dampschiffahrts AG, Hamburg, and renamed *Petropolis*. 29.4.1945: badly damaged by an Allied air raid upon Hamburg and subsequently broken up where she lay.

Meropi
Steel steamship.
In the fleet: 1922–9.
Official number: 145707.
Tonnage gross: 3445.
Tonnage nett: 2159.
Length: 346.0 x beam: 48.1 x depth: 23.0 feet.
Machinery: T. 3-cyl. by the North Eastern Marine Engineering Co. Ltd, Newcastle-upon-Tyne.
History: 12.1908: completed by Societé Anonyme Chantiers Navals Anversois, Antwerp, as *Oppurg* for Dampschiffs-Reederei Union AG, Hamburg. 1912: sold to Rhederei AG von1896, Hamburg, and renamed *Olga*. 8.1914: seized by the Russians at Odessa and renamed *Sukum*. 1919: surrendered to the UK shipping controller as a prize. 1919: reallocated to France. 1920: sold to C. D. Calaftis, Syra, Greece and renamed *Meropi*. 1921: sold to Smith & Fletcher, Cardiff. 1922: sold to the Unity Shipping & Trading Co. Ltd (Sir W. R. Smith & Sons, managers), Cardiff. 1929: sold to C. M. Lemos, Chios, Greece and renamed *Taxiarchis*. 28.3.1931: wrecked on Lundy Island whilst bound from Barry to Rosario with a cargo of coal; she was refloated and subsequently broken up.

Welsh City
Steel steamship.
In the fleet: 1922–38.
Official number: 144722.
Tonnage gross: 6303.
Tonnage nett. 3997.
Length: 411.7 x beam: 54.5 x depth: 33.6 feet.
Machinery: T. 3-cyl. by Blair & Co., Stockton-on-Tees.
History: 1.1922: completed by Ropner Shipbuilding & Repairing Co. Ltd, Stockton-on-Tees for the St Just Steamship Co. Ltd (Sir W. R. Smith & Sons, managers), Cardiff. 1928: transferred to the Reardon Smith Line Ltd (same managers), Cardiff. 1938: sold to G. N. Statathos, Athens, Greece and renamed *Maria Statathos*. 26.4.1941: sunk by Axis air attack at Milos.

York City

Steel steamship.
In the fleet: 1922–37.
Official number: 144723.
Tonnage gross: 6397.
Tonnage nett: 4054.
Length: 411.8 x beam: 55.0 x depth: 33.6 feet.
Machinery: T. 3-cyl. by Blair & Co., Stockton-on-Tees.
History: 1.1922: completed by Joseph L. Thompson & Sons Ltd, Sunderland for the St Just Steamship Co. Ltd (Sir W. R. Smith & Sons, managers), Cardiff. Transferred to the Reardon Smith Line Ltd (same managers), Cardiff. 1937: sold to N. G. Nicolaou (Georgios Nicolaou (Hellas) Ltd, manager), Piraeus and renamed *Nicolaou Ourania*. 16.5.1941: bombed and sunk by Axis air attack at Suda Bay; later salved by the Germans, repaired and renamed *Nikolaus*. 9.1943: torpedoed and sunk by the Royal Navy off Bastia.

General Smuts

Steel steamship.
In the fleet: 1923–34.
Official number: 144726.
Tonnage gross: 4365.
Tonnage nett: 2698.
Length 386.7 x beam: 52.8 x depth: 26.3 feet.
Machinery: T. 3-cyl. by the builders.
History: 3.1921: completed by Palmer's Shipbuilding and Iron Co. Ltd, Jarrow as *Phoebus*, for Soc. Les Affréteurs Réunis (Jean Stern, manager), Rouen. 1923: sold to the Oakwin Steamship Co. Ltd (Sir W. R. Smith & Sons Ltd, managers), Cardiff and renamed *General Smuts*. 1926: transferred to the St Just Steamship Co. Ltd (same managers), Cardiff. 1928: transferred to the Reardon Smith Line Ltd (same managers), Cardiff. 1934: sold to the Alexandria Navigation Co. SA, Alexandria, Egypt (Watts, Watts & Co., managers), London, and renamed *Star of Egypt*. 1950: broken up at Milford Haven by T. W. Ward Ltd.

Buchanness (2)

Steel steamship.
In the fleet: 1924–48.
Official number: 144727.
Tonnage gross: 4573.
Tonnage nett: 2841.
Length: 401.6 x beam: 54.3 x depth: 25.3 feet.
Machinery: T. 3-cyl. by the builders.

History: 11.1924: completed by Workman, Clark & Co. Ltd, Belfast for the Oakwin Steamship Co. Ltd (Sir W. R. Smith & Sons Ltd, managers), Cardiff. 1926: transferred to the St Just Steamship Co. Ltd (same managers), Cardiff. 1928: transferred to the Reardon Smith Line Ltd (same managers), Cardiff. 1931: renamed *Imperial Valley*. 1946: transferred to the Leeds Shipping Co. Ltd (same managers), Cardiff. 1948: sold to the Memphis Shipping Co. Ltd (Phocean Ship Agency Ltd, managers), London and renamed *Memphis Town*. 1951: sold to Cia. de Nav. Oriental de Panama SA, Costa Rica and renamed *Marinella*. 11.9.1959: arrived at La Spezia for breaking up.

Cragness (2)

Steel steamship.
In the fleet: 1924–42.
Official number: 144728.
Tonnage gross: 4809.
Tonnage nett: 2980.
Length: 412.1 x beam: 55.0 x depth: 25.1 feet.
Machinery: T. 3-cyl. by Blair & Co., Stockton-on-Tees.
History: 11.1924: completed by Joseph L. Thompson & Sons, Sunderland for the Oakwin Steamship Co. Ltd (Sir W. R. Smith & Sons Ltd, managers), Cardiff. 1926: transferred to the St Just Steamship Co. Ltd (same managers), Cardiff. 1928: transferred to the Reardon Smith Line Ltd (same managers), Cardiff. 1931: renamed *Queen City*. 21.12.1942: sunk by torpedo and gunfire from Italian submarine *Tazzoli* in a position 00.49S, 41.34W; six lives were lost.

Skegness (2)

Steel steamship.
In the fleet: 1924–41.
Official number: 144729.
Tonnage gross: 4573.
Tonnage nett: 2842.
Length: 401.6 x beam: 54.3 x depth: 25.3 feet.
Machinery: T. 3-cyl. by the builders.
History: 12.1924: completed by Workman, Clark & Co., Belfast for the Oakwin Steamship Co. Ltd (Sir W. R. Smith & Sons Ltd, managers), Cardiff. 1926: transferred to the St Just Steamship Co. Ltd (same managers), Cardiff. 1928: transferred to the Reardon Smith Line Ltd (same managers), Cardiff. 1931: renamed *Sacramento Valley*. 6.6.1941: torpedoed and sunk by German submarine U106 west of the Cape Verde Islands in a position 17.10N, 30.10W; three lives were lost.

Margherita
Steel auxiliary yacht/training vessel.
In the fleet: 1925–32.
Official number: 132010.
Tonnage gross: 204.
Length: 160.7 x beam: 25.8 x depth: 16.5 feet.
Machinery: (from 1925) two 4-cyl. 2 SC SA by L. Gardner & Sons, Patricroft.
History: 8.5.1913: launched and 6.1913: completed by Camper & Nicholsons
Ltd of Gosport as a two-masted schooner yacht for Major G. Cecil Whitaker.
Post-1919: appeared under the ownership of Solomon Barnato ('Solly') Joel.
2.1925: sold to Sir William Reardon Smith & Sons, Cardiff, rerigged as a three-
masted schooner and equipped with auxiliary diesel engines. 15.9.1932: sold
to David Ernest Townsend, Jersey. 21.12.1932: Renamed *Davida*. 1939: owner
recorded as Mrs I. Townsend.

(Unfortunately, it has not proved possible to trace the full history of this vessel and her ultimate fate; if any readers can help in this matter, the author
would be glad to hear from them.)

1935

Great City – see 1915 fleet list.

Orient City – see 1925 fleet list.

Indian City (2) – see 1925 fleet list.

Atlantic City (2) – see 1925 fleet list.

Jersey City – see 1925 fleet list.

Paris City – see 1925 fleet list.

Welsh City – see 1925 fleet list.

York City – see 1925 fleet list.

Imperial Valley – see *Buchannness* (2) in 1925 fleet list.

Queen City – see *Cragness* (2) in 1925 fleet list.

Sacramento Valley – see *Skegness* (2) in 1925 fleet list.

Leeds City (3)

Steel steamship.
In the fleet: 1927–51.
Official number: 148831.
Tonnage gross: 4758.
Tonnage nett: 2884.
Length: 400.5 x beam: 58.2 x depth: 37.2 feet.
Machinery: T. 3-cyl by Central Marine Engineering Works Ltd, West Hartlepool.
History: 10.1927: completed by William Gray & Co. Ltd, West Hartlepool for the St Just Steamship Co. Ltd (Sir W. R. Smith & Sons Ltd, managers), Cardiff. 1928: transferred to the Reardon Smith Line Ltd (same managers), Cardiff. 1946: transferred to the Leeds Shipping Co. Ltd (same managers), Cardiff. 1951: sold to Lino Kaiun KK, Tokyo, Japan and renamed *Terushima Maru*. 20.8.1952: ran aground in the River Hooghli. 23.8.1952: broke in two and became a constructive total loss.

Quebec City (2)

Steel steamship.
In the fleet: 1927–42.
Official number: 148833.
Tonnage gross: 4745.
Tonnage nett: 2877.
Length: 400.5 x beam: 54.3 x depth: 25.6 feet.
Machinery: T. 3-cyl. by Central Marine Engineering Works Ltd, West Hartlepool.
History: 12.1927: completed by William Gray & Co. Ltd, West Hartlepool for St Just Steamship Co. Ltd (Sir W.R. Smith & Sons Ltd, managers), Cardiff. 1928: transferred to the Reardon Smith Line Ltd (same managers), Cardiff. 19.9.1942: sunk by torpedo and gunfire from German submarine U156 north of Ascension Island in a position 02.16N, 17.36W; one life was lost.

Braddovey

Steel steamship.
In the fleet: 1927–38.
Official number: 148832.
Tonnage gross: 3359.
Tonnage nett: 2045.
Length: 340.2 x beam: 48.7 x depth: 23.2 feet.
Machinery: T. 3-cyl. by D. Rowan & Co. Ltd, Glasgow.
History: 10.1927: completed by Napier & Miller Ltd, Glasgow for the Leeds Shipping Co. Ltd (Sir W. R. Smith & Sons Ltd, managers), Cardiff.

1938: sold to Sosyotesilop Turk Anonim Sirkoti, Istanbul, Turkey and renamed *Krom*. 1940: sold to T. C. Munakalat Vekaleti Devlet Denizyollari Isletme UM, Istanbul, Turkey. 30.3.1944: torpedoed and sunk off Fethiye, Turkey.

Bradesk

Steel steamship.
In the fleet: 1927–36.
Official number: 148830.
Tonnage gross: 3352.
Tonnage nett: 2039.
Length: 340.2 x beam: 48.7 x depth: 23.2 feet.
Machinery: T. 3-cyl. by D. Rowan & Co. Ltd, Glasgow.
History: 9.1927: completed by Napier & Miller Ltd, Glasgow for the Leeds Shipping Co. Ltd (Sir W. R. Smith & Sons Ltd, managers), Cardiff. 1936: sold to J. W. Paulin, Wiborg, Finland and renamed *Nagu*. 2.1945: taken as a prize by the USSR and renamed *Petrozavodsk*. 1970: deleted from *Lloyd's Register* due to lack of current detail.

Bradfyne

Steel steamship.
In the fleet: 1928–40.
Official number: 148834.
Tonnage gross: 4740.
Tonnage nett: 2872.
Length: 400.2 x beam: 54.2 x depth: 25.6 feet.
Machinery: T. 3-cyl. by the Central Marine Engineering Works Ltd, West Hartlepool.
History: 3.1928: completed by William Gray & Co. Ltd, West Hartlepool for the Leeds Shipping Co. Ltd (Sir W. R. Smith & Sons Ltd, managers), Cardiff. 22.11.1940: torpedoed and sunk by German submarine U100 south of Rockall, in a position 55.04N, 12.15W; thirty-five lives were lost.

King City (2)

Steel steamship.
In the fleet: 1928–40.
Official number: 148835.
Tonnage gross: 4744.
Tonnage nett: 2879.
Length: 400.5 x beam: 54.3 x depth: 25.6 feet.

Machinery: T. 3-cyl. by the Central Marine Engineering Works Ltd, West Hartlepool.

History: 5.1928: completed by William Gray & Co. Ltd, West Hartlepool for the Reardon Smith Line Ltd (Sir W. R. Smith & Sons Ltd, managers), Cardiff. 22.11.1940: shelled and sunk by the German commerce raider *Atlantis*, N of the island of Rodriguez in the Indian Ocean in an approximate position 17S, 66E; six lives were lost.

Santa Clara Valley

Steel motor vessel.
In the fleet: 1928–41.
Official number: 148836.
Tonnage gross: 4665.
Tonnage nett: 2845.
Length: 401.1 x beam: 54.3 x depth: 24.1 feet.
Machinery: 4-cyl. 2 SC SA oil engine by the builders.
History: 8.1928: completed by William Doxford & Sons Ltd, Sunderland as *East Lynn* for the Oakwin Steamship Co. Ltd (Sir W. R. Smith & Sons Ltd, managers), Cardiff. 1931: renamed *Santa Clara Valley*. 24.5.1937: transferred to the Reardon Smith Line Ltd (same managers), Cardiff. 23.4.1941: bombed and sunk in a raid by German aircraft at Nauplia Bay, Greece; one life was lost. 1.10.1952: wreck refloated by salvors. 14.11.1952: arrived under tow at Trieste for breaking up.

Willamette Valley

Steel motor vessel.
In the fleet: 1928–40.
Official number: 148837.
Tonnage gross: 4702.
Tonnage nett: 2865.
Length: 401.1 x beam: 54.2 x depth: 25.8 feet.
Machinery: 6-cyl. 4 SC SA by J. G. Kincaid & Co. Ltd, Glasgow.
History: 10.1928: completed by Napier & Miller Ltd, Glasgow as *West Lynn* for the Oakwin Steamship Co. Ltd (Sir W. R. Smith & Sons Ltd, managers), Cardiff. 1931: renamed *Willamette Valley*. 21.4.1937: transferred to the Reardon Smith Line Ltd (same managers), Cardiff. 1939: taken over by the Admiralty for use as a 'Q-ship' and renamed *Edgehill*. 1940: became Royal Fleet Auxiliary X39 and renamed *Willamette Valley*. 29.6.1940: torpedoed and sunk by German submarine U51 in a position 49.20N, 15.30W. No lives were lost.

New Westminster City

Steel steamship.
In the fleet: 1929–42.
Official number: 148838.
Tonnage gross: 4747.
Tonnage nett: 2882.
Length: 400.0 x beam: 54.3 x depth: 25.6 feet.
Machinery: T. 3-cyl. by Central Marine Engineering Works Ltd, West Hartlepool.
History: 7.1929: completed by William Gray & Co. Ltd, West Hartlepool for the Reardon Smith Line Ltd (Sir W. R. Smith & Sons Ltd, managers), Cardiff. 3.4.1942: bombed and sunk by German aircraft at Murmansk; two lives were lost. 3.1947: raised by the USSR and towed to Penarth for repairs. 1948: sold to Irish Bay Lines Ltd (H. Lenaghan & Sons, managers), Belfast and renamed *Dingle Bay*. 1951: sold to Nakamura Kisen KK, Kobe, Japan and renamed *Asakaze Maru*. 1965: broken up in Sakai, Japan.

Prince Rupert City

Steel steamship.
In the fleet: 1929–41.
Official number: 148839.
Tonnage gross: 4749.
Tonnage nett: 2876.
Length: 400.5 x beam: 54.3 x depth: 25.6 feet.
Machinery: T. 3-cyl. by the Central Marine Engineering Works Ltd, West Hartlepool.
History: 8.1929: completed by William Gray & Co. Ltd, West Hartlepool for the Reardon Smith Line Ltd (Sir W. R. Smith & Sons Ltd, managers), Cardiff. 2.6.1941: bombed and sunk by German aircraft NE of Cape Wrath in a position 58.46N, 04.41W; four lives were lost.

Tacoma City

Steel steamship.
In the fleet: 1929–41.
Official number: 148840.
Tonnage gross: 4738.
Tonnage nett: 2871.
Length: 400.4 x beam: 54.2 x depth: 25.6 feet.
Machinery: T. 3-cyl. by the Central Marine Engineering Works, West Hartlepool.
History: 10.1929: completed by William Gray & Co. Ltd, West Hartlepool for the Reardon Smith Line Ltd (Sir W. R. Smith & Sons Ltd, managers), Cardiff. 13.3.1941: mined and sunk off Rock Ferry in the River Mersey; four lives were lost.

Vernon City
Steel steamship.
In the fleet: 1929–43.
Official number: 161612.
Tonnage gross: 4748.
Tonnage nett: 2875.
Length: 400.5 x beam: 54.3 x depth: 25.6 feet.
Machinery: T. 3-cyl. by the builders.
History: 11.1929: completed by William Gray & Co. Ltd, West Hartlepool for the Reardon Smith Line Ltd (Sir W. R. Smith & Sons Ltd, managers), Cardiff. 28.6.1943: torpedoed and sunk by German submarine U172 in the south Atlantic, in a position 04.30S, 27.20W. No lives were lost.

Fresno City
Steel motor vessel.
In the fleet: 1929–40.
Official number: 161613.
Tonnage gross: 4955.
Tonnage nett: 3004.
Length: 415.6 x beam: 55.0 x depth: 24.5 feet.
Machinery: 4-cyl. 2 SC SA oil engine by the builders.
History: 12.1929: completed by William Doxford & Sons Ltd, Sunderland for the Reardon Smith Line Ltd (Sir W. R. Smith & Sons Ltd, managers), Cardiff. Originally, it was intended that the vessel should bear the name *San Francisco City*, but on 18.4.1929, Sir William telegraphed from California, where he was on a business trip at the time, ordering the change of name. 5.11.1940: shelled by the German battleship *Admiral Scheer* SE of Greenland, in a position 51.47N, 33.29W; one life was lost and the vessel sank the following day.

Victoria City
Steel steamship.
In the fleet: 1929–40.
Official number: 161614.
Tonnage gross: 4739.
Tonnage nett: 2876.
Length: 400.4 x beam: 54.2 x depth: 25.6 feet
Machinery: Q. 4-cyl. by the Central Marine Engineering Works Ltd, West Hartlepool.
History: 12.1929: completed by William Gray & Co. Ltd, West Hartlepool for the Reardon Smith Line Ltd (Sir W. R. Smith & Sons Ltd, managers), Cardiff.

2.12.1940: torpedoed and sunk by German submarine U140 in a position 55.00N, 11.00W; her entire crew of forty-three was lost.

Vancouver City
Steel motor vessel.
In the fleet: 1930–9.
Official number: 161615.
Tonnage gross: 4995.
Tonnage nett: 3005.
Length: 415.6 x beam: 55.0 x depth: 24.5 feet.
Machinery: 4-cyl. 2 SC SA by the builders.
History: 1.1930: completed by William Doxford & Sons Ltd, Sunderland for the Reardon Smith Line Ltd (Sir W. R. Smith & Sons Ltd, managers), Cardiff. 14.9.1939: torpedoed and sunk by German submarine U38 NW of Land's End in a position 51.23N, 07.03W; three lives were lost.

Bradglen
Steel steamship.
In the fleet: 1930–41.
Official number: 161616.
Tonnage gross: 4741.
Tonnage nett: 2874.
Length: 400.4 x beam: 54.2 x depth: 25.6 feet.
Machinery: Q. 4-cyl. by the Central Marine Engineering Works, West Hartlepool.
History: 2.1930: completed by William Gray & Co. Ltd, West Hartlepool for the Leeds Shipping Co. Ltd (Sir W. R. Smith, Popham & Liley, managers), Cardiff. 19.9.1941: mined and sunk in the Thames estuary, two miles from B3 buoy, Barrow Deep; nine lives were lost.

Bradburn (2)
Steel steamship.
In the fleet: 1930–51.
Official number: 161617.
Tonnage gross: 4736.
Tonnage nett: 2872.
Length: 400.4 x beam: 54.2 x depth: 25.6 feet.
Machinery: Q. 4-cyl. by the Central Marine Engineering Works, West Hartlepool.

History: 5.1930: completed by William Gray & Co. Ltd, West Hartlepool for the Leeds Shipping Co. Ltd (Sir W. R. Smith, Popham & Liley, managers), Cardiff. 1951: sold to Taiheiyo Kaiun KK, Tokyo, Japan and renamed *Kaiyo Maru*. 1956: sold to Nichiro Gyogyo KK, Tokyo, Japan. 1967: broken up in Yokosuka, Japan.

Devon City (2)
Steel motor vessel.
In the fleet: 1933–58.
Official number: 161620.
Tonnage gross: 4928.
Tonnage nett: 3007.
Length: 425.5 x beam: 56.3 x depth: 25.4 feet.
Machinery: 4-cyl. 2 SC SA by William Doxford & Sons Ltd, Sunderland.
History: 12.1933: completed by the Furness Shipbuilding Co. Ltd, Haverton Hill for the Reardon Smith Line Ltd (Sir W. R. Smith & Sons Ltd, managers), Cardiff. 1958: sold to the Maritime & Industrial Corp., Monrovia, and renamed *Cinderella*. 1965: sold to the Cheyenee Cia. Nav. SA, Monrovia, and renamed *Oinoussai*. 28.6.1967: wrecked thirty-five miles north of the mouth of the Orange River, South West Africa in a position 28.08S, 15.50E.

Houston City
Steel motor vessel.
In the fleet: 1934–40
Official number: 161621.
Tonnage gross: 4935.
Tonnage nett: 3009.
Length: 425.5 x beam: 56.3 x depth: 25.4 feet.
Machinery: 4-cyl. 2 SC SA by William Doxford & Sons, Sunderland.
History: 1.1934: completed by the Furness Shipbuilding Co. Ltd, Haverton Hill for the Leeds Shipping Co. Ltd (Sir W. R. Smith & Partners Ltd, managers), Cardiff. 21.10.1940: mined and sunk half a mile from the East Oaze light vessel. No lives were lost.

Francisco
Steel steamship.
In the fleet: 1935.
Official number:132209.
Tonnage gross: 6272.

Tonnage nett: 4746.

Machinery: T. 3-cyl. by Earle's Shipbuilding & Engineering Co. Ltd, Hull.

History: 12.1910: completed by the Northumberland Shipbuilding Co. Ltd, Newcastle-upon-Tyne for Thomas Wilson, Sons & Co. Ltd, Hull. 1916: owners restyled Ellerman's Wilson Line Ltd. 1935: sold to the Leeds Shipping Co. Ltd (Sir W. R. Smith & Partners Ltd, managers), Cardiff, and immediately resold to Trieste-based shipbreakers under a 'Scrap and Build' contract to build the motor vessel *Cornish City*, completed by the Furness Shipbuilding Co. Ltd, Haverton Hill, in November 1936 for the Reardon Smith Line Ltd, Cardiff.

Salient

Steel steamship.

In the fleet: 1935.

Official number: 119210.

Tonnage gross: 3879.

Tonnage nett: 2419.

Length: 364.3 x beam: 49.6 x depth: 25.5 feet.

Machinery: T. 3-cyl. by G. Clark Ltd, Sunderland.

History: 3.1905: completed by Short Bros Ltd, Sunderland for James Westoll, Sunderland. 1928: transferred to Westoll Steamships Ltd (James Westoll, Ltd, managers), Sunderland. 1935: sold to the Leeds Shipping Co. Ltd (Sir W. R. Smith & Partners, managers), Cardiff, and immediately resold to Hughes Bolckow Shipbreaking Co. Ltd, Blyth, under a 'Scrap and Build' contract to build the motor vessel *Cornish City*, completed by the Furness Shipbuilding Co. Ltd, Haverton Hill, in November 1936 for the Reardon Smith Line Ltd, Cardiff.

Key to machinery types

T. 3-cyl. – three cylinder triple expansion steam engine.

C. 4-cyl. – four cylinder double compound steam engine.

Q. 4-cyl. – four cylinder quadruple expansion steam engine.

4-cyl. 2 SC SA – four cylinder, two stroke cycle, single-acting oil engine.

6-cyl. 4 SC SA – six cylinder, four stroke cycle, single-acting oil engine.

Statistical summary of fleet lists

Year	Number of vessels	Average age	Total gross tonnage	Average gross tonnage
1905	1 (under construction)	N/A	3089	3089
1915	10	2.3	45,820	4582
1925	38 (i)	5.5	188,183	4951
1935	30 (ii)	9	182,970	6099

(i)   Excluding the yacht/training vessel *Margherita*.
(ii) Excluding the *Francisco* and the *Salient*, bought for 'Scrap & Build' purposes.

Appendix 5

SAILING SHIP RIGS

Drawn by Richard Jenkins

(These diagrams are intended to provide the layman with a basic guide to the outline of the various rigs mentioned by WRS in his text.)

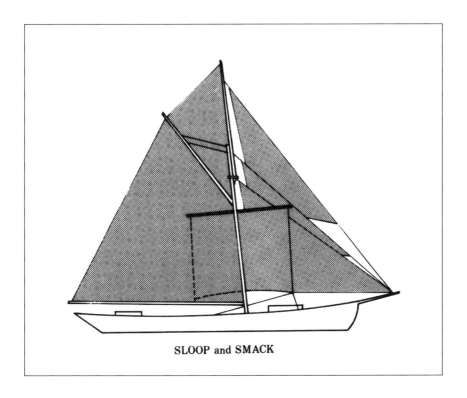

SLOOP and SMACK

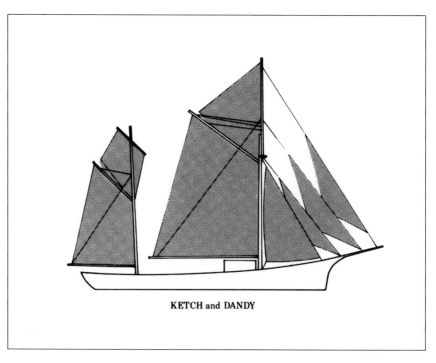

KETCH and DANDY

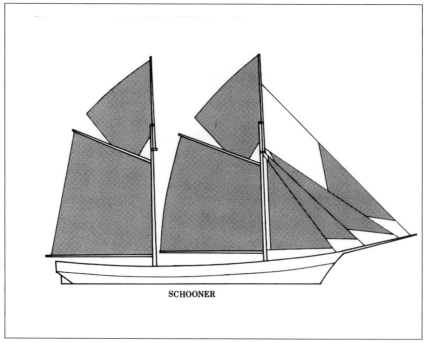

SCHOONER

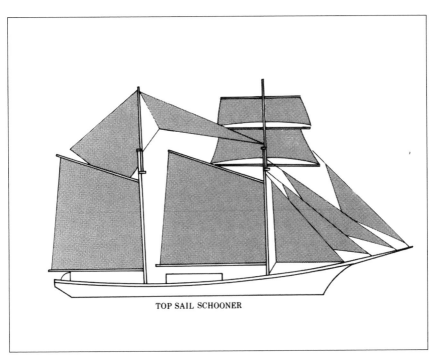

TOP SAIL SCHOONER

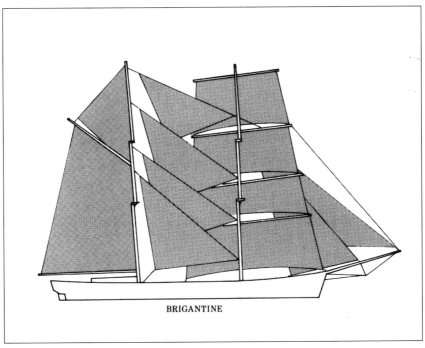

BRIGANTINE

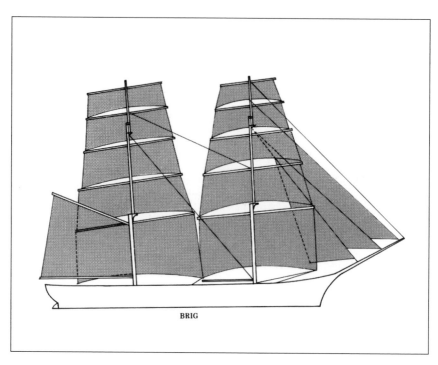

BRIG

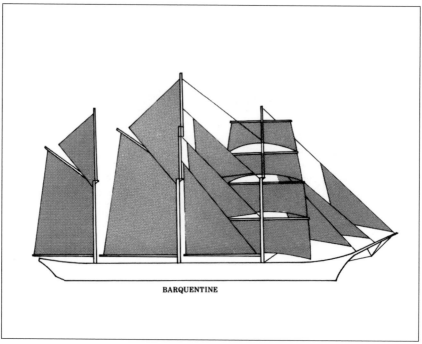

BARQUENTINE

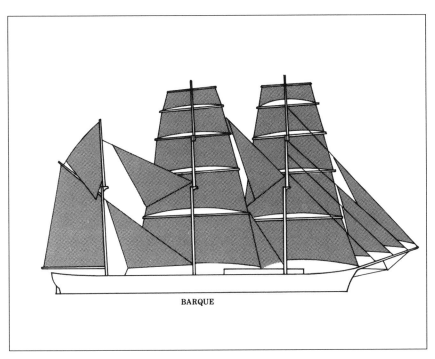

BARQUE

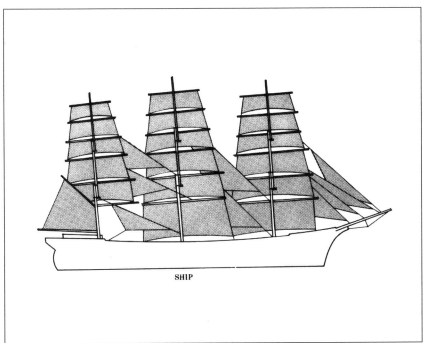

SHIP

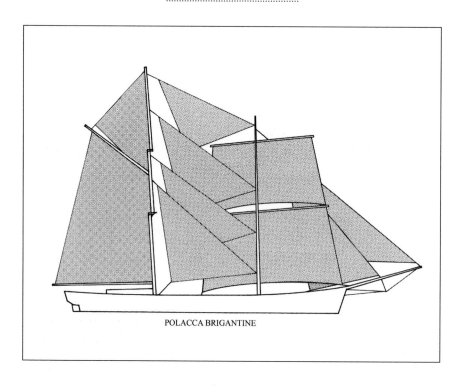

POLACCA BRIGANTINE

Appendix 6

PORTS WORLD-WIDE TO WHICH REARDON SMITH SAILED DURING HIS SEAFARING CAREER, c.1870–1900.

Maps drawn by Linda Norton, cartographer, Dept of Geology,
Amgueddfa Cymru – National Museum Wales.

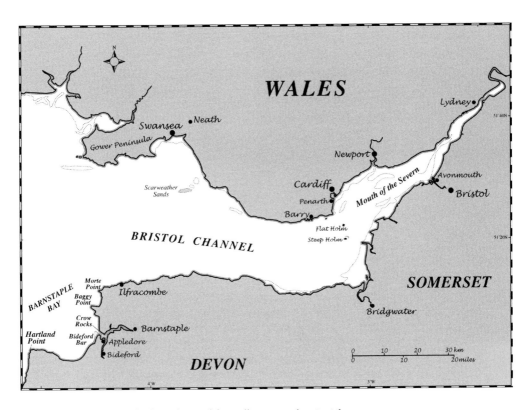

Ports in the Bristol Channel visited by William Reardon Smith

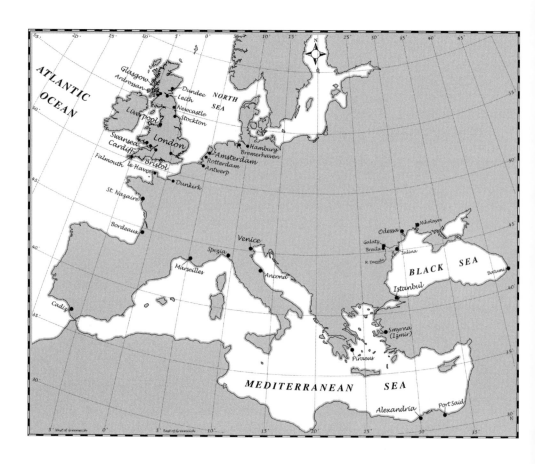

European and Mediterranean ports visited by William Reardon Smith

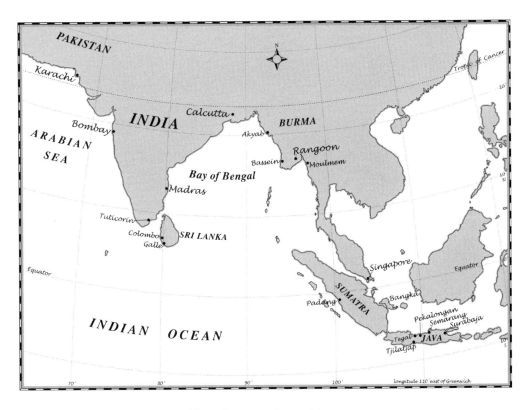

Ports in south-east Asia visited by William Reardon Smith

South American ports visited by William Reardon Smith

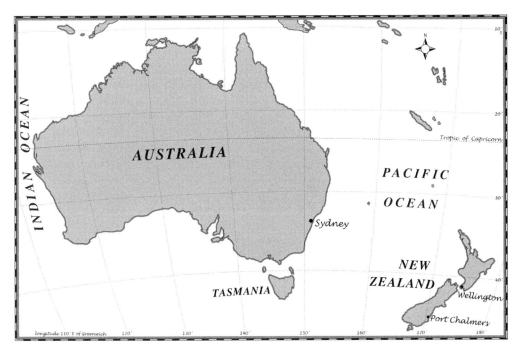

Ports in Australasia visited by William Reardon Smith

African and Arabian ports visited by William Reardon Smith

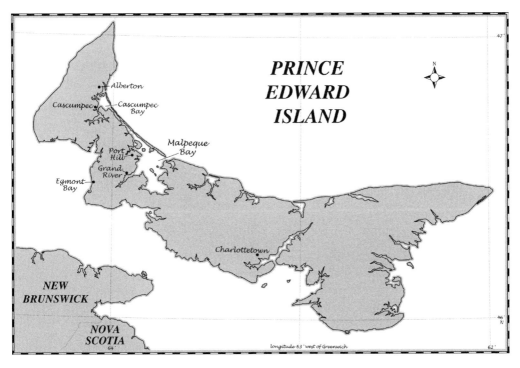

Locations on Prince Edward Island, Canada, where William Reardon Smith was involved
in rigging vessels in 1875

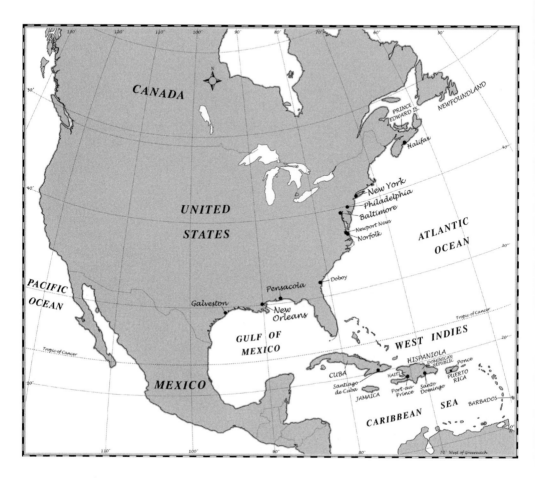

North American Ports visited by William Reardon Smith

BIBLIOGRAPHY

ARCHIVAL AND DOCUMENTARY SOURCES

Amgueddfa Cymru – National Museum Wales
Dept of Art – correspondence files.
Dept of Industry – Chairman's Archive, Reardon Smith Line.

Glamorgan Record Office, Cardiff
Annual reports.
Cardiff and Bristol Channel Incorporated Shipowners' Association records.
Crew agreements.
Reardon Smith Line records.
South-East Wales Pilotage Authority records.
Statutory shipping registers of the port of Cardiff.

Guildhall Library, City of London
Lloyd's Captains' Registers.

National Maritime Museum, Greenwich, London
Crew agreements.

North Devon Record Office, Barnstaple
Statutory shipping registers of the port of Bideford.

National Archives, Kew, London
Defunct companies files.

West Glamorgan Record Office, Swansea
Crew agreements.

World Ship Society
Shipyard construction lists.

NEWSPAPERS AND JOURNALS

Bideford and North Devon Weekly Gazette
Cardiff and South Wales Journal of Commerce
Daily Gleaner (Kingston, Jamaica)
Daily Telegraph
Houston Press
Journal of Commerce
Lloyd's Daily Shipping Index
Lloyd's List
Maritime Review
New York Times
North Devon Journal
Patriot (Charlottetown, Prince Edward Island)
Shipbuilding and Shipping Record
Shipmates – Reardon Smith Seafarers' Newsletter
Shipping World
South Wales Echo
Syren & Shipping Illustrated
Times
Western Mail
Western Morning News

ACADEMIC AND HISTORICAL JOURNALS

Atlantic Reporter
Cymru a'r Môr/Maritime Wales
Journal of Economic History
Journal of European Economic History
Journal of Transport History
Mariner's Mirror
North Devon Heritage
Ships in Focus Record
Transactions of the Honourable Society of Cymmrodorion
Welsh History Review

PRINTED BOOKS

Annual Reports, Chamber of Shipping, London (various dates).

British Vessels lost at Sea, 1914–1918 (London: HMSO, 1919).

Burke's Peerage and Baronetage (various dates).

Lloyd's Book of Houseflags and Funnels, 1912 (London: Lloyd's of London, 1912).

Lloyd's Register of Shipping (various dates).

Lloyd's Register of Yachts (various dates).

Mercantile Navy List (various dates).

Oxford Dictionary of National Biography.

Western Mail Cardiff Directory (various dates).

Who was Who, 1941–50 (London: Adam and Charles Black, 1952).

Anon., *Cardiff, a commercial and industrial centre* (Cardiff: Western Mail, 1919).

Anon., *Cardiff 1921* (London: The Syren & Shipping Illustrated, 1921).

Anon., *Exhibition of Cargo-carrying steamers – Catalogue* (Cardiff: National Museum of Wales, 1933).

Allen, Edward L., *Pilot Lore from Sail to Steam: and Historical Sketches of the Various Interests Identified with the Development of the World's Greatest Port* (New York: United New York and New Jersey Sandy Hook Pilots' Benevolent Associations, 1922).

Boyle, Vernon C. and Donald Payne, *Devon Harbours* (London: Christopher Johnson, 1952).

Brock, Bob and Ann, *HMS Weazle, 1782–1799* (Appledore: North Devon Museum Trust, 1998).

Burrell, David, *Scrap & Build*, (Kendal: World Ship Society, 1983).

Carter, David, *Illustrated History of Appledore, including an account of one of its families* (Swindon: David Carter, 2000).

Clement, David B., *Holman's: a family business of shipbuilders, shipowners and insurers from 1832* (Topsham: Topsham Museum Society, 2005).

Colledge, J. J., *Ships of the Royal Navy* (London: Greenhill Books, 3rd edn, 2003).

Craig, Robin, *Steam Tramps and Cargo Liners* (London: HMSO, 1980).

Davies, John, *A History of Wales* (London: Allen Lane, 1993).

Disney, M. H., *The Honourable Company* (London: Honourable Company of Master Mariners, 1974).

Doe, Helen, *Enterprising Women and Shipping in the Nineteenth Century* (Woodbridge: Boydell Press, 2009).

Eames, Aled, *Ventures in Sail* (Caernarfon, Liverpool and London: Gwynedd Archive and Museum Service, Merseyside Maritime Museum and National Maritime Museum, 1987).

Evans, Charles E., *Memoirs of Lieutenant-Commander Charles E. Evans* (Cardiff: Western Mail, 1946).

Farr, Grahame, *Shipbuilding in North Devon* (London: National Maritime Museum, 2nd edn, 1980).

Fayle, D. E., *The War and the Shipping Industry* (London: Humphrey Milford, 1927).

Forde, Captain Frank, *Maritime Arklow* (Dun Laoghaire: Glendale Press, 1988).

Grant, A. and P. Walters, *Salmon Netting in North Devon* (Appledore: North Devon Museum Trust, 1998).

Gray, Leonard, H. *Hogarth & Sons Ltd – Baron Line* (Kendal: World Ship Society, 1976).

Greenhill, Basil, *The Merchant Schooners* (London: Percival Marshall and Co. Ltd, 2 vols, 1951)

Greenhill, Basil and Ann Giffard, *Westcountrymen in Prince Edward's Isle* (Newton Abbot and Toronto: David and Charles and the University of Toronto, 1967)

Hawkes, Jacquetta, *Mortimer Wheeler: Adventurer in Archaeology* (London: Weidenfeld and Nicolson, 1982).

Heaton, Paul M., *Reardon Smith Line: the History of a South Wales Shipping Venture* (Risca: Starling Press, 1984).

Heaton, Paul M., *Tatems of Cardiff* (Risca: Starling Press, 1987).

Hope, Ronald, *A New History of British Shipping* (London: John Murray, 1990).

Hughes, Barry D., *Rolle Canal and the North Devon Limestone Trade* (Bideford: Edward Gaskell, 2008).

Jeffreys, Captain D. E., *Maritime Memories of Cardiff* (Risca: Starling Press, 1978).

Jenkins, David, *Jenkins Brothers of Cardiff: a Ceredigion family's Shipping Ventures* (Cardiff: National Museum of Wales, 1985).

Jenkins, David, *Owen & Watkin Williams of Cardiff: the Golden Cross Line* (Kendal: World Ship Society, 1991).

Jenkins, David, *Shipowners of Cardiff, a Class by Themselves: a History of the Cardiff and Bristol Channel Incorporated Shipowners' Association* (Cardiff: National Museum of Wales and University of Wales Press, 1997).

Jenkins, J. Geraint, *Evan Thomas, Radcliffe, a Cardiff Shipowning Company* (Cardiff: National Museum of Wales, 1982).

Jenkins, J. Geraint and David Jenkins, *Cardiff Shipowners* (Cardiff: National Museum of Wales, 1986).

Jong, N. de and Marven Moore, *Shipbuilding on Prince Edward Island* (Quebec: Canadian Museum of Civilisation, 1994).

Larn, Richard and Clive Carter, *Cornish Shipwrecks – the South Coast* (Newton Abbot: David and Charles, 1969).

Lloyd, J. E., *Wales and the Past – Two Voices* (Cardiff: National Museum of Wales, 1932).

Lubbock, Basil, *The Last of the Windjammers*, Vol.1 (Glasgow: Brown, Son and Ferguson, 1927).

MacGregor, David R., *Merchant Sailing Ships* (London: Conway Maritime Press, 1984).

Nasaw, David, *Andrew Carnegie* (New York: Penguin Books, 2006).

Nicholson, John, *Great Years in Yachting* (Lymington: Nautical Publishing Co. Ltd, 1970).

Ritchie, Carson, *Q-ships* (Lavenham: Terence Dalton and Co. Ltd, 1985).

Runciman, Walter, *Windjammers and Sea Tramps* (Newcastle upon Tyne: Walter Scott Publishing Co. Ltd, 2nd edn, 1905)

Runciman, Walter, *Before the Mast – and After: the Autobiography of a Sailor and Shipowner* (London: Ernest Benn Ltd, 1924).

Slade, W. J., *Out of Appledore* (London: Conway Maritime Press, 4th edn, 1980).

Tennent, A. J., *British Merchant Ships sunk by U-boats in the 1914–1918 War* (Newport: Starling Press, 1990).

Underhill, H. A., *Masting and Rigging – the Clipper Ship and Ocean Carrier* (Glasgow: Brown, Son and Ferguson, 1946).

Wheeler, Sir Mortimer, *Still Digging: Interleaves from an Antiquary's Notebook* (London: Michael Joseph, 1955).

Wignall, T. C., *The Life of Commander Sir Edward Nicholl* (London: Mills and Boon, 1921).

Williams, Desmond I., *Seventy Years in Shipping* (Cowbridge: Graig Shipping plc, 1989).

ARTICLES, LETTERS TO THE PRESS AND STORIES

Appleyard, Harold, 'Ropner trunk-deck steamers', *Ships in Focus Record*, 1/ 2, 3 (1996–7).

Baillie, Jess, 'Board of Trade Shipping Inquiries, 1875–1935', *Annual Report of the Glamorgan Archivist* (1989).

Bassett, Douglas A., 'The Making of a National Museum' (part 2), *Transactions of the Honourable Society of Cymmrodorion* (1983).

Boswell, J. S. and B. R. Johns, 'Patriots or Profiteers? British Businessmen and the First World War', *Journal of European Economic History*, 11 (1982).

Boyce, G., '64thers, Syndicates and Stock Promotions: Information Flows and Fund Raising Techniques of British Shipowners before 1914', *Journal of Economic History*, 52/1 (1992).

Boyle, C. Vernon, 'The Bideford Polackers', *Mariner's Mirror*, 18/2 (April 1932).

Craig, Robin, 'British Shipping and British North American Shipbuilding in the Early Nineteenth Century, with special reference to Prince Edward Island', in H. E. S. Fisher (ed.), *The South West and the Sea*, (Exeter: Exeter University Press, 1968).

Craig, Robin, 'The Ports and Shipping, *c.*1750–1914' in Glanmor Williams (ed.), *Glamorgan County History*, Vol. 5, *Industrial Glamorgan* (Cardiff: University of Wales Press, 1980).

Craig, Robin, 'Trade and Shipping in South Wales – the Radcliffe Company, 1882–1921', in Colin Baber and L. J. Williams (eds), *Modern South Wales: Essays in Economic History* (Cardiff: University of Wales Press, 1986).

Fletcher, Max E., 'From coal to oil in British shipping', *Journal of Transport History*, New Series, 3/1 (February 1975).

Greenhill, Basil and Michael Nix, 'North Devon Shipping, Trade and Ports, 1786–1939' in Michael Duffy et al. (eds), *The New Maritime History of Devon: Vol. II, From the Late Eighteenth Century to the Present Day* (London: Conway Maritime Press and the University of Exeter, 1994).

Hughes, Captain William, 'My fifty years at sea' (part 1), *Cymru a'r Môr/ Maritime Wales*, 6 (1981).

Jenkins, David, 'Sir William Reardon Smith and the St Just Steamship Co. Ltd, 1912–22', *Cymru a'r Môr/Maritime Wales*, 10 (1985).

Jenkins, David, '*Llongau y Chwarelwyr*? Investments by Caernarfonshire slate quarrymen in local shipping companies in the late nineteenth century', *Welsh History Review*, 22/1 (June 2004).

Morgan, D. Jeffrey, 'Boom and Slump – shipowning at Cardiff, 1919–1921', *Cymru a'r Môr/Maritime Wales*, 12 (1989).

Osborne, Alec, 'St Just Steamship Company Limited', *Shipmates*, 11 (June 1999).

Smith, Sir William Reardon, 'The only cure for depression', *Western Mail*, 8 January 1921.

Smith, Sir William Reardon, 'Trade chaos in the USA', *Western Mail*, 12 February 1921.

Smith, Sir William Reardon, 'Changes in Shipping Conditions', *Shipping World – Jubilee Supplement*, 3 May 1933.

Walsh, John, 'John Wesley and the community of goods', in Keith Robbins (ed.) *Protestant Evangelicalism: Britain, Ireland and America, c.1790–1860. Essays in Honour of W. R. Ward* (Oxford: Oxford University Press, 2001).

Whitlock, John, 'Appledore lifeboat's first coxswain', *North Devon Heritage*, 7 (1995).

Williamson, Henry, 'The Crake', in *Tales of Moorland and Estuary* (London: Macdonald, 1953).

INDEX